PORTLAND ROCK CLIMBS

YOUR AVENUE TO ADVENTURE

PORTLAND ROCK CLIMBS

FOURTH EDITION

THE COMPREHENSIVE
AND
INFORMATIVE GUIDE TO
LOCAL AND CLASSIC ROCK CLIMBS
IN PORTLAND, OREGON

Book Design: Image One C&D
Technical Maps and Illustrations: Tim Olson
Copy Editor: Debra Peterson
Cover Design: Kerry Crow
Cover Photograph: *Nate Farr leading Borderline at Beacon*
Frontispiece list:
F1a: *Mike leading Classic Crack, Broughton*
F1b: *Dave leading May Day, Ozone*
F2a: *Rian Ashford leading Gandalf's Grip*
F2b: *Climber at Red Wall, Broughton*
F3a: *Nate on Borderline, Beacon*
F4a: *Ian Goss on Angular Motion*
F4b: *Jim Toon on Dod's Jam, Beacon*

To order PRC or the Beacon Rock climbers map at the source: PortlandRockClimbs.com

Library of Congress Card Number: 2007904209
Portland Rock Climbs 4th Edition (4.1)
PRC 1st edition 1993, PRC 2nd edition 2001
PRC 3rd edition 2007, PRC 4th edition 2011

Portland Rock Climbs & Mr Piton are trademarks

Manufactured in the United States of America

ISBN-10: 0-9635660-3-2
ISBN EAN-13: 978-0-9635660-3-4

CONTENTS

INTRODUCTION

CLIMBING CRAGS

CHAPTER 1

CHAPTER 2

CHAPTER 3

APPENDIX

CAUTION

Rock climbing contains certain inherent risks that may be dangerous to your health. The sole purpose of this book is to inform rock climbers of the many wonderful crag climbing opportunities available in and around our corner of northwest Oregon. Before attempting any climb described in these pages, you should first be proficient in the use of modern rock climbing equipment. These climbs, for the most part, are not for beginners.

This guidebook is not a substitute for personal insight, time-learned skills, or lessons taught by climbing instructors. There are no warranties, neither express nor implied, that this book contains accurate or reliable information. As the user of this or any guidebook, you assume full responsibility for your own safety. Because the sport is constantly evolving, the author cannot guarantee the accuracy of any of the information in this book, including the location of bolts, pitons (or other hardware), route names and route ratings, route descriptions, or approach trails. No one can offer you any assurance against natural hazards such as lightning or other weather phenomena, loose or poor quality rock, or the risk of equipment failure.

Only you can know the scope and the upper limit of your rock climbing abilities. Assess your prospective climb shrewdly, and make prudent decisions based on your strengths and weaknesses. If you have any doubt concerning your ability to safely ascend a climbing route today, then stop and consider a climb that is less difficult or dangerous.

This is not a how-to guide but rather a where-to book. *Portland Rock Climbs* explains where to rock climb, but you must honestly determine whether you have mastered the most important aspects of the sport before embarking on any rock climbing adventure. Before you use this book:

Consult other climbers about the adventure or rock climb you are planning to embark upon. A skilled climber who knows the crag can give quality advice and insight as to proper gear placement as well as impart ideas about climbing technique and balance that will surely be beneficial to you.

Wisely seek assistance, and attain good instruction from others, such as a diligent climbing instructor who will teach you how to become a safe, intuitive climber.

Consider with suspicion all fixed protection, such as bolts and pitons. Weathering, metal quality, and impact stress loading are some of the variants that can cause fixed gear to fail. Placing additional equipment, such as cams or wires as your safety backup, is a good precaution.

Exercise good judgment as to where the climbing route ascends the cliff face, and learn to quickly perceive subtle variants you will likely encounter in route difficulty. Ask yourself if the route is an off-width, or has run-out sections, or are portions of the wall damp? Know your own strengths and weaknesses; develop a competent understanding of your route-finding abilities and safety skills, for these and the right equipment are your best protection against the hazards of climbing. Never climb beyond your strengths. Confidence and ability gained through many hours of physical and mental preparation are perhaps the most valuable skills you and your climbing partner will need when managing the degree of risk you both are willing to accept.

The graphical designs and imagery are an expression of art.

To attain a full spectrum of rock climbing diversity in western Oregon these select guidebooks are a must-have for any dedicated rock climber who relishes 'sport' or 'traditional' climbing, as well as the raw edge of adventure found deep in the heart of the Oregon Cascade range.

- *Rock Climbing Western Ore., Greg Orton*
- *Ozone, Kevin Evansen & Associates*
- *Weekend Rock-Oregon, Ron Horton*
- *Rock Climbing Oregon, Bolf & Ruef*
- *NW Oregon Rock, Olson*
- *Gorge Classic Climbs, Olson*

PREFACE

This edition of *Portland Rock Climbs* fulfills requests from close friends who expressed their desire for a truly diversified guidebook that covers the entire scope of rock climbing with articulate precision. Their words of encouragement provided the motivation to achieve that goal.

Their invaluable ideas and fruitful suggestions were essential in helping to bring this project to the light. From a large collection of maps, illustrations, and climbing related documents that lay deep upon my desk, came this reformulated guidebook that I hope you find useful for many years to come.

Ideally, this edition will encourage you to seek your own bold new frontier. A world full of discovery and possibilities awaits the adventurous climber, and these pages reveal but a tiny fragment of the whole.

Throughout your quest, remember that our rock climbing actions today impact and influence the future decisions of property owners and land managers alike. We are responsible for keeping ours a friendly, self-managed sport and for interactive cooperation with land managers so that rock climbers will continue to be welcomed for generations to come. By developing a perceptive, respectful awareness of the environment around us, from the peregrine falcon to *Sedum integrifolium*, we ultimately discover that we are entrusted with the keys to provide a legacy for tomorrow.

DEDICATION

Many years ago, while solo rock climbing at Rocky Butte, I had the good fortune of meeting Robert McGown and Wayne Wallace, two remarkably talented climbers whose expertise and insights helped transform the direction and expectations concerning the sport of rock climbing in Portland. These extraordinary men have impacted and shaped the core values of not one but two sports in the Northwest: rock climbing and mountaineering.

Robert McGown's imprint on the sport has spanned many years, from the early 1970s into the 1990s. Bob's vibrant enthusiasm for the hunt in those early climbing days was inspirational, and his is a truly remarkable legacy. I wish him continued success as he reaches for the most distant stars.

Wayne Wallace is known for his savvy adventures along the crest of the Picket Range in northern Washington State. Wayne's boldness throughout his quest to conquer the vast unknown and his seemingly endless strength are in a universal first degree of their own.

With gratitude I thank both Wayne and Bob for their amazing friendships and for providing the courage to develop this edition of *Portland Rock Climbs*.

Mike Schoen has been another courteous and ardent fellow adventurer—one who has excelled far beyond many of us and is worthy of the highest respect. Mike's creative short stories enlivened each climbing adventure, and his timeless wit and humor have made each enjoyable outing even more memorable. Because of his friendship I have learned to understand the brilliant nature of the "Light" more clearly. I wish him strength and fortitude in his ongoing quest for discovery!

All three of these climbers know how to enjoy each adventure to the fullest. They all possess scholarly intuition, strength, and discipline, yet each has a boldness that we all may aspire to.

To my beloved Dad, who taught us how to walk with vitality so our heart would reach for the highest goal. Thank you for the knowledge you have given!

ACKNOWLEDGMENTS

During the long hours of formulating a giant project of this kind, I learned that the end result, which you now see, can only come into existence through the shared knowledge and guidance of many individuals. Thank you all for sharing your expertise and wisdom.

The authors of earlier Portland rock climbing guidebooks provided the foundation upon which this book is founded. Bob McGown, Mike Pajunas, Jeff Thomas, and Nicholas Dodge shared the beginning histories of local rock climbing. Wayne Wallace's infinite knowledge of Broughton Bluff provided crucial details, while Dave Sowerby's small *Portland Rock Update Guide* offered vital clarification to certain aspects of Broughton.

Gary Rall has made great strides toward establishing a long-term liaison with the owners of Carver Bridge Cliff. His invaluable time and commitment has kept this favorite little crag open for all. Special thanks to the Carver Climbing Club directors for striving to maintain a strong working relationship with the owners of the Carver site. Though it was many years ago, I am still grateful for the graphic design talents of Terri Walker, who expertly brought the original 1993 edition of *Portland Rock Climbs* to light. I hope her design career has proved successful.

Many others graciously shared information for this guide as well. Greg Lyon, Bob McGown, Steve Mrazek, Nathan Charlton, Jim Opdyke, Mark Cartier, Scott Tracy, Phillip Hranicka, Chad Franklin, and Eric Vining provided crucial analogies for various routes at Beacon Rock, Broughton, Rocky Butte, Carver and Madrone. Chuck Buzzard shared an extensive data list on certain routes at Madrone Wall. Shane Polizzano and Eric Linthwaite helped with various route details on the northwest section of Beacon Rock.

Jon Bell offered his excellent skills to write the introduction for both the Ozone crag and the Far Side crag. Very high regards to Kevin Evensen, Bryan Smith, Jon Stewart, Mark Deffenbaugh, Jon Bell, Kevin Rauch, Tymun Abbott, and others for granting use of their vast Ozone beta list. Bill Coe, Bryan Smith, Jon Stewart and Jim Opdycke provided an excellent analysis of The Far Side climbing site. Tymun Abbott and John Rust provided pertinent details concerning new route activity at French's Dome. Greg Murray's openness helped solve the riddles at Broken Rock and New Frontier. Various loaned photographic credits: Hugh Brown page 255; Dave Sowerby page 50-51; Bill Coe page 200.

Mike Schoen generously granted permission for the use of several of his photographs—and always without strings attached.

Freelance editor Debra Peterson skillfully revised the opening text and chapter introductions. To various business associates who gave generously of their time to produce this finished product, thank you. Your expertise is the best!

Wayne leading Carrots For Everyone 5.10a

"To rest is not to conquer."
From the movie 'The White Spider'

Linda Schneider climbing the
classic *Dracula* 5.12a on Bat Wall

Ryan Palo powering the stellar
route *Dark Tower* 5.13 at
Broughton Bluff

PORTLAND ROCK CLIMBS
ALL FOR THE SPORT OF CLIMBING

INTRODUCTION

This fourth edition of *Portland Rock Climbs* provides a fresh look at the sport of rock climbing in the Portland area. This edition is intended to bridge the gap between old information and new as well as provide the skilled climber with a valuable tool to use throughout his or her quest in the sport of rock climbing. It is my sincere hope that it serves you well.

Our corner of the Pacific Northwest offers numerous tantalizing climbing destinations, and several of the finest little crags are readily accessible in or very close to Portland. Many of the climbs available in the Portland area transcend well beyond the ordinary scope of rock climbing. I encourage you to explore these favorite crags and experience the unique treasures right here in our region. Crags like Broughton Bluff and Carver Bridge Cliff are prime reasons that the sport of rock climbing continues to be popular in the Portland area.

At the heart of this guidebook is the latest climbing information and it's presented in a new way. Previous authors have laid the groundwork for making this a successful guidebook. Carl A. Neuberger's "A Climbers Guide to the Columbia Gorge," was published in the December 1958 issue of the *Mazama Annual* Volume XL, Number 13. Neuberger's article provided the first comprehensive guide detailing the great Columbia River Gorge classics. He described key features of the gorge that were of great interest to climbers—objectives like St. Peter's Dome, Rabbit Ears below Table Mountain, Little Cougar Rock, and other famous Columbia River Gorge climbs—all within a compact, well-written guide.

The next Oregon guidebook with a compilation of climbing history and route statistics was the twice published *A Climber's Guide to Oregon* by Nicholas Dodge. Printed in 1968 and 1975, Dodge's book contains a wealth of interesting content from the earlier years of climbing and mountaineering and describes many fascinating areas in Oregon from Illumination Rock to Wolf Rock.

In 1983, after years of prolific mountaineering and rock climbing, Jeff Thomas compiled and published *Oregon Rock: A Climber's Guide*. Chock-full of excellent photos and descriptions, the broad scope of Thomas' guide allowed for its marketing success while focusing attention on two of Portland's great climbing areas: Broughton Bluff and Beacon Rock.

The *Rocky Butte Quarry: A Climber's Guide to Urban Rock*, published in 1987 by Mike Pajunas and Bob McGown, contributed equally toward filling in the gaps in crag information and made a reasonable comeback with an updated edition in 1989.

The 1993 and 2001 edition of *Portland Rock Climbs* took that next step and incorporated information about all the local rock climbing areas in one publication.

These guidebook authors have helped to

Paul Couser on *Bloodline* at Broughton Bluff

draw considerable climber and community attention to our favorite local crags, not only for access but also for their natural preservation.

Portland Rock Climbs encompasses a select group of our favorite crags. These are the crags that stand well above other climbing areas (no pun intended) by providing consistent rock climbing opportunities. These are: Broughton Bluff, Rocky Butte, Carver Bridge Cliff, the Madrone, Ozone, Far Side, Beacon Rock, and French's Dome. The Madrone Wall, at the time of this printing, is still closed but is being developed into a county park that will be accessible to all visitors. When this park does open, it will quickly become a premier year-round climbing area. For the latest information about the scheduled opening date of the Madrone Wall contact the Access Fund: Portland Chapter (more information at: www.accessfund.org/regions/state/or, the Madrone Wall Preservation Committee at their Web site, www.savemadrone.org, or contact Clackamas County directly.

GENERAL HISTORY

Every generation of rock climbers strives to reach out and discover bold new horizons that prove both challenging and rewarding. Rock climbers today have great access to a myriad of cragging opportunities. There are over 700 rock climbs available locally to test your endurance and skill, many of which are steep, multi-pitch climbs, some of them located in the very heart of the spectacular Columbia River Gorge.

Exploring and scrambling has been a gratifying pursuit in northwest Oregon since before the turn of the twentieth century. In the Columbia River Gorge, interest for exploration expanded in part because of the building of the Columbia River Highway, which began in 1913. Recreational pursuits in northwest Oregon have continued to become focused and energized ever since.

From the early 1950s onward, rock climbers have consistently shown great interest in the local crags such as Broughton Bluff and Rocky Butte. As the resilience of rock climbing equipment improved, and as lead climbers' skills began to reach well above the 5.9 level, these crags soon became favorite focal points for practicing the sport of climbing. The old classic climbs of the gorge became less popular. For example: the number of summit ascents on St Peters Dome in 1963–64 was five groups; from 1965–68 just three groups; in 1972 one group; in 1977 one group; and in 1994 one person (Wayne Wallace's roped solo ascent)! In early 2008 Radek & Shirley Chalupa, and Jeff Thomas accomplished another rare ascent of this summit. At that rate of diminishing ascents we must wonder if anyone is interested in ever climbing to the summit of St Peters Dome again.

The trend toward climbing on solid rock is in many ways a great benefit to the sport, for over time these places have developed into excellent, high-quality cragging sites, perfect for testing rock climbing skills and endurance. Most present-day climbers visiting these favorite crags find great satisfaction when free-climbing there. The old classic gorge summits still do exist, of course. To truly experience the wild edge of raw adventure you will probably have to do as the early explorers did, and take to the hills.

BRIEF HISTORY OF THE CRAGS

Broughton Bluff is the most frequented climbing crag in Portland, especially during spring, summer, and fall. It is the one place that has enjoyed continuous popularity ever since the 1960s. The area is protected by a canopy of Douglas fir trees that provide excellent shade on hot and sometimes humid summer days. Poison oak and nettles

Nick Sommerhiser on *Orient Express*

grow prolifically here, but year-round use at the popular sections of the crag has generally kept them pushed back.

Rocky Butte Quarry is a unique crag located in northeast Portland near the junction of I-205 and I-84. This easily accessible crag is a great place to top-rope or to learn the sport. As the name implies, it was a rock quarry site prior to 1956, but now trees envelop the crag in a canopy of cool shade, perfect for summer climbing.

Climbers visited this north-facing crag during the 1960s and '70s to practice their free- and aid climbing skills, but only a few of those early climbers' ascents are known. It was not until the mid to late 1980s that the crag was thoroughly explored for climber use. Video Bluff, Toothpick Wall, and Breakfast Cracks have become favorite areas to climb on a hot summer afternoon. If you can overlook the rough outer appearance—such as the freeway, spray paint, broken glass, and other litter—you will begin to see the inner beauty of this favorite haunt.

Carver Bridge Cliff is a small, secluded, and perpetually shaded basalt cliff of intricate beauty deep in a forest of fir and maple trees. This crag offers very steep and mostly difficult rock climbing for the skilled climber. The best season for climbing here is usually mid-April through October. It is a great place to climb on a summer morning when the temperature at the crag is cool and comfortable.

The Madrone Wall is the best year-round climbing crag in Portland. Thanks to concerted efforts by people involved with the Madrone Wall Preservation Committee and the local chapter of the Access Fund, we will soon have renewed access to this superb, year-round haven along the Clackamas River. The planning and park development process for this site are under way, but until Clackamas County officially opens the crag to public access, please respect the closure signs and climb elsewhere.

This crag offers a southwest facing orientation, which is perfect for those mid-winter sunshine days. During the summer it can be quite hot and humid, especially on sunny afternoons. But, overlooking the biting red ants and the minor amount of poison oak, this place is hauntingly beautiful. The reddish-orange rock walls and the stately Pacific madrone (Arbutus menziesii) trees combine to create a wonderful forested setting.

The Ozone Wall is one of Portland's newest additions and certainly one of the better sites for multi-season climbing. With great south facing exposure directly overlooking the Columbia River the steep andesitic bluff provides a great user friendly place to climb in a forest canopy that softens the notorious Gorge winds.

Beacon Rock, the great monolith of the Columbia River Gorge, is situated among some of the most vivid scenery in the Pacific Northwest. This is a favorite well-traveled climbing site during the summer months. Strong winds and cold temperatures keep Beacon Rock nearly void of rock climber presence in the winter months, except for an ardent select core of individuals who relish nailing in the late Fall and early winter season.

The best months to climb here are normally mid-April through September, but the south face of Beacon Rock is closed to climbing (except the northwest

Kim Crihfield at *Horsethief Butte*

section near the main highway) from February 1ˢᵗ until approximately July 15ᵗʰ due to peregrine falcon nesting. Contact Washington's Beacon Rock State Park manager for the specific seasonal closing and opening dates of this crag.

Beacon Rock offers steep, highly sustained, full pitch and multi-pitch, technically demanding rock climbs at varying levels of difficulty. This is bold climbing! Beacon's easiest route (SE Face route) is 5.7, but it involves nearly 600 feet of multi-pitched leads and requires considerable route-finding skill. The majority of the more frequently ascended climbing routes here range from 5.10 to 5.11+ in difficulty. To date the most difficult lead climbs established are 5.12+ with virtually unlimited potential beyond that, whether free climbing or nailing.

The climbing routes are of the highest standard, easily taking first place locally in bold, technical rock climbs. Many of the dihedral systems were nailed in the 1960s and '70s. Later, many of these nailing routes were free climbed at surprisingly moderate ratings, thus establishing some of the finest stemming and jamming problems in the entire Columbia River Gorge basin.

NW OREGON CLIMATE

The Oregon climate west of the Cascade Range is predominantly wet for most of the year. Pacific marine air weather systems bring an abundance of rainfall that saturates the region, especially from late-October through May. Most rock climbers in northwest Oregon generally seek the local crags during the warm season (May through September). During this portion of the year mild marine air often mixes with inland Great Basin hot weather to bring a climber-friendly cycle that keeps the region quite comfortable.

During the summer months, temperatures will average in the seventies to mid eighties (Fahrenheit) with occasional short peaks of hot, sunny days in July and August reaching the nineties. Temperatures above 100°F are infrequent.

By late October, the Pacific marine air storm tracks become more active, usually bringing a consistent series of rain showers. The typical winter storm systems generate frequent cold, rainy days with average temperatures in the 35–50°F range. Occasional strong low weather systems sweep south from the inland polar region to produce short periods of intense cold in the twenties to mid-thirties east of the Cascade Range, but these brisk temperatures seldom penetrate into the valleys of western Oregon. Average annual precipitation in the Willamette Valley near Portland is about 40 inches; at times the winter weather is prohibitively wet. During these periods, most rock climbers seek the refuge of a local rock gym or sports gym for fitness continuity.

Although the winter may seem long in Oregon, virtual year-round rock climbing is readily available and without driving all the way to Smith Rock. Broughton Bluff and the Madrone Wall (opening date not yet confirmed) both offer a southwesterly orientation. With a little winter sunshine these crags quickly dry out and both provide a respite from the notorious howling east winds of the Columbia River Gorge.

Most of the crags around Portland may be utilized during May through October. In spite of the typical rain showers, the cliffs are generally vertical enough to quickly dry out during seasonally mild temperatures. Several popular sites at the crags are so precipitous (such as the Bat Wall) they seldom get damp from rainfall except in the depth of winter.

How does this data break down for quick use by a rock climber? If it is not raining, go climbing; if it is raining, go east to fascinating, sunny places such as Pete's Pile, or the remote, well-concealed Bulo Point climbing crag.

GEOLOGY OF NW OREGON

A formative discussion on the physical geology and natural processes of rock structures is beneficial to all climbers by providing a better understanding of the cliffs and mountains we climb on. This analysis is a brief summary of plate tectonics and continental volcanism designed to enhance your understanding of localized geologic characteristics of rock stratum and lava formation.

THREE TYPES OF ROCK

Rock formations are classified geologically into three main groups to emphasize the mode of origin: igneous, metamorphic, and sedimentary.

Plutonic rock forms from magma migrating toward the earth's surface, cools slowly underground, and hardens to form rock masses known as intrusive igneous rock. Volcanic rock forms when the magma breaks out upon the earth's surface and cools quickly as extrusive igneous rock. The principal forms of hardened extrusive igneous rock are basalt, andesite, dacite, and rhyolite, while the intrusive igneous forms are granite, diorite, and gabbro.

Metamorphic rock is formed when deeply buried, then folded and compressed by stresses, high temperatures, and chemical conditions. Sedimentary

Dave Sowerby at *The Rat Cave*

rocks are formed by processes that are active at the earth's surface. These are usually formed by erosion, decay, breakdown of other rock material, or an accumulation or buildup of rock, shells, or corals that over time are compacted and hardened to form sedimentary rocks. Examples are limestone, gypsum, flint, conglomerate, sandstone, and shale.

BORING LAVA FORMATION

The basalt lava cliff formations in and around Portland were deposited from a flow called the Boring Lava Flow. Prominent hills such as Mount Scott, Mount Tabor, Rocky Butte, Chamberlain Hill, and buttes near the town of Boring are cinder cone volcanoes part of the Boring Lava Field formation which generally deposited cinder, ash and lava flows. Larch Mountain, further to the east is a shield volcano which allowed for fluid lava to travel along a gentle gradient slope to deposit alternating layers of basalt and debris.

The degree to which the Boring Lava formation congealed resulted in deep layers of compact basalt with broad smooth surfaces with widely-spaced generally vertical joint cracks. The flow was deposited upon the Troutdale Conglomerate formation, a mixture of well-rounded pebbles of stream transported volcanic material. The slope below the north face of Broughton Bluff reveals some of this layer of pebbled product. Thick sheets of this low silica basaltic lava flow also exist on Mount Sylvania, as well as near Oregon City. Broughton bluff, Carver cliff, and Madrone wall are part of this extensive formation. Surface color striations, such as at the Madrone Wall show a distinctly golden-tan undertone with a smattering of artistic yellowish-brown, red, orange, and gray painted upon the surface of the rock cliff caused from iron oxidation interaction with water. The cliff scarp at Ozone is likely a short distance andesitic lava flow from nearby Zion Mtn.

COLUMBIA GORGE BASALT GROUP

The Columbia River Basalt flow formation is visible throughout the gorge. This basalt formation, when deposited, cooled quickly into dark, dense, and frequently tightly columnar jointed features from 6 inches to 2 feet in diameter capped with an entablature. The cliffs in the Gorge near Yeon Mountain reveal well over 2,000 feet of horizontal layered bands of this basalt flow, bringing beauty and rugged harmony to this scenic area. The vertical beauty of the Gorge terrain was enhanced by Columbia River erosion processes, by multiple Missoula Flood inundations, and a gradual uplift of the Cascade Range.

Although some rock climbing is possible on these flood basalt formations the nature of the narrow columnar rock formations, decomposition, and weathering processes tends to limit rock climber interest.

The outstanding exception in the gorge of course is Beacon Rock, an old volcanic neck core that is the second largest monolith in the world after the Rock of Gibralter. The volcano, erupted and built in a distant Epoch, was weathered by erosional processes and flood waters of ancient Lake Missoula, leaving this prominent remnant pillar in the central Gorge. The 848-foot-high monolith is composed of a medium-colored, vesicular an-

Kay Kucera on Bloodline

desite and is steeply featured on all sides. On the south face massive vertically-jointed columns make this site a perfect haven for skilled rock climbing enthusiasts. Today, the mile-long zigzag trail leading to the top of Beacon provides hikers with one of the finest panoramic views of the Columbia River Gorge.

CLIMBING ROUTE RATINGS

This guide uses the well-known Yosemite Decimal System (YDS) as the standard method for rating rock climbs. This system, first developed at Tahquitz in the 1950s, is a two-system concept connecting a Difficulty Grade and a Free Climbing Class.

Difficulty Grades

A Difficulty Grade (Roman numerals I through VI) indicates how long it will take to climb a route and is determined by the difficulty, the involvement, and the length of a route. For example:

- **Grade I**   Can be climbed in a few hours.
- **Grade II**   Can be climbed in a half day or less.
- **Grade III**   Can be done in less than a day.
- **Grade IV**   One long, hard day. The hardest pitch is no less than 5.7 in free climbing difficulty.
- **Grade V**   In one long day if the climbers are experienced and fast, otherwise 1½ days plus should be expected while the hardest pitch is usually at least a 5.8 difficulty.
- **Grade VI**   Requires multiple days to ascend and often includes extreme mixed free climbing and/or difficult nailing.

The Yosemite Decimal System concept, though designed to assist, is highly subjective and will vary from area to area. Some climbers may be able to climb very efficiently on two Grade IV routes while others may barely manage a Grade II without bivouacking. Most of the climbs found in this guide are Grade III or less in difficulty.

Free Climbing Difficulty Class

The Free Climbing Difficulty Class is based on an ascending scale from 1 to 5 and is then subdivided into an open-ended scale from 5.0 to 5.15 and beyond. This scale is designed to reflect the hardest free move on a pitch or the overall sustained character of the pitch. See the graph in Appendix C for detailed comparisons with other international ratings.

This open-ended scale allows for future routes of increasing difficulty. If a particular pitch contains a series of moves of the same difficulty, a higher rating is usually assigned. Further sub-grading separates the easier 5.10s from the harder 5.10s by using the letters A, B, C and D. Occasionally a slightly broader definition is applied with a minus (-) or a plus (+) emblem after the numeral. For example: 5.10a/b (**.10-**), 5.10b/c (**.10**), 5.10c/d (**.10+**). Some free-climbing routes at the local crags are underrated due to top-roping before leading. The best solution is to rate the climb according to an on-sight lead by a climber unfamiliar with the route in question.

Aid Climbing Difficulty

The art of modern nailing, Aid Climbing Difficulty or Class 6, is quite unlike its neighbor mentioned above. Both the technical severity of the piton or pro (protection) placement and the climber's security are linked to the same rating. In the sport of nailing, the letter A indicates aid climbing, while the number, (0 through 6 and higher), indicates the degree of nailing. The letter C indicates that it can be ascended clean without the need for pitons or other gear driven with a hammer. All of Class 6 aid climbing uses equipment as the means for progressing up the rock scarp to a higher point.

- ✦ **A0** Pendulum, shoulder stand, tension rest, or a quick move up by pulling on protection.
- ✦ **A1** Solid equipment placements.
- ✦ **A2** Is more difficult to place but offers some good protection.
- ✦ **A3** Involves marginal placements and the potential for a short fall.
- ✦ **A4** Frequent marginal placements; will only hold body weight.
- ✦ **A5** Pro supports body weight only; risk of 50-foot-plus fall.
- ✦ **A6** Involves full pitch leads of A-4 and serious ground fall potential.

Modern nailing equipment has profoundly changed the way in which climbers approach a prospective route. Knifeblades, RURPs, Bird Beaks, and a variety of hooks and ultrathin wires offer new ways to aid climb at the extreme edge. Since free climbs are often maintained as free climbs,

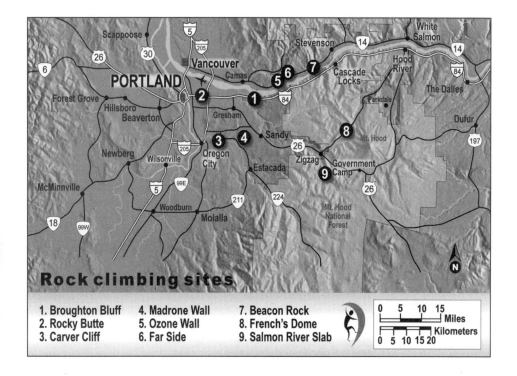

Rock climbing sites

1. Broughton Bluff	4. Madrone Wall	7. Beacon Rock
2. Rocky Butte	5. Ozone Wall	8. French's Dome
3. Carver Cliff	6. Far Side	9. Salmon River Slab

certainly some nailing routes should be maintained as nailing routes.

For those routes requiring a "seriousness" rating, they are as follows:

- **PG**: Protection may be adequate near the difficult sections, yet involve risky or runout sections which can increase the potential for an accident.
- **R**: A bold lead with a serious fall potential; may involve questionable or poor protection; serious injury is possible.
- **X**: Involves high risk of ground fall potential; very poor to no protection available; serious or fatal injury possible.

The climbing difficulty class rating listed in this guide is not to be considered as absolute. All climbing routes are subject to unforeseen challenges that can quickly make the climb inherently dangerous.

Confidence, ability, intuition, and good judgment are crucial for managing the degree of risk that you and your climbing partner are willing to accept. Develop those invaluable skills so that you can foresee your risks or liabilities, because careless judgment becomes a harsh learning curve. Proceed with caution; climb at your own risk!

An additional concept utilized frequently in this guide:

- **TR**: Indicates the route is generally a top-rope climb, although the climb may have been free climbed in the past.

The "Star" or Quality Rating used throughout this book is designed to help climbers selectively choose the more aesthetic climbs. This is a highly subjective system for many of the un-starred routes are worthy of attention, so be sure to check out some of the lesser-known climbs as well.

- **No Stars**: An average route.
- **One Star** (★): Good quality route, better than the usual.
- **Two Stars** (★★): Excellent route, good position with quality rock climbing, a highly recommended route.
- **Three Stars** (★★★): Superb position, a classic line on excellent rock, a must-do route on everyones list.

Of these starred routes, not all will be bolted face climbs. Some will be crack climbs, several will be short but worthy, and a few will be two routes connected together making an even better classic climb.

The star ratings for a climb at Broughton Bluff will vary from the quality routes at Beacon Rock or Smith Rock as they represent the favorable, interesting routes at that particular cliff.

Hard or Soft Ratings

If Portland area ratings for rock climbs seem a bit skewed you're not alone in this analysis, and perhaps they really are to some extent. As one local climber once said, "If you can climb 5.12 in Portland you can climb 5.12 anywhere."

Each local climbing site tends to reflect a slightly different rating scale. Some sites tend to have ratings that are **HARD** for that specific grade (5.10b may seem like a 5.10c), while other crags tend to be slightly **SOFT** for that grade. The following analogy should provide a quick means to compare overall ratings at the local Portland area crags: *Broughton* routes are typically hard for the grade; *Carver* is usually hard; *Madrone* is solid; and *Beacon* is hard for the grade. Possible reasons? The slick surface texture of local basalt, inobvious moves that involve diligence to solve, or climbers who tend to rate a new route hard or soft.

VISUAL BIO

These quick and convenient graphical emblems provide a fast visual bio to basic site characteristics that we seldom think to ask. The emblems cover basics such as effects of localized weather on each crag or route, cliff orientation, shaded by trees or directly facing the full sunshine.

In simple terms the upper emblem string conveys a message: The site is open or climbable for 8-months (depending on weather or regulations), it is five minutes to the nearest section of cliff, the cliff orientation is west facing, receives afternoon sunshine, it is shaded by a forest of trees, and has special regulations. A cam emblem is for trad gear route, while the carabiner emblem indicates sport routes. If the site is forested (no sun) such as Carver it will be simply a 'Trees' emblem. The last emblem (umbrella) will be found next to certain actual route names. The umbrella emblem will help to point you to rock climbs that may be dry even if it has rained or is raining lightly, although extended heavy winter rains will soak most crags.

Keith Campbell

EQUIPMENT

Both personal safety and your quality of enjoyment depend on your being adequately prepared with the appropriate gear when rock climbing at the local Portland crags. Essential equipment such as locking carabiners, belay-rappel devices, and even double ropes will help to ensure that your outing is a successful one.

In recent years, climbers have seen quality improvements in rock climbing equipment, both innovative and beneficial to the sport. Standard rock gear protection ("pro") such as spring-loaded camming devices (Camalots, Friends, TCUs, etc.), HBs, RPs, curved wired stoppers or nuts (or wires), bolts, and tailored rock shoes have contributed greatly to climbers' overall safety and climbing enjoyment . The following gear recommendations should be used as a broad list from which you can generally determine your needs for a specific climb. Gear sizes appear under each route name as a guideline, but choose your gear by analyzing your skills and needs for each rock climb *before* ascending it. Ask other climbers what they may have used for route protection, and be willing to take extra equipment and perhaps even larger-sized gear.

For traditional free climbing at Portland area crags you will likely need a variety of the following gear: A single 60-meter rope, helmet, a set of 12–15 quick draws (QDs), wired stoppers up to 1½ inches, small camming devices like TCUs up to 1½ inches, and larger spring-loaded camming devices ranging from 1–4 inches.

It is wise to bring extra slings as well as some of the big stuff like Hexcentrics or Big Bro, especially if a particularly fine offwidth crack is your challenge. Tiny specialized pro (like HBs, RPs, or Steel Nuts) may be useful

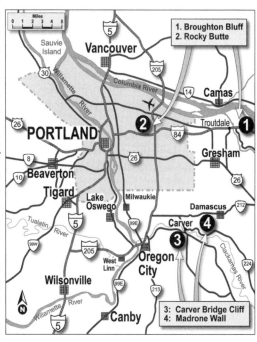

on a few of the desperately thin routes. You can go with a rather lean rack of the above gear when visiting Carver Bridge Cliff, while a more comprehensive gear rack, including two ropes, would prepare you nicely for the long, steep leads at Beacon Rock.

For those interested in pursuing a career in nailing, a number of outrageous routes are available at all the local crags. Consider some of the following to assist you in your climb: Knifeblades, Hooks, RURPs, bashies, tie-off loops, etc.

For the climbing enthusiast who needs the latest new gear products (or even quality used equipment) there are many local retail outdoor stores available that offer competitive prices.

Remember, wherever you climb, always exercise good judgment before and during the climb. Practice route analysis, ask for consultation and advice from others, develop foresight, and when you begin your ascent, climb with a reasonable degree of caution, fully aware of the risks of this sport!

❋ BOTANICAL ELEMENTS

Our northwest Oregon crags are saturated with diverse botanical flora enhanced by the north pacific weather systems that impact this region each year. Tall canopied forests of Douglas fir, Western Red Cedar, White Oak, Red Alder and Bigleaf Maple are dominate trees in our lower elevation forests. In addition, Oregon Ash, Vine Maple, Pacific Dogwood, Hazelnut, and a few Cascara Buckthorn add vibrance to the beauty and dimension of the forest structure.

Moss clings to the edge of steep cliffs, hanging from branches of trees like a thick beard. Common low growing shrubs and plants such as Saskatoon, Solomon Seal, Mahonia, Yarrow, Miner's Lettuce, and a veritable family of fern varieties create a dense layer of ground foliage. Other unique varieties are Oregon Stonecrop, Woolly Eriophyllum, Penstemon (p. ovatus) and of course the unfriendly ever-present Poison Oak.

A magnificent broadleaf evergreen tree with reddish peeling bark called Pacific Madrone (arbutus menziesii) grows on the sunny slopes of the Madrone-Hardscrabble Wall complex.

Carver Bridge Cliff holds a unique treasure of Trillium that bloom in Spring. The deep shade is also home to Three-leaved Anemone, Alumroot (micrantha), Thimbleberry, Currant, Salal and Sword Fern.

Next time you are heading to the crag bring a flora book to peruse, and take time to enhance your awareness of the local flora habitat at our crags.

⬡⬡ CLIMBING STYLE AND ETHICS

Contemporary climbing ideology consists of two forces: style and conceptual ethics. Style is how you climb on the rock while climbing ethics are what you do to the rock. Conceptual patterns in rock climbing develop into presently accepted style trends such as toproping, rappel inspection, pre-placed natural protection, and free-soloing, but these styles are likely to continue to change in the future. Will bolting, or gardening con-

Driving From	Driving To	Total Miles	Est. Time
Seattle, WA	Portland, OR	180 miles	3.5 hours
Tacoma, WA	▲	150 miles	3 hours
Yakima, WA		185 miles	3.75 hours
Hood River, OR		56 miles	1 hour
The Dalles, OR		81 miles	1.5 hours
Pendleton, OR		210 miles	3.5 hours
Redmond, OR		130 miles	3 hours
Bend, OR		163 miles	3.5 hours
Salem, OR		51 miles	1 hour
Albany, OR		73 miles	1.5 hours
Eugene, OR		115 miles	2.25 hours
Roseburg, OR		185 miles	3.75 hours
Grants Pass, OR		253 miles	5 hours
Lincoln City, OR		83 miles	1.75 hours
Astoria, OR	▼	98 miles	2.25 hours
Driving time from city center Portland to the crag listed in PRC			
Broughton Bluff			20 minutes
Rocky Butte Quarry			10 minutes
Carver Bridge Cliff			20 minutes
Madrone Wall			25 minutes
Ozone Wall			30 minutes
Beacon Rock			45 minutes

DOD'S JAM ROUTE

In 1961 Eugene Dod, Bob Martin, and Earl Levin teamed up to explore a particularly steep crack system near the third tunnel at Beacon Rock leading up to Big Ledge.

The development of "Dod's Jam" route is particularly interesting in that it began as a mixed aid and free climb from the railroad tracks at the bottom of the face. On one of the early attempts (in 1961) Earl Levin recalled evaluating a 65-foot overhanging jam crack, which would probably have been aided, but for Eugene Dod, who insisted on flailing away at it, with all his might.

"Starting out was most difficult, as Eugene had to stand on my shoulder to work his way into the crack. Up he went and struggling every inch of the way. At the halfway point he was almost completely exhausted and felt that he would fall any moment. Somehow he made his way to the top where he rested before setting up a third belay position on a tiny ledge appropriately named "The Perch". At the same time I belayed Bob Martin to my position. Bob then decided to go on to Eugene and received a belay to "The Perch". He was so tired at this point that Eugene took the next lead. Through a tree growing inconveniently in our path and sixty-five feet higher up an overhanging face (A1) we found ourselves on 'Big Ledge' and peaceful serenity. Nick Dodge, *A Climbing Guide to Oregon* (1975), pg 26.

tinue to be part of the ethical choices of the future? Only time will tell.

In order for new climbs to attain an acceptable rating there must be another unchanging point of reference nearby for comparison. For example: Classic Crack at Broughton is considered to be an accepted 5.9 rating, therefore, ratings for new rock climbs nearby could be established based on a comparison with its rating criteria.

Several simple examples of locally accepted trends are route cleaning, bolting, and pre-inspection. Climbers at crags like Beacon Rock are more inclined toward the traditional "ground up" climbing method, where a number of the rock climbs were established when the first ascent party placed the fixed gear while on lead. Certain crags have government-mandated bolt and route development rulings that apply in order to assure adequate management of the public resource.

Placing additional rappel anchors or more fixed gear on established routes is atypical, although it is considered acceptable to upgrade the old fixed gear on rock climbs, such as upgrading ¼-inch bolts to ⅜-inch bolts. Anchors are usually replaced by local climbers because our moist climate tends to heavily corrode most fixed metal products within twenty years. Any route, whether established via free or nailing, is usually considered as such; it is the first ascent party's present choice. Chiseling is uncharacteristic. People will continue to climb at very high standards in the years to come.

The advent of power drills has

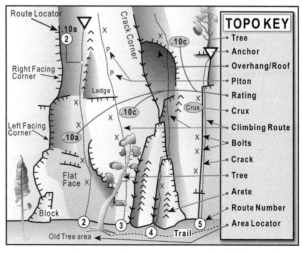

Route Locator

Crack Corner

TOPO KEY
- Tree
- Anchor
- Overhang/Roof
- Piton
- Rating
- Crux
- Climbing Route
- Bolts
- Crack
- Tree
- Arete
- Route Number
- Area Locator

Right Facing Corner

Left Facing Corner

Ledge

Flat Face

Block

Old Tree area ← — — — Trail

transformed the sport by allowing easier route development. Yet restraint should be exercised when bolting, because every route does not necessarily need a bolt. Vandalism of climbing routes fixed with bolts or pitons has occasionally occurred. This is neither style nor ethics. Just be aware that some climbing routes you may wish to climb may not be available as a lead route due to missing fixed gear.

Ongoing community involvement in caring for the crags—including all of us—will help keep these places available in the years to come. Enjoy the sport of rock climbing for its social and outdoor benefits by respecting others as well as the rock.

ABOUT THIS GUIDEBOOK

This books purpose is to provide information that will help influence rock climbing for the public good with the goal to educate users about long-term stewardship of our natural resources we enjoy climbing upon, while offering insight about the nuances of each different climbing site, route development limitations, private property or ownership issues, provide a written communication bridge to rock climbers with the hope of eliminating or reducing potential friction with area residents, and encourages users to become involved in trail maintenance and other crag stewardship opportunities. This book is all about creating a good public resource that will be helpful toward preserving access in both public and private venues, brings crucial reference material forward for public officials, and is highly useful with emergency response agencies for developing emergency rescue or evacuation plans. You are not merely a visitor, but a valued partaker with an interest in how public lands are being managed.

"It is a long road that leads to the peaks."
~Gaston Rebuffat

PORTLAND ROCK CLIMBS

CHAPTER 1
BROUGHTON BLUFF

· ·

P ERCHED MAJESTICALLY ALONG THE EASTERN SHORE of the Sandy River is a rock climbing paradise that has provided years of enjoyment for all who visit. This steep-walled crag, with its close proximity to the City of Portland, is one of the best local crags to offer an excellent variety of climbing opportunities for every rock climber.

Located just minutes east of Troutdale at the entrance of the majestic Columbia River Gorge, Broughton Bluff offers great rock climbs on an extensive and secluded 160-foot-high series of cliffs on Oregon State Parks land. This excellent year-round rock climbing crag provides individuals of all ages the opportunity to explore the intriguing facets of rock climbing.

In the late 1950s Broughton Bluff was approached by a few dedicated rock climbers who began to utilize this crag, often for aid climbing but also to refine essential rock skills in order to succeed on the great walls and mountains in other states. Broughton is a great place to learn new climbing skills, develop physical strength, challenge your ability to persevere, and even excel beyond your greatest climbing aspirations.

⬛ BRIEF HISTORY OF THE AREA

The broad sweep of this heavily forested bluff, located at the Lewis and Clark State Park, was named after Lieutenant Broughton. As a member of the Captain George Vancouver expedition of 1792, he had traveled up the Columbia River to a place just east of the Sandy River. The honorary name was bestowed in 1926 by the Scouts and accepted by the U.S. Board of Geographic Names.

The crag, which is bordered on the west by the Sandy River, continues to be historically important, especially to rock climbers. Of the earliest known ascents at Broughton Bluff, most were done using a variety of mixed aid and free climbing. One of those early ascents to become established was the Hanging Gardens II 5.6 A1 (now a free climb at 5.10a) route ascended by Bob Waring, John Wells, and Bruce Holcomb in 1965. Today, it is considered a trade route classic. This climb stands as a tribute to those early days of exploratory aid climbing. Perhaps the finest achievement at Broughton took place in 1968 when Steve Strauch and Jim O'Connell ascended the North Face via the superb classic and ever-popular Gandalf's Grip (5.9+). This route is one of the best crack climbs of this rating at Broughton Bluff.

In the 1970s a small number of active climbers established many more routes. Jim Mayers,

Drew Hansen leading *Loose Block Overhang*

Gail Van Hoorn, Alan Campbell, Dave Jensen, Talbot Bielefeldt, Dean Fry, and others "opened the door" by aid climbing routes like Peach Cling (now a free climb at 5.11b), Mr. Potato (5.11a), and Sesame Street (5.9+), all of which were ascended in 1972; Peer Pressure (5.10d) in 1973, Face Not Friction (5.11d) in 1975, as well as ever-popular Classic Crack.

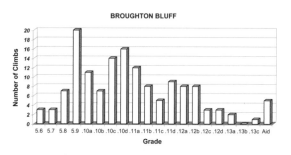

The mid-1970s brought serious free climbers who began to push beyond the known boundaries of their time, firmly establishing a whole new dimension of free climbing adventure. Many of the older routes were now being ascended free without the use of direct aid, while the latest climbs were pushed considerably beyond the 5.9 realm.

Red Eye (5.10c) and Sheer Stress (5.10a) were done in 1976; Sandy's Direct (5.10c) and Physical Graffiti (5.10d), a short, difficult roof problem, were put up in 1977. Beyond the Red Wall stands the superb cliff known as the Bat Wall, where climbers established Superstition (5.11a) and Hanging Tree (5.10d) in 1977 as well. It was this massive and secluded wall that became the key to the next generation.

Some of the climbers who were instrumental here in the 1970s are Doug Bower, Monty Mayko, Bruce Casey, Robert McGown, Mike Smelser, Jeff Thomas, Ken Currens, Mark Cartier, Jay Kerr, and Dan Foote. They and others focused their energy toward free climbing the untapped routes.

Nearly ten silent years descended upon Broughton Bluff but the summer of 1990 brought another group of climbers who noticed a realm of blank space waiting to be conquered. A few extra bolts quickly unraveled the final mysteries of Broughton, firmly bringing the 5.12 rating to the crag.

The Unnamed Aid Route on the Bat Wall quickly fell from its old aid status. After numerous free climbing attempts by several local climbers, Gary Rall finally succeeded beyond this key rock climb. Afterward, a name with real bite stood out: Dracula (5.12a). A virtually endless series of climbs soon followed. Bela Lugosi (5.12c), Bad Omen (5.12b), and Kashmir (5.12b) were all established in 1990. In 1991, Heart of Darkness (5.12b) brought renewed interest to the Jungle Cliff, while Bloodline (5.12b) continued the legacy in 1992 at the Bat Wall.

Gary Rall, Wayne Wallace, Dave Sowerby, Jay Green, and many others have helped to push the standards of the 1990s. The mysteries of Broughton met a new destiny.

Compositionally, Broughton Bluff is a form of

Climber leading *Edges & Ledges 5.8*

blocky, densely compacted volcanic basalt, very dark in color, and occasionally stained with brilliant hues of reddish-orange sections on its surface. From a climber's perspective, the entire bluff formation is composed of thirteen aptly named walls, ten of which are detailed in this guide with climbing topographical reference maps. The sections of cliff at Broughton that offer the greatest variety of free climbing opportunities lay north from the Bat Wall. The access trail south of the Bat Wall is a bit rough and the rock climbs tend to receive less attention. Several other cliffs even farther to the south (Aerie, Perihelion, and Eclipse Wall) are located on private land and are not available for climbing purposes. Detailed route information provided on the ten cliffs are from left to right: North Face, Hanging Gardens Wall, Red Wall, Bridge Cliff, Spring Rock, Bat Wall, Trinity Wall, Berlin Wall, Jungle Cliff, and New Frontier Cliff.

VISUAL BIO

12 Month 5 Mins W PM Shade **Trad** **Sport**

These emblems represent most of Broughton Bluff. The North Face is fully shaded, but does receive minor late afternoon sunshine in the summer. The Hanging Gardens Wall receives some mid-morning sunshine that filters through a tall canopy of fir trees. The southern-most cliffs (Berlin Wall, Jungle Wall and New Frontier) will take about 15 minutes to approach. Broughton offers considerable variety for traditional gear leads, but also a respectable amount of sport routes particularly on the Red Wall and Bat Wall. There are a few nocturnal scorpions (as the route name Scorpion Seams can attest) at Broughton, but you may not see one unless you climb there frequently.

HOW TO GET THERE

From the city center of Portland, drive east on I-84 toward the town of Troutdale. Continue on the interstate highway until you cross the Sandy River, then take exit #18 onto the Historic Columbia River Highway. (This is a popular scenic river road that curves south along the river before heading east through Corbett.) At exit #18 drive south a very short distance until you cross under a railroad trestle that spans the Sandy River. Just beyond (on the east side of the road and river) is the Lewis and Clark State Park. This wayside facility offers ample free parking and is used by boaters, hikers, and climbers. Take note of the curfew hours on the entrance sign. The park rangers will lock the gate at dusk and vehicles remaining in the parking lot after closing will be cited.

APPROACH

From the parking lot walk south along the gravel path to the base of the steep hillside, then up the climber-maintained zigzag path. This trail angles around onto the south slope then continues up to meet the cliff base near the south edge of the Hanging Gardens Wall. The trail to the right quickly leads to the Red Wall, while the left path meanders along the base of Hanging Gardens Wall then around the

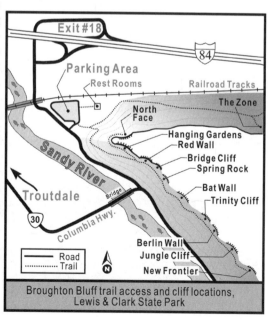

Broughton Bluff trail access and cliff locations, Lewis & Clark State Park

corner farther to the North Face.

If you plan to top out from a rock climb on either the North Face or the Hanging Gardens Wall, the best option for a scrambling descent is down a third-class ridge crest between these two cliff formations. Most of the rock climbs at Broughton have excellent established belay anchors from which you can rappel back down to the ground near your original starting point without actually topping out on the climb. An emergency rescue gurney is located at the base of the Red Wall.

NORTH FACE

1. Frodo's Journey   5.9+   ★★

60' (13m) in length, QD's and Pro to 2"

Start up left from the cave and clip the first bolt on Traffic Court. Then step left and climb directly up over a small roof and V-shaped slot to a small perch. Continue up the slab (3 bolts) to a slight overhang. Clip the 4th bolt then surmount the bulge, and continue up several face moves to a bolt anchor up high on the left face.

2. Traffic Court   5.9   ★★ 🌂

60' (18m) in length, Thin Pro to 2", TCU's suggested

Start as for Gandalf's left variation and climb past a bolt to a stance. Ascend a vertical corner till it eases to a slab. Muscle over a final bulge directly above then step right to rejoin with Gandalf's Grip at the belay.

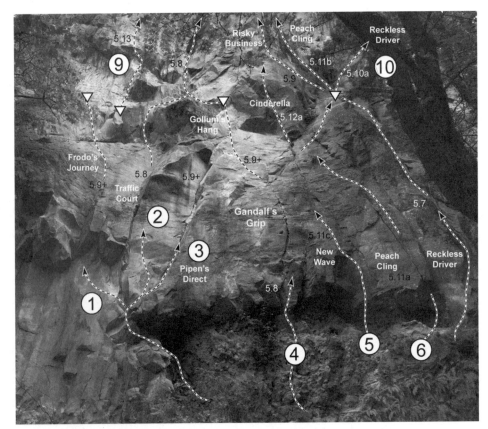

North Face from *Frodo's Journey (#1)* **to** *Reckless Driver (#10)*

3. **Pipen's Direct   5.9+** ☂ ̄ʲ

Pro to 1½"

Start up left from the cave past a bolt to a small ledge. Continue up the right leaning dihedral to rejoin the regular route.

4. **Gandalf's Grip   II 5.9+   ★ ★ ★** ☂ ̄ʲ

Multi-pitch, Pro to 3½", TCU's or small wires suggested

This route is a Broughton super classic.

Pitch 1: Commence up steep ground to the right of the alcove using a vertical crack. At a small narrow stance move up left (bolts) via tiny edges and sloping insecure holds (5.9+) to the Gollum's Hang. Surmount the bulge (bolt) and belay on a sloping ledge.

Pitch 2: Move left and climb a steep crack corner through two small overhangs (5.8) then

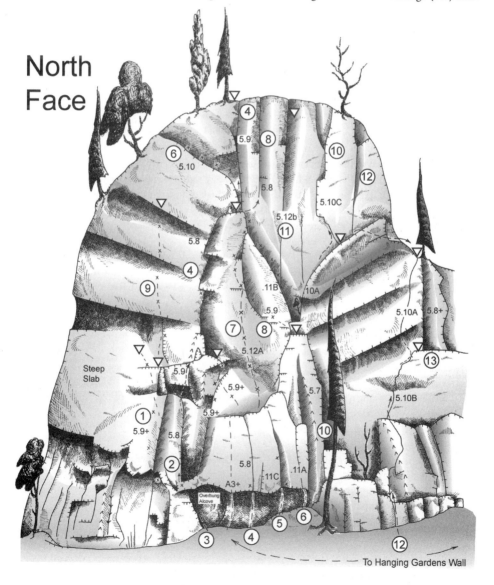

North
Face

angle up right to a belay on a nice small flat ledge.

Pitch 3: Above is an obvious wide crack. Climb this to the top and walk off, or rappel from here to the previous anchors.

5.   New Wave   II 5.11c   ★★
30' (9m) for the 1ˢᵗ Pitch, Pro to ¾"
A thin seam to the right of Gandalf's Grip start. P2 is now called Skullduggery.

6.   Peach Cling   II 5.11b PG   ★★
Multi-pitch, Pro to 2", mostly small wires
Excellent route. Starts 15' right of Gandalf's. Layback up a desperate thin left-leaning tips flake until it ends in a shallow corner. Continue up to a good belay on a ledge. Move up left via strenuous and off-balance moves (bolts) ending on a ledge and bolt belay (2ⁿᵈ anchor on Gandalf's). Continue up leftward (pitons) on down sloping smears (5.10) to the top. Walk off.

7.   Cinderella   5.12a   ★★
30' (9m) in length, QD's and pro to 1½"
Excellent quality route ascending the center bulge on the North Face between Gandalf's Grip and Peach Cling. Joins with Risky Business. Either rappel from Gandalf's second belay anchor with two ropes or climb up and walk off.

8.   Risky Business   5.9   ★★
40' (12m) in length, QD's and pro to 1", cams recommended.
The first pitch is a great climb! Start at the first belay on Peach Cling. Step left onto a sloping series of ledges (5.9) passing several bolts. Continue up good holds until able to join with Peach Cling then to the belay anchor on Gandalf's Grip. A surprisingly quality climb of only moderate difficulty. The 2ⁿᵈ pitch turns immediately right from the belay stance, around a corner (5.8) to a hidden jug, then ascends a mossy crack dihedral leading to the summit.

9.   Dark Tower   5.13a/b
102' (31m) in length when starting from the ground to the top anchor
Sport route using 5 QD's from lower belay to upper belay
Difficult route that ascends the slightly overhung left side of the north face wall. Start from a belay anchor (see diagram), move up a left facing corner, then surmount the first roof. Continue up the headwall on crimpers to a crux move just below the belay anchor. Located immediately left of the 2ⁿᵈ pitch of Gandalf's Grip.

10.   Reckless Driver   II 5.10c
Multi-Pitch, Pro to 3", cams or TCU's helpful
No traffic jam on this route. Start 5' right of Peach Cling. Move up an easy corner to a ledge then up a right-facing corner (5.6) then leftward to the Peach Cling belay. Up to the right is a bush. Thrash over the bush past a crux (5.10a) up an easy right angling ramp system to a belay anchor. Exit off down right to a large fir tree (rappel), or from the top of the ramp step left and climb up a thin crack system (5.10c) to the summit.

11.   Skullduggery   5.12b
165' (50m) in length, Pro to 2" small cams and nuts
A stout thin seam up right of P2 Peach Cling. Eases to a 5.7 dihedral near upper anchor.

12.   Sweet Emotion   II 5.10b PG
165' (50m) in length, Pro to 2½", Needs bolts on 2nd pitch

13.   American Graffiti   5.8+
30' (9m) in length, Pro to 2"
Climb the crack just below the large fir tree on the west edge of the North Face.

HANGING GARDENS WALL - LEFT HALF

14. Giant's Staircase   5.6

15. Edges and Ledges   5.8   ★ ★ ★

60' (18m) in length, 4 QD's and pro to 2"

Start right of Giant Staircase, but on the left side of a large detached top heavy column of rock. Climb up the left corner of this detached block, and step onto a large ledge, then embark up left onto the bolted prow and face climb on interesting edges to the belay anchor above.

16. The Sickle   5.8   ★ ★ ★

60' (18m) in length, Pro to 4"

This popular climb is the obvious curving wide crack about 30' up the wall, and just above a large ledge. This area has numerous cracks and ledges that offer climbers an excellent area to top-rope with relative ease.

17. The Hammer   5.9   ★

60' (18m) in length, Pro to 3"

A rather difficult, short jam crack high step crux problem off the upper main ledge leads to

Left aspect Hanging Gardens Wall, *Giant's Staircase* **(#14) to** *The Hammer* **(#17)**

easier jams and smears near the anchor.

18. Prometheus Slab 5.7
60' (18m) in length

An original 1960s climb. There are several additional TR climbs near PS and Spud using a fixed anchor accessible from the trail above the wall.

19. Spud 5.9+
60' (18m) in length, Pro to 3"

A bit thin at the start.

20. Tip City 5.10c ★★
60' (18m) in length, Pro to 1½"

An excellent thin crack. Locate two parallel cracks that join with Chockstone Chimney at a ledge. The left crack is Tip City and the right is Lean Years. The climb is slightly easier if you utilize both cracks.

21. Lean Years 5.10c ★★
60' (18m) in length, Pro to 1½"

The right parallel crack. Both routes make excellent options to practice thin crack climbing.

22. Hangover 5.11
40' in length (TR)

23. Chockstone Chimney 5.9
80' (24m) in length, Pro to 4"

An original 1960's climb.

24. Milestone 5.7
80' (24m) in length, Pro to 3"

Leading Hit The Highway 5.10a

HANGING GARDENS WALL - RIGHT HALF

25. Loose Block Overhang 5.9 ★★★
120' (36m) in length, Pro to 2½"

This very popular climb offers several optional starting points. You may climb a corner to an offwidth fist crack (5.8) for 25' to the top of a large block and then belay at a bolt anchor. Or ascend on the left via steep steps into a weird tight corner capped by an overhang. Surmount this hang on the right by using hand edges and fist jams till you can smear onto the top of the block to the bolt anchor. On the 2nd pitch, jam up a slightly overhung crack (5.9 crux) until it eases onto a ledge and bolt belay. Maneuver up a very short 5.8 left-facing corner, swing right onto a slab (piton) then up an easy blocky section and walk off left. Or from the same belay exit up a left slanting crack (20') on steep rock and thin holds as an odd alternative.

26. Grace and Danger 5.11b R
25' (7m) in length, Pro to 1½" Cams recommended

Ascend the outside arête next to the 1st pitch of Loose Block.

27. Slapfest 5.12b ★★
40' (12m) in length, 6 QD's and minor pro to 1"

Climb the superb bolted face immediately right of the crux pitch of Loose Block Overhang. A rather stiff, unusual route. Joins with Least Resistance at its crux move.

28. Least Resistance 5.10a
30' (9m) in length, Pro to 1"

Climb the first 50' of Hanging Gardens route but angle up left to a left-leaning seam (bolts) that pulls around an outside corner up to a stance at the second bolt anchor on the Loose Block Overhang.

29. Dynamic Resistance 5.10d ★★

80' (24m) in length, QD's and Pro to 1½"

Climb the first 50' of Hanging Gardens route and move up left to a steep corner between Least Resistance and Sandy's Direct. Power up the strenuous tight corner (bolts), move right around an odd bulge, then exit up left over a final crux roof to a bolt anchor. Rappel. An excellent climb.

30. Sandy's Direct 5.10c PG ★

120' (36m) in length, Pro to 2" including small wires

A challenging lead climb. Climb the first 50' of Hanging Gardens route (stay left of the maple tree belay) and continue straight up a vertical corner system 80' to a sloped ledge with a belay anchor. Rappel.

31. Face Not Friction 5.11d ★★

60' (18m) in length, QD's and minor pro to start

Tip City (#20) and Lean Years (#21)

Quality climbing, worth the effort. Up and left of the maple tree belay is a partially fixed face-seam problem on vertical rock. Climb this to a bolt anchor at a small ledge. Rappel or continue up left on steep, bushy cracks to an upper ledge, then exit left to walk down.

32. Hanging Gardens Route II 5.10a (or 5.6 A0) ★★★

Multi-pitch, Pro to 1½"

One of the original Broughton favorites put up in 1965. This very popular climb offers multiple optional starting points.

Pitch 1: The standard route ascends a wide 3-4" crack with edges (5.8) to a stance, then [or angle up left to a corner with ledges] directly up over several balanced blocks. Move right to the bolt belay next to the small tree. Reference photo for other options that lead directly to the first belay anchor via some wide cracks (5.8).

Pitch 2: From the tree move right across a steep slab (5.6) and jam up a slightly overhung bulge (5.7) to a narrow crawl. The original route traverses right passing the Mr. Potato anchor then up a short corner and bolt belay on the left (or go up left from the pitons to the Sesame Street belay anchor on a large ledge about 20' higher up).

Pitch 3: Move right and up around a blind corner. Free climb (5.10a) or A0 (fixed bolts & pitons) diagonally right 20' along the "bicycle path" to a stance on a small ledge at a bolt anchor belay. A vertical 80' rappel takes you directly to the ground just to the right of Shining Star.

Bryan Smith leading *Sesame Street*

Hanging Gardens Wall
Left Half

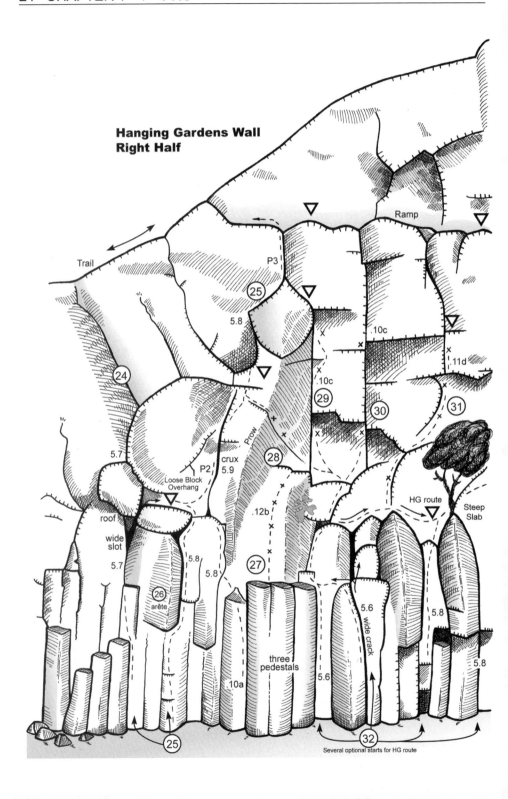

**Hanging Gardens Wall
Right Half**

Ramp

Trail

P3

㉕ 5.8

⑳ 5.7

.10c

.11d

.10c

㉙

㉚

㉛

Prow

crux
5.9

P2

Loose Block
Overhang

.12b

㉘

HG route

Steep
Slab

roof

wide
slot

5.7

5.8

5.8

㉖ arête

5.6

wide crack

5.8

㉗

.10a

three
pedestals

5.6

5.8

㉕

㉜
Several optional starts for HG route

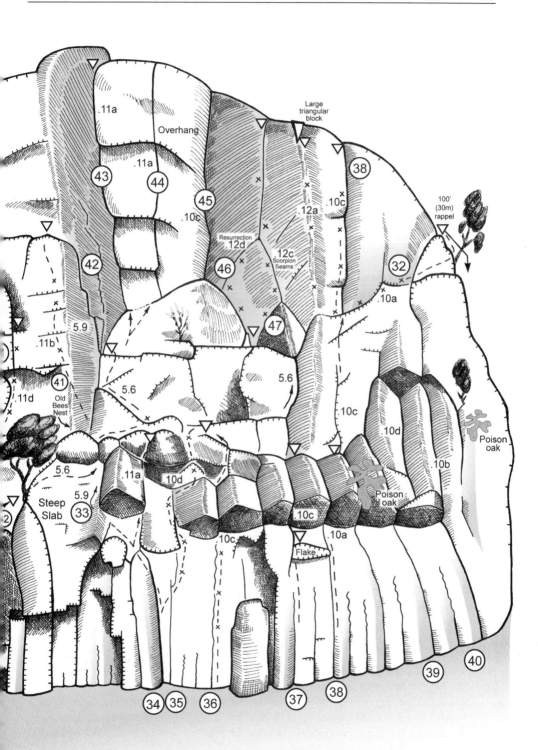

.11a

Overhang

43

.11a

44

45

.10c

Large
triangular
block

38

.12a

.10c

100'
(30m)
rappel

42

5.9

.11b

Resurrection
.12d

46

.12c
Scorpion
Seams

47

32

.10a

41

.11d

Old
Bees
Nest

5.6

5.6

5.6

.10c

.10d

Poison
oak

.10b

Poison
oak

5.6

5.9

Steep
Slab

33

.11a

.10d

.10c

.10c

.10a

Flake

.10c

34 35

36

37

38

39

40

33. BFD   5.9
30' (9m) in length, Pro to 1"
A short challenging climb. Small cams can be quite helpful for the crux section.

The following 5 routes have belay anchors located on a narrow series of sloped ledges about 40' up the cliff.

34. Mr. Potato   5.11a
40' (12m) in length, Pro to ¾"
Unusual yet interesting climb. Start up the same crack as you would for BFD, but continue directly up a right facing near vertical corner. Pull over several bulges to join with Hanging Gardens route where two pitons are secured at a small stance.

35. From Something to Nothing (aka Something)   5.10d   ★★
40' (12m) in length, Pro to 1" and QD's
A very popular face and corner problem immediately right of Mr. Potato. Climb up the same crack corner as Mr. Potato, but move up right (bolts) on face edges to an awkward stance at a slot with a bulge above. From the slot work left onto the steep face around the slight bulge to another tenuous stance on an arête. Surmount the next bulge on thin face edges (crux) to a bolt anchor.

36. Fun in the Mud   5.10c   ★★
40' (12m) in length, Pro to 1" and QD's
This is a good route with a stiff bulge problem involving thin jams to surmount the crux. Starts up a steep bolted slab, pulls the overhang then steps right slightly and up a corner step, then move directly left to catch the "Something" bolt anchor.

37. Circus Act   5.10c   ★
40' (12m) in length, Pro to 1" including TCU's

38. Shining Star   5.10a
140' (42m) in length, Pro to 2"
A good first pitch. Located on the right side of Hanging Gardens Wall. Climb a crack on a mossy slab immediately right of a maple tree. Pull through the bulge (5.10a) and continue up to a stance on sloping ledges. Step left to join Hanging Gardens route or step right and climb a broken crack system (5.10c) via edges and corners. Crosses over the Hanging Gardens route at the "bicycle path". Note: immediately left of the second portion of Shining Star is a minor prow with bolts called **Show Me The Money** 5.11. It can be used to access certain upper routes such as The Black Prow or upper Hanging Gardens route.

39. Hung Jury   5.10d
130' (39m) in length, Pro to 2½" including pitons

40. Hang 'Em High   5.10b
130' (39m) in length, Pro to 2"

The following seven routes are located in a overhanging amphitheater above the second pitch of the Hanging Gardens route. Refer to Map #1 for a visual tour.

41. Main Vein   5.11b
30' (9m) in length, Pro to 2"
This is the obvious prow right of Face Not Friction and above the maple tree belay. Follow the standard Hanging Gardens route past the tree, but at the old bees nest move up left around the corner by way of a crack. Once on the steep slab angle left then right and finish up a bolted arête until it joins with Sesame Street.

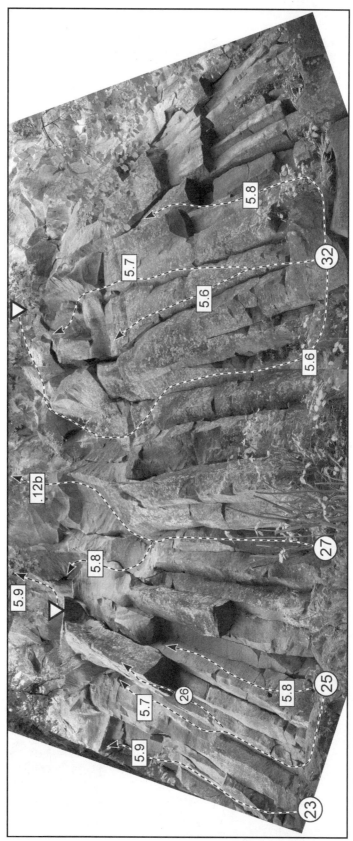

Chockstone Chimney to Hanging Gardens Route

42. Sesame Street 5.9 ★★

Pro to 3"

Excellent but short. Climb the first pitch of Hanging Gardens. At the piton anchor for Mr. Potato step up left on easy ledges to a bolt belay. To your left is a slightly overhung zigzag jam crack. Climb this 15' to another belay. Rappel with two ropes or traverse left along ledges to the descent trail.

43. Demian 5.10d PG ★★

30' (9m) in length, Pro to 3" TCU's optional

Superb, strenuous route ascending a desperate overhanging crack.

44. Endless Sleep 5.11a R

30' (9m) in length, Pro to 2"

45. Peer Pressure 5.10c R

30' (9m) in length, Pro to 2'

Poorly protected at the start but exciting stemming above. From the bolt anchor at the base of Scorpion Seams angle up let on slabs then ascend the overhung corner (pitons) to the top.

46. Scorpion Seams 5.12c ★★

30' (9m) in length, 6 QD's

On the right face of the overhanging alcove are two bolted seams that merge halfway up the route and finish to the same belay anchor. The left start is called **Resurrection** (5.12d) while the right start is called **Scorpion Seams** (5.12c).

47. Black Prow 5.12a

30' (9m) in length, Pro to 2"

A rescue gurney is located near the base of the Red Wall for emergency use.

RED WALL

48. Arch de Triumph 5.7

20' (6m) in length Pro to 4"

49. Arcturas 5.10d

20' (6m) in length (TR)

50. Anastasia 5.9 ★

25' (7m) in length (TR)

Climb a thin crack to a flared crux problem on a steep slab.

51. Dry Bones 5.10+/.11- ★

25' (7m) in length (TR)

52. On the Loose 5.11a ★★

30' (9m) in length (TR)

An excellent top-rope problem left of Classic Crack.

Broughton Bluff
Map 1: Upper Right section
of the Hanging Gardens Wall

53. _____ 5.13 (?)
   30' (9m) in length (TR)
54. Classic Crack 5.9+ ★★★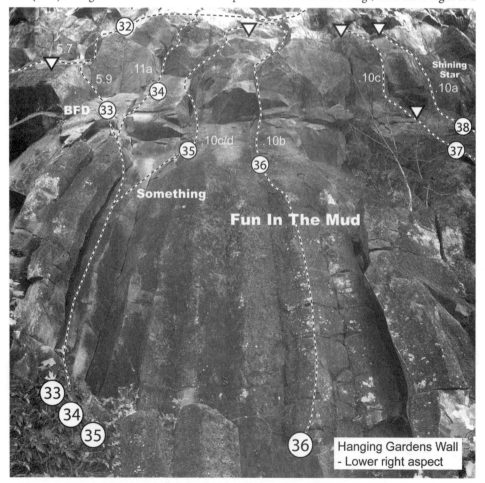
   30' (9m) in length, Pro to 2"
   Classic...that's exactly what it is! A beautiful jam crack that splits a smooth wall. A well-traveled slippery route. Can be top-roped by scrambling up an access trail to the left.
55. Thai Stick 5.10d ★★★
   30' (9m) in length, QD's
   A very popular lead climb. Climbers often combine this with Critical Mass for a stellar full power packed lead.
56. Mr. Bentley 5.11+ ★★
   30' (9m) in length (TR)
   Excellent top-rope route involving sequential endurance.
57. Sheer Stress II 5.10a PG ★★★
   Multi-pitch, Pro to 2½"
   Very popular route. One of the super classics. Commence up the shallow left-facing corner (crux) 15' right of Classic Crack. Climb up until it eases under a bulge, then move right to a

Hanging Gardens Wall - Right section showing _BFD_ (#33) to _Shining Star_ (#38).

bolt anchor. Belay. Move right to a semi-detached block, and then climb up over a bulge, then up a steep jam crack (5.10a) until possible to exit right on good holds to a ledge. Rappel with 2 ropes from bolt anchor.

The following routes are located generally above Classic Crack or Sheer Stress and can be accessed by most of the previous routes on the Red Wall.

Red Wall routes from *Arch de Triumph* (#48) to *On the Loose* (#52).

58. Physical Graffiti II 5.10d ★★★

Multi-pitch, Pro to 2"

A fascinating route highlighted by a hand jam roof problem. Move up an easy corner (5.7) on the left corner of Red Wall and above Arch De Triumph. Upon reaching a roof traverse right to a ledge and bolt belay. Jam a crack busting through a big overhang. The climb eases onto a steep crack and an anchor. Rappel or finish up one of the upper variations (5.10a and dirty).

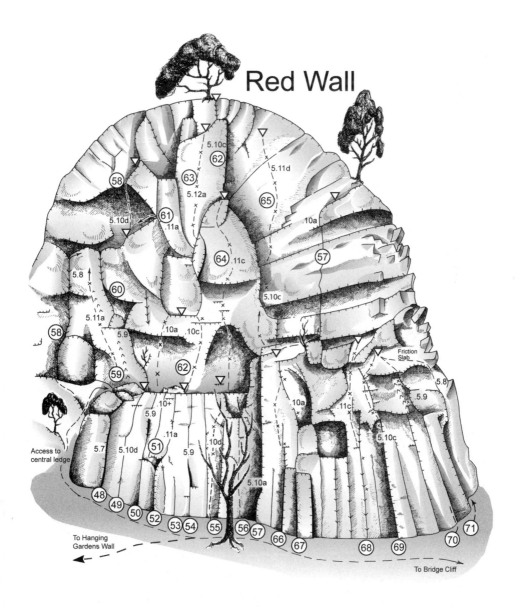

Red Wall

59. Habitual Ritual   5.11a

30' (9m) in length, 4 QD's and minor pro to 2"

60. Physical Direct   5.9

30' (9m) in length, Pro to 2" TCU's recommended

61. Hit the Highway   5.11a   ★

30' (9m) in length, Pro to 1½"

Good yet surprisingly hard lead. Begin on the intermediate ledge at the top of Classic Crack, but left of the anchor. Ascend directly up a steep bolted face (5.10a) then move right to the Red Eye belay. Step right and up (5.10a) a few moves until possible to move left to an ominous looking steep corner. Climb this and exit left to join with Physical Graffiti or jam directly up a vertical crack to a ledge. Angle up left to a bolt belay. Rappel.

62. Red Eye   II 5.10c   ★★

Multi-Pitch, Pro to 2½" (1ˢᵗ pitch is 4 QD's)

A very popular route, especially the first pitch. Lead Classic Crack or start at the ledge above Classic, and climb a bolted face past a round red "eye" to a bolt anchor on a ledge to your left. Belay, then step right and up a crack system to easier ground. Belay at stance. Finish up a wide off width corner (5.10c) with numerous edges. Exit left and up to the tree at top of bluff. Rappel with two ropes or walk off.

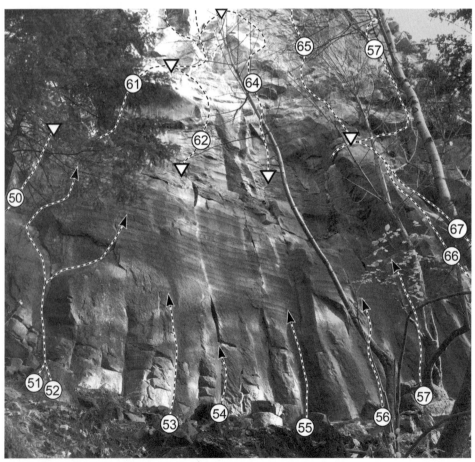

Red Wall routes from *Anastasia* (#50) to *Sheer Energy* (#67).

Note: **The Conspiracy** (5.11c/d) is a minor squeeze job variation between Red Eye and Critical Mass. The difficulty depends upon whether you reach out right to Critical Mass, but it is an alternative connector to get up onto the stellar Kashmir route if you are climbing Thai Stick.

63. Kashmir 5.12a ★★★
40' (12m) in length, 5 QD's and minor pro to 2½" (#5 Rock and 2½" Friend)
This superb line is located on the brilliant orange face in the upper amphitheater. Ascend Red

Red Wall Far Right Section, from *Opus* (#66) to *Friction* (#70)

Eye approximately 30' until possible to enter onto the steep bolted Kashmir face on the left. Rappel from bolt anchors with 2 ropes unless you rappel to the Red Eye anchor. See the note below for an alternative connector route variation to get to Kashmir.

64. Critical Mass 5.11c ★ ★ ★
80' (24m) in length, 8 QD's and optional pro to 1½"
Impressive bolted climb on a steep orange wall. Originally this route powered out the 5.11a scoop then exited up left into a corner crack. Redirecting it focuses you on a balancy 5.11c crux at the final bulge above the initial overhung scoop.

Start by ascending Sheer Stress or Thai Stick, then power out the upside down scoop on positive holds, then dance over the thin crux bulge to a sloping stance. A few more tenuous moves end when you grasp a large block. The bolt anchor is at the top of the large block and below the prominent off width.

65. Pinhead (E. Pluribus Pinhead) 5.11d ★ ★ ★
100' (30m) in length, 8 QD's and minor pro to 1½"
A fabulous route ascending the beautiful upper orange face of the Red Wall. Commence up the first pitch of Sheer Stress to the bolt anchor. From the anchor continue up left (bolts) on a steep section that eases to a minor stance. Step up right and climb a vertical bright reddish-orange colored face to a bolt anchor.

Hugh on upper Hanging Gardens 5.10a

The next several routes are just to the right of Sheer Stress on a darker shaded section of wall.

66. Opus 5.11+ R
45' (13m) in length, 3 QD's to 1st anchor

67. Sheer Energy 5.10a ★ ★
45' (13m) in length, Pro to 1½"
A great climb and surprisingly popular. Step to the top of several free-standing columns of basalt, then climb a short crack and face climb up left (bolts) to the Sheer Stress belay anchor.

Classic Crack 5.9

68. Hard Body 5.11b/c ★ ★ ★
50' (15m) in length, 6 QD's
Very popular route with an unusual crux. Commence up a shallow corner to a strenuous move, then pull through a bulge and up steep rock to an anchor capped by a roof. Rappel.

69. Shootin' (aka Shoot from the Hip) 5.10c ★ ★
45' (13m) in length, Pro to 1" and QD's
Fun climb with big holds and a crack to start.

70. Friction 5.9 ★
45' (13m) in length, Pro to 1" and QD's
A tenuous crux move but still a popular climb.

71. That's the Way 5.8
45' (13m) in length, Pro to 2"

Kerry Metlen on Sheer Stress

BRIDGE CLIFF

72. Under Your Belt 5.9+ R

165' (50m) in length, Pro to 2"

A little known climb ascending the blocky 5th class section on the lower left. From a belay ledge 2/3 up the wall, step left and finish up a clean dihedral to the top. Rappel or walk off.

73. Walk on the Wild Side 5.10c/d PG ★★

45' (13m) in length, Pro to 2"

The standard approach to this classic begins via the first pitch of Fruit Bat. Belay on the half-way ledge, then traverse left roughly 15' past a central corner (Spider Monkey) to a second left-leaning corner. Ascend this to the top. Rappel or walk off.

74. Edge of Eternity II 5.11c ★

Multi-pitch, Pro to 2"

A long climb that begins on the lower section of wall. Climb the dihedral and move right around a difficult corner (5.11) to dirty ledges. Above an easy wide corner is a clean angular face with bolts. Climb this (crux) to a big ledge. Belay. Step right and climb (bolts and pitons) the right face of an arête (5.10a) to a tiny ledge, then a short face to the tree belay. Rappel or walk off.

75. Eagle's Wing 5.12a

Pro QD's

Climbs the face to the right of the start of Edge of Eternity.

76. Spider Monkey 5.9 ★

40' (12m) in length, Pro to 3"

This is the large, dark dihedral on the upper face above the belay ledge.

77. Fruit Bat II 5.10b ★

Multi-pitch, Pro to 2"

This is the best option for approaching all the upper tier routes. Start past a bolt into a sloping corner. Exit up left via grassy ledges and corners to a ledge belay. On the right face of the deep dihedral is a thin finger crack. Ascend this and top out. *Note:* several of the previous routes have original start points but are heavily vegetated and dirty.

78. Seventh Sojourn 5.9

Pro unknown

79. Shandor 5.9

Pro to 3"

SPRING ROCK

80. Toe Cleavage 5.8+

30' (9m) in length, Pro to 1"

A minor route with a tricky crux

smear move to easier climbing.

81. Velcro Fly   5.10d PG

30' (9m) in length, QD's and minor pro to 1"

The route is highlighted by a thin crux move in a shallow corner at a bulge. Wander up easier slabs to a bolt belay.

82. Free Bird   5.11a   ★★

40' (12m) in length, Pro to 1"

Excellent route. Step up to a small corner, reach left, then climb a second corner to a roof. Exit left onto slabs that lead up left to a bolt anchor.

83. Ground Effects   5.12a/b   ★★

40' (12m) in length, 4 QD's

Probably the most unusual and fascinating route on Spring Rock. The climb involves two roof moves using very unorthodox technique. Solve the puzzle.

84. Jumping Jack Thrash   5.11d R   ★★

40' (12m) in length, Pro to 1"   TCU's and RP's recommended

A great climb, but it is usually TR due to a very risky landing on large rocks. Ascend a thin crack in the center of the face to a bolt anchor under an overhang. Rappel.

85. The Spring   5.10b/c   ★★

40' (12m) in length, Pro to 3"

This punchy little flared crack climb is great for strong climbers who like powerful moves in a moderate sense. Takes good camming unit protection.

Climbing routes on *Spring Rock* from *Toe Cleavage* (#80) to *Dyno-mite* (#88).

86. Short Fuse 5.10c ★★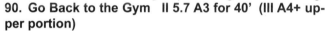

35' (10m) in length, QD's and minor pro to ½"

Yes, it is quite short, but it is still a worthy climb. Ascend the blank face and exit right to a ledge, step up left to a bolt anchor. Remember to bring a small selection of gear!

87. Short Circuit 5.10b

35' (10m) in length, QD's

88. Dyno-mite 5.10b

35' (10m) in length, Pro to 1½"

BAT WALL

89. Hanging Tree III 5.11a R ★

Multi-pitch, Pro to 3" including KB, LA, Rurps

Notoriously loose and dirty in places, yet the upper portion of the climb offers excellent quality stemming and face climbing.

90. Go Back to the Gym II 5.7 A3 for 40' (III A4+ upper portion)

40' (12m) in length, Pro to 1" includes TCU's, KB, LA, Leepers, Hangers, Bathooks

Great aid route. The second part (II A3), branches onto a ¼" deep tied-off pin stack seam, then up to a hanging belay. Die in the Gym (III A4+) goes over the smooth bulge on hooks (seven in a row) and bad pins to a sloping stance belay at 65'. Finish up the upper wall by criss-

Climber leading *Shootin'* on Red Wall

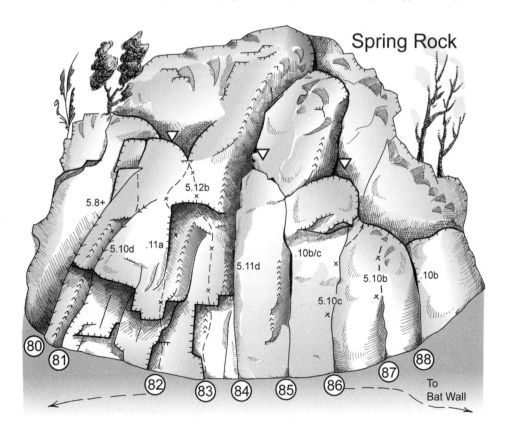

Spring Rock

5.8+

5.12b

5.10d .11a

5.11d

.10b/c

5.10b

.10b

5.10c

80 81

82 83 84 85 86 87 88

To
Bat Wall

crossing the Hanging Tree route to the summit anchor (160').

91. Dracula 5.12a ★ ★ ★

65' (19m) in length, 10 QD's

The premier Broughton Bluff classic rock climb! A very difficult free climb of the highest standard. Originally called the Unnamed Aid Route. Commence up a small right-facing corner to the right of the dead leaning tree. From a small ledge embark up a diagonal right leaning hand ramp, then up left, then right to a seam. Balance up the seam and surmount the final obstacle, a flared pea-pod corner. Bolt belay anchor.

92. Bela Lugosi 5.12c ★ ★

65' (19m) in length, 10 QD's

Fascinating route to climb. Ascend a shallow corner gracefully to a thin stance. Pull through a desperately thin crux then up left via a zigzag seam (crux) until it joins with Dracula to the pea-pod finish.

Bat Wall from the route *Hanging Tree* (#89) to *Bad Omen* (#95)

93. Fright Night 5.13c PG
65' (19m) in length, 8 QD's

A serious and committing climb. Presently the most difficult route at Broughton Bluff. Local climbers make the climb a bit more rewarding by exiting left to Dracula at the second to last bolt. This avoids the difficult crux on Fright Night but still commits you to stellar climbing and the opportunity to send the Dracula 'pod' one more time.

94. The Haunting 5.12b ★
65' (19m) in length, 5 QD's and pro to 2"

Originally called Snap, Crackle, Pop (aid climb), this fascinating vertical seam has yielded a sequential and difficult free climb of modern standards. Ascend the seam 25', then angle right across Bad Omen and enter a fist jam that eases to a hand crack (5.9) corner ending at

Dave S. on *Bad Omen*

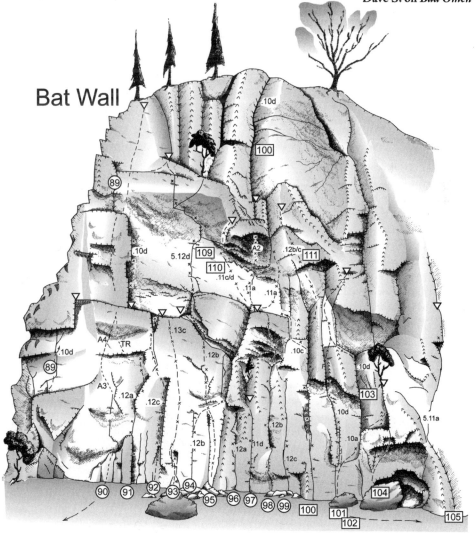

Bat Wall

Bat Wall routes from *Bad Omen* (#95) to *Well Hung* (#104)

the Superstition belay anchor.

95. Bad Omen   5.12b   ★ ★ ★

65' (19m) in length, 10 QD's

Superb! Another Broughton super classic. Begin up a steep face via side pulls to a thin stance, move over the bulge (crux) and up small edges to an unorthodox high step (crux). Carefully work up a left leaning flared slot until a protruding roof forces you left and up to a sloping ledge and bolt belay. Rappel.

96. Danse Macabre   5.12a

40' (12m) in length, 3 QD's

97. Bloodsucker   5.11d

40' (12m) in length, 3 QD's

98. Bloodline   5.12b   ★ ★ ★

65' (19m) in length, 7 QD's

Originally called Beeline, this gusto climb offers the local rock jock a bold start and a fantastic roof to exit through. One of the most exciting and interesting routes on the Bat Wall. Layback up an overhung face to several natural pockets then crack up to a stance. Balance up a smooth section then up a thin crack to a stance below a large roof. Start on the right and power up left then over the lip and finally to the ledge and bolt belay for Superstition.

David working on *Lost Boys*

99. Predator 5.12c

60' (19m) in length, QD's

100. Superstition III 5.11a ★★★

Multi-pitch, Pro to 2"

First pitch QD's and minor pro to 1"

A great route and quite popular, particularly the first pitch. Step up onto an outside corner and ascend a shallow groove corner system until possible to smear left via under clings (5.10+). Move up a thin crack then crawl left along on a narrow ledge to a bolt anchor. Rappel, or [option #1] continue up the old route on bad rock, and bad pins up a vertical face above to the roof (the ¼" bolt line out the large

Stephanie D'Cruz, *Superstition 5.11a*

roof is "Snap, Crackle, Pop"), then fight (5.11a) rightward around a corner up to a belay ledge. Or [option #2] step to the right from this first belay and climb a better second pitch option. This is a good climb that ascends up 4 bolts (5.11a) to an anchor. From the second belay, continue up the crack corner above to a steep, nettle filled and surprisingly strenuous wide crack problem (5.10d). Rappel with 2 ropes to the ground.

101. Lost Boys 5.10d ★★

70' (21m) in length, 8 QD's

A fun climb and an excellent warm-up. On the right side of the Bat Wall are several large boulders in front of a cave. Begin behind the left one, face climb up to an overhang (crux) with a slot. Move up, then right, mantle, then up until you can exit right via an under cling and reach (crux) around a corner to a bolt anchor on a ledge. Rappel.

102. Mystic Void 5.10a

45' (13m) in length, Pro to 1"

Ascends the face left of, then joins with Well Hung just above the large roof. Rappel from bolts at the maple tree.

103. Mystic Pizza 5.10d

70' (21m) in length, QD's and pro to 1½"

An interesting variation with good pro. Start as for Mystic Void; instead of traversing to the right to join Well Hung, continue up the obvious corner system then exit up left (crux) to join Lost Boys.

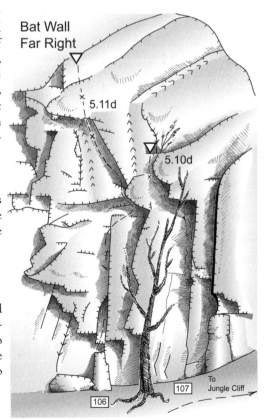

Bat Wall
Far Right

5.11d

5.10d

To
Jungle Cliff

107

106

Ten Great Trad Routes Under 5.10

For those who relish the challenge of placing pro while on lead, here is a great selection of stellar gear routes under 5.10.

1. Gandalf's Grip, 5.9, Broughton
2. The Sickle, 5.8, Broughton
3. Loose Block O., 5.9, Broughton
4. Classic Crack, 5.9, Broughton
5. Free For All, 5.8, Beacon Rock

6. Jill's Thrill, 5.9, Beacon Rock
7. SE Face Route, 5.7, Beacon Rock
8. Cruisin', 5.7, Beacon Rock
9. New Generation, 5.8 P1, Carver
10. Cornicks Corner, 5.9, Madrone

---

104. Well Hung   5.10b   ★★
45' (13m) in length, Pro to 1"
An original Bat Wall favorite, even if it is a bit dirty. Step directly off the large boulders onto the face under the large roof. Traverse right then swing onto the roof via jug holds to a stance. Move up the corner to the bolt anchor at the maple tree. Rappel.

105. Gold Arch   5.11a
70' (21m) in length, Pro to 3"
At one time a fantastic line, but getting dirtier every year due to soil erosion from the field above the cliff. Start 30' right of Well Hung and ascend a slab then a strenuous barn door lie back on a gold-streaked wall to a belay. The second pitch leads to easier ground above.

The next climbs are found at the extreme southern end of the Bat Wall.

106. The Hunger   5.11d
55' (16m) in length, Pro to 1½" and cams suggested
Physically difficult route, but a little dirty.

107. Dark Shadows   5.10d   ★
40' (12m) in length, Pro to 1½"
TCU's recommended
Originally called Shadow Dancing (5.8 A2), this climb was easily freed to produce a unique problem. Ascend a face to a left facing corner capped by a large roof. Step left, then up, then left (crux) past fixed pitons and up to a belay anchor on a small ledge. Rappel.

108. _____

The following routes are located on the upper headwall of the Bat Wall.

109. MF Reunion   5.12d   ★★
60' (18m) in length, 7 QD's
A high quality route that is located above Fright Night. Though seldom climbed, this route ascends a surprisingly stunning sec-

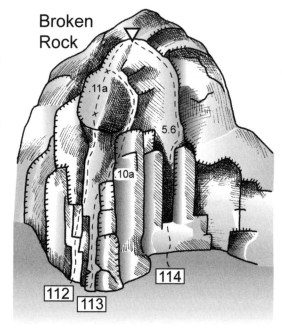

Broken Rock

tion of the Bat Wall. From the Bad Omen anchor climb up a short corner to a stance, then crimp up past a blank crux section. Embark up left on incut crack edges out a smooth round overhang to a belay at a ledge.

110. Vampyr   5.11c/d

Pro QD's

This bolt route climbs up left from the first pitch belay on Superstition. There are four bolts to the next belay anchor.

111. Remain in Light   5.12 b/c

Pro QD's

Where Superstition moves left on the first pitch crux, this route instead continues up the corner, then steps right onto Lost Boys, then continues up a slightly hung section and eventually steps left to merge again with Superstition at the next belay. If you climb straight up past the last bolt to the anchor it is 5.12b/c, but if you move left and climb up 5' before moving back right to the last bolt it is considered 5.11d/12a.

Immediately south of the Bat Wall are several outcrops of rock. The first small bluff is a blocky short vertical chunk known as Broken Rock. The trail beyond this outcrop contains the remaining hidden walls of Broughton Bluff, steeped in mysterious lore.

BROKEN ROCK

112. Static Cling   5.11a

35' (10m) in length, pro to ¾", small TCU's

Height is a factor when moving past the first bolt. A variation using part of Plan B route is 5.10d.

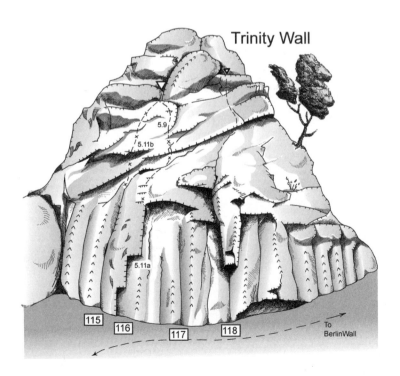

113.   Plan B   5.10a

35' (10m) in length, Pro to 2", 1½" Friend and #0 TCU recommended

114.   Lickity Split   5.6   ★

35' (10m) in length, Pro to 2", including a 3½" Friend

An interesting route.

TRINITY WALL

115.   Bust A' Move   5.11b   ★

40' (12m) in length, 4 QD's and pro to 1"

Terrific climb with a surprising crux. Commence up a shallow corner then over a minor bulge. Angle rightward via thin holds and under clings (crux), then up an easy corner to a bolt anchor. Rappel.

116.   Father   5.11a

40' (12m) in length, Pro to 1½"

Quality climb. Ascend the strenuous right-facing corner until possible to exit up left onto a slab. Move up right on easy ground then up left (bolt) in the center of the face, and left to the bolt anchor in a corner. Rappel.

117.   _____

40' (TR)

Berlin Wall

118. _____

40' (TR)

BERLIN WALL

119. Closet Nazi 5.12a ★★ 🌂

45' (13m) in length, 5 QD's

Remarkable and highly challenging route. Climb the bolt line on the left side of the wall up very clean, overhung rock. Can be a virtual stream of water during the winter months.

120. Recipe for Airtime II A3 🌂

30' (9m) in length, Pitons and natural pro

121. Twist and Crawl 5.11d 🌂

40' (12m) in length, 5 QD's

Located in the center of the wall directly under the huge roof. Unusual yet quite good. Move up a dihedral around a crux corner then up and out the overhang to the anchor.

122. Genocide 5.12d / 5.13a 🌂

40' (12m) in length, 5 QD's (1" nut or cam to start)

To the right of Twist and Crawl is another route on this virtually upsidedown wall. Start up a crack on a slab then up via physically articulate moves out the overhang to a bolt anchor.

123. Pride and Joy 5.10a

40' (12m) in length, Pro to 1", Small wires recommended

On the far right side of Berlin Wall is a smooth vertical section of rock broken with several thin cracks. The left is a 5.10a, the right is a top-rope. Takes good pro. Rappel from the tree anchor directly above the top-rope problem.

124. _____ 5.10

40' (12m) in length (TR)

The next two crags are located on private land. The Jungle Cliff has a layer of thinly caked dirt due to water runoff from the field above the wall, especially from the center of the wall to the right side.

JUNGLE CLIFF

125. Zimbabwe II 5.10a

Multi-pitch, Pro to 3", Cams recommended

Ascends the steep face on the far left corner of Jungle Cliff via numerous ledges.

126. Slash and Burn 5.12a

60' (18m) in length, QD's and minor pro to 2"

A good route on fantastic steep rock. Begin at the cave, pull up (5.9), move up the slab to the right, then up the face to an anchor. Continue up the overhanging corner above, move left at difficult section and finish up a vertical dihedral to a final crux move. Rappel from bolt anchor.

127. Under the Yum Yum Tree 5.10d

50' (15m) in length, Pro to 2", Needs bolts

Fun climb with an appropriate name. Start to the right of the cave and ascend a dusty slab via a thin crack and corner system to a bolt anchor.

128. Tarzan 5.12d

50' (15m) in length, 7 QD's

The obvious and impressive arête. Tarzan is definitely one of the most unusual routes of this kind at Broughton Bluff. Worth the blast.

129. Crime Wave 5.10c PG

50' (15m) in length, QD's, TCU's, #2 Friend recommended

A slightly awkward variation next to Gorilla Love Affair.

130. Gorilla Love Affair 5.10d ★★★

50' (15m) in length, 6 QD's, optional TCU's

A very exhilarating climb. Stem up to a small roof, move left, then up to another roof. Step right and up a smooth dihedral (crux) until possible to step left to finish up a crack leading to the bolt belay for Under the Yum Yum Tree. Rappel.

131. Out of Africa II 5.9 A3

132. Heart of Darkness 5.12b ★★

80' (24m) in length, 10 QD's

A beautiful route that leads up an overhung arête in the heart of Jungle Cliff country. Desperately struggle out the overhung start to a stance, then up and left along a hand ramp. Pull through the crux (thin) then up the right side of the arête to a stance. Make a quick move up a smooth face and up to a tiny stance belay. Proceed up left out the fiercely overhung headwall (5 bolts and 5.11d) via face and jug holds. Rappel with 2 ropes.

133. Mowgli Direct 5.12b

40' (12m) in length, QD's

Located between Heart of Darkness and Mowgli's Revenge.

134. Mowgli's Revenge 5.11b

40' (12m) in length, 4 QD's

Underneath a large roof to the right of Heart of Darkness, you will find two bolt routes. The left one is Mowgli's Revenge. An interesting climb that exits the roof on the left side. Rappel from bolt anchor.

135. Amazon Woman 5.10d ★

40' (12m) in length, 4 QD's and minor pro to 1½" Cams recommended

Commence up a vertical stem problem via small edges to a stance. Reach up right under the roof, then traverse right and exit to a good stance. Step up a wide crack to a huge ledge and bolt belay. Rappel.

136. Amazon Man 5.11d (or III 5.11 A3) ★★★

Multi-pitch, Pro to 3", Bring KB & LA

This formidable achievement, put up in 1979, penetrates through the heart of Jungle Cliff. Begin up a corner (immediately right of Amazon Woman) past a fixed piton to a stance, then up a wide crack to a big ledge with a good anchor. Mowgli's Revenge joins here. Continue up by one of two cracks to a stance, then delicately traverse left via sloping ledges (bolts) to the Heart of Darkness belay. Ascend directly above you (5.10+) to another belay then move right around the sweet headwall and up a difficult section. Belay at bolts on Skull Ledge. Storm the dihedral (5.11 D) directly above that leads to the summit. Monkey Paws route (5.11b) is the face climb at right side of skull ledge. Rappel with 2 ropes.

137. Killer Pygmy   III 5.10+ A4   ★

Multi-pitch, Pro to 4", Cams, TCU's, KB, LA, Angles and bolts

Outrageous aid line that boldly pushes up the smooth center face to Skull Ledge. The final pitch angles up right via two optional cracks (A2).

138. Mujahadeen   II 5.10d A3

80' (24m) in length, Pro to 4", including KB, LA, and Angles

The entire right side of Jungle Cliff has a thin layer of dried mud on the surface which makes free climbing illogical. But nailing is another story...dirt, dust and all.

NEW FRONTIER CLIFF

139. Luck of the Draw   5.11a

80' (24m) in length, QD's and pro to 1"

140. Touch and Go (variation)   5.10c

80' (24m) in length, QD's and pro to 1"

141. Alma Mater   5.10d   ★ ★ ★

80' (24m) in length, QD's

Beautiful steep slab on the left side of New Frontier Cliff. Commence up an odd balance start (5.10d) until it eases to a continuous, fun 5.8 climb ending on a ledge. Rappel.

142. Split Decision   5.8

30' (9m) in length, Pro to 4"

Climb the wide crack immediately right of Alma Mater.

143. Tin Star   5.8

60' (18m) in length, Pro to 1½"

Climb the outside of the block to the belay ledge, then continue up left onto a face (bolts) and up to an anchor.

144. True Grit   5.9

80' (24m) in length, Pro to 2"

From the top of the block step up left into dihedral and up this to top.

145. Pony Express   5.6

30' (9m) in length, Pro to 2"

This is the route on the right side of the block.

146. Happy Trails II 5.10a

Multi-pitch, Pro to 3"

Interesting climb with some grungy, loose sections. Walk to the right side of the wall (trail's end). Above is a

Jungle Cliff
Map 2: Amazon Woman

132 Heart of Darkness

133 Mowgli Direct

134 Mowgli's Revenge

135 Amazon Woman

136 Amazon Man

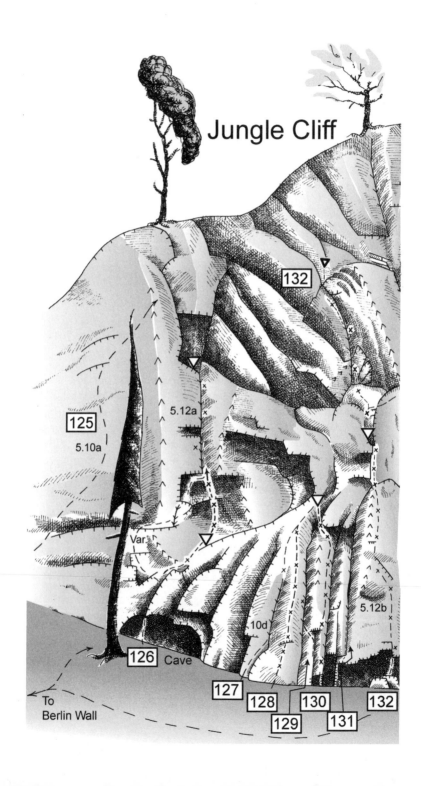

Jungle Cliff

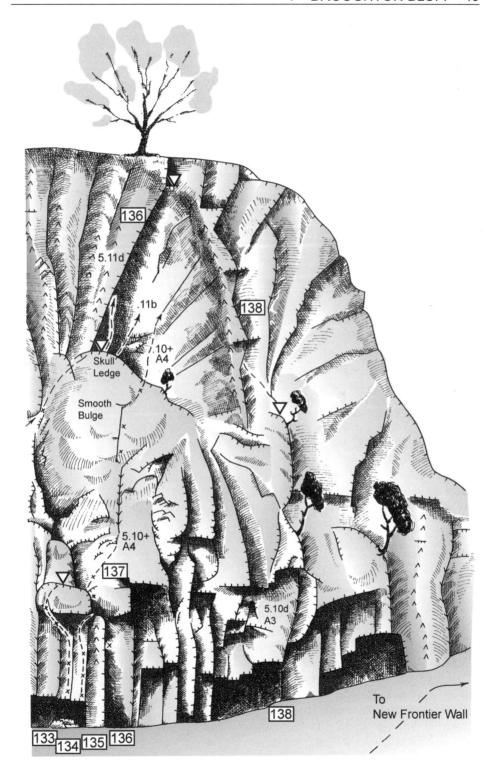

136

5.11d

.11b

138

.10+
A4

Skull
Ledge

Smooth
Bulge

5.10+
A4

137

5.10d
A3

To
New Frontier Wall

138

133 134 135 136

The List

This list provides a diverse selection of challenging routes from traditional gear climbs to mixed climbs, as well as sport climbs. This is not a beginners list, but a base from which to refine your strengths and to carry your skill to a new level. The lowest rated climb is 5.9 and the peak rating is a mere 5.12a. This well-rounded spectrum progressively encourages you to strengthen your core leading abilities in the 5.10-/5.11+ range.

Broughton Bluff
1. Gandalf's Grip (complete) 5.9+ ☐
2. Classic Crack 5.9 ☐
3. Sheer Stress (complete) 5.10a ☐
4. Free Bird 5.11a ☐
5. Dracula 5.12a ☐
6. Superstition (complete) 5.11a ☐
7. Lost Boys 5.10d ☐

Rocky Butte Quarry
8. Phylynx 5.11b ☐

Carver Bridge Cliff
9. Uncola 5.11c ☐
10. Smerk (complete) 5.11a ☐
11. New Generation 5.9 ☐
12. Angular Motion 5.12a ☐

Madrone Wall
13. Where The Wild Things Roam 5.11d ☐
14. Beam Me Up Mr. Scott 5.11c ☐
15. Ant Abuse 5.10a ☐
16. Mr. Noodle Arm 5.11b ☐
17. Nouveau Riche 5.10c ☐

Ozone Wall
18. Snake Roof 5.10a ☐
19. Masterpiece Theater 5.11c ☐
20. Carrots For Everyone 5.10a ☐
21. May Day 5.10c ☐
22. Chain Mail 5.11b ☐
23. High Plains Drifter 5.10d/.11a ☐
24. Stepchild 5.10a ☐

Beacon Rock
25. Jill's Thrill 5.9 ☐
26. Fear of Flying 5.10b ☐
27. Blownout (complete) 5.10b ☐
28. Borderline (second pitch) 5.11b ☐
29. Flying Swallow (complete) 5.10d ☐
30. Blood, Sweat and Smears 5.10c ☐
31. Steppenwolf (to Big Ledge) 5.10c ☐
32. Free for Some (complete) 5.11a ☐
33. Pipeline 5.11b ☐

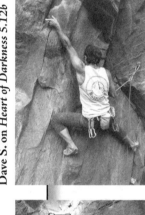

Dave S. on *Heart of Darkness* 5.12b

Kay Kucera climbing *Lost Boys* 5.10d

The Spring 5.10a/b

Chris on *Shoot from the Hip*

Heart of Darkness 5.12b

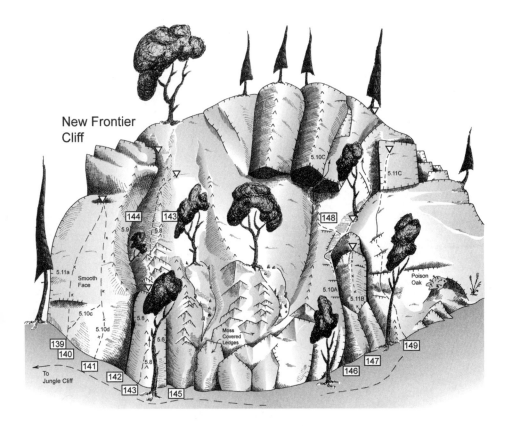

short clean jam crack that pulls through a slot to a left-facing slab corner. Climb this and enter into a loose chimney then belay at the oak tree. Continue up right a few moves until you can under cling left then up a broken slab above to top out. Rappel or walk off.

147. Wild Wild West 5.10c

60' (18m) in length, Pro to 3", cams suggested

Climb the first pitch of Happy Trails. From the oak tree, step left to a crack then up to a large roof. Under cling out right (crux) and around corner (rope jams easily) then up easy cracks to the top.

148. Pioneer Spirit 5.11b

45' (13m) in length, 4 QD's and minor pro to 1"

Climb the short, clean jam crack of Happy Trails. Step right and then up this tantalizing face climb. The crux is a blind lunge. Rappel from bolt anchor.

149. Promised Land 5.11c R

80' (24m) in length, Pro to 3", cams and small wires, RP's recommended

Superb climb on beautiful rock, yet located virtually "at the end of the Broughton world." Start to the right of Happy Trails and behind several trees. Pull up an easy bulge, move up left on a slab to a vertical step. From a ledge, climb the exciting and steep crack system to a huge block. Lean out right (bolt) and layback up the arête to a bolt anchor. Route is totally overgrown.

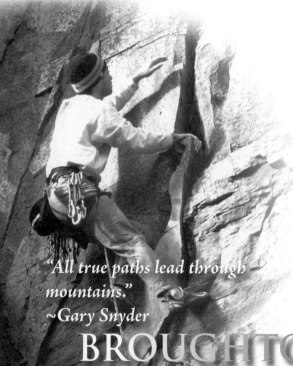

"All true paths lead through mountains."
~Gary Snyder

Monty Mayko climbing the popular
Sheer Energy 5.10a

BROUGHTON BLUFF

CHAPTER 2

ROCKY BUTTE QUARRY

THIS UNIQUE INNER CITY CRAG located in northeast Portland provides enjoyable roadside rock climbing opportunities for all age groups. Whether your rock climbing skill level is beginning, intermediate, or advanced, the one-hundred-plus crack and face climbs on this steep basalt crag provide excellent scope and variety that will challenge you on to ever greater goals in the sport of rock climbing.

North facing, and overlooking a distant Columbia River, the surprisingly extensive and tall Rocky Butte Quarry is the ideal place for rappelling, top-roping, or lead climbing. With just a one-minute walk from the parking area you can access the upper edge of this crag to explore some of these favorite climbs.

Though the cliffs of the main quarry are located close to the busy I-205 freeway corridor, a canopy of trees provides ample cool and comfortable shade as well as a green barrier from the nearby freeway. Even during hot summer days this enjoyable crag continues to be a popular climbing area offering a great respite from the humid summer temperature.

The Joseph Wood Hill Park on the very top of Rocky Butte is a great place to view the city of Portland as well as a perfect site for instructing beginning climbers the "ropes" of climbing. Park along the west side of the loop road at the top of Rocky Butte. Along the inner side of the loop road is the "castle," a majestic, circular-shaped stone walled platform that was at one time rumored to be part of the defenses for the Bonneville Dam in the late-1930s.

A low, angled roadside retaining wall *above* the road partially encircles the upper "castle." This slab offers the novice rock climber a great place to grasp the basic techniques of balance, top-roping, and simple rappelling. The vertical short wall of the upper main fortress provides excellent and challenging horizontal bouldering, including several fun corner problems.

On the west side of this fortress and *below* the road is a vertical 20-foot-high, 200-foot-wide retaining wall. A sawdust platform trail runs along the entire base of this wall creating quick access to a great bouldering area for climbers of all skill levels.

Bri Stekly on *Orient Express 5.8*

⊟ BRIEF HISTORY OF THE AREA

In 1931, Rocky Butte was purchased by Joseph Wood Hill where he built and operated a military academy. Portions of land on the butte were donated to Multnomah County in 1935. With federal funding through President Roosevelt's administration, the New Deal idea promoted a Work Project Authority (WPA) to start construction of a road to the top of the butte.

Rock from the quarry on the north side of the butte was used for road abutments and retaining walls. With the guidance of an Italian stone mason the scenic road and the castle-like formation at the top of the butte proved a resounding success for the people of the area. The west side road project, started in 1938, now provides tourists a unique road

Rocky Butte Quarry: The Heart of Urban Climbing

with the turn enclosed entirely inside the tunnel.

The scenic views of the Columbia River Gorge and the evening lights of the City of Portland from the heights atop Rocky Butte are splendid.

Today, the Portland Bible College and City Bible Church with its large round church domes are now located at the site of the old Hill Military Academy. Other stonework facilities, such as the Rocky Butte Jail, were built from locally quarried material. The old jail site on the east side of the butte is now part of the I-205 freeway corridor.

After rock quarrying at the butte ended in 1956, the Mazamas and other groups began frequenting the north-facing bluff to practice rappelling. Numerous old bolt lines and ring pitons provided evidence of those early years of aid climbing at the quarry.

The late 1970s brought a new era to the quarry: the sport of free climbing. Some of those early free climbs quickly attained popular recognition, such as Blackberry Jam (5.10a), first ascended in 1974 by Jim Davis and T. Crossman. Other climbs such as Espresso (5.9) and White Rabbit (5.10b) in 1977; Bird of Paradise (5.10c) in 1979; and Toothpick (5.11c), Close to the Edge (5.11+), and Blueberry Jam (5.10a) were soon to follow.

Those young people who proved instrumental during the 1970s phase were key to the future of climbing here. Doug Bower, Bill Coe, Jay Kerr, Robert McGown, Mike Smelsar, John Sprecher, Scott Woolums, and others continued to expand the scope of rock climbing at Rocky Butte. Though climbing activity at the crag fell quiet from 1979 to 1984, these same people as well as Mike Pajunas, Wayne Wallace, Joe Parsley, Gary Rall, and others eventually tamed the Rocky Butte "frontier" in the late 1980s.

Scores of urban classic climbs were produced: Bite the Bullet (5.11a), Fandango (5.10c), Live Wire (5.11a), Edge of Might (5.11b), Stranger than Friction (5.10a), Zeeva's (5.10b), Phylynx (5.11b), Crack Warrior (5.11b), Emotional Rescue (5.10b), Vertical Therapy (5.9), Red Zinger (5.11c), and many more.

Rock climbers who frequent the quarry these days generally use it as a top-rope climbing area. The popular rock climbs have fixed bolt anchors or tree affixed top-rope chains near the top of the route. There are a number of routes that are still leadable climbs, such as Emotional Rescue or Flakey Old Man, if you are so inclined.

The close proximity to the city and the increased presence of human traffic unfortunately brought several environmental drawbacks. Spray-painted graffiti on the walls, garbage dumped over the cliff edge, broken glass, and traffic noise from the busy I-205 freeway are the most obvious. Most of these can be easily overlooked by using a ground tarp. The pesky plant *Rhus diversiloba* (poison oak) is prevalent throughout the area and grows along the access trails and on some of the climbs, but it is generally kept beaten back by regular climber presence. This crag is very accessible to the public, especially for the local rock climber seeking a quick escape from the office blues.

On a positive note, the Oregon chapter of the Access Fund promotes a Bi-Annual Rocky Butte

Tyler leading *Flakey Old Man 5.7*

Quarry Cleanup day. You are welcome to join the work party to help remove junk and clean up the access trails. For many years now this event has provided the positive means for us to keep this city park a climber-friendly environment.

At the top edge of the quarry cliff, numerous trees offer a convenient means for climbers to set up a strong top-rope anchor belay point. Many of the popular climbs also have excellent fixed bolt anchors near the upper edge of the climbs, but be cautious when accessing these anchors as they tend to be very near to the edge of the precipice. In certain places these anchors were established on the vertical face at the top of the climb. In all cases, use additional precautionary measures when approaching the edge of the cliff to locate and set up your top-rope anchor.

Thanks to the interest sparked by the *Rocky Butte Quarry: A Climber's Guide to Urban Rock* (1987) by Mike Pajunas and Bob McGown, climber activity at this crag has increased rapidly. The trails have improved with use, while the overall image of our Rocky Butte Quarry has changed for the better.

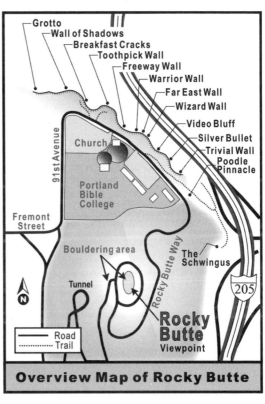

Overview Map of Rocky Butte

This chapter on the quarry describes thirteen sections of wall in detail with topographical reference maps for the areas that are most frequently visited by rock climbers. Only a few of the climbs west of the Breakfast Cracks area are mentioned here. The following are described from right to left as you would encounter the bluff from above. They are: Poodle Pinnacle, Trivial Wall, Silver Bullet Bluff, Video Bluff, Dream Weaver Wall, Wizard Wall, Far East Wall, Warrior Wall, Freeway Wall, Mean Street, Easy Street, Toothpick Wall, and Breakfast Cracks. The Wall of Shadows and the Grotto area have not been detailed.

VISUAL BIO

These emblems represent virtually all of the Rocky Butte Quarry climbing site when accessed from NE Rocky Butte road. If you plan to start your proposed climb at the bottom of the bluff (such as Emotional Rescue) it will take about five minutes to descend to the base on one of the nar-

David leading *Emotional Rescue*

row steep trails.

📓 🚴🏂 HOW TO GET THERE

The Rocky Butte Quarry is located quite near the intersection of the I-84 and I-205 freeways. To visit this Portland climbing crag, take exit #5 eastbound off I-84 (or exit #23 from I-205 at Sandy Blvd). Once you are on NE 82nd Avenue, drive to the point where it intersects with NE Fremont Street. Turn east and drive approximately ½ mile until the road curves north to become 91st Avenue. Shortly the road curves east again and becomes NE Rocky Butte Way. The quarry cliff is accessed on your immediate left or northeast side of the road across from the City Bible Church domes. Parking is available for 0.3 mile along the road shoulder from the last house (Breakfast Cracks area) to the stone retaining wall (Video Bluff area) at the eastern end of this short stretch of road. Do NOT park in the Bible College parking area.

To reach the bouldering areas, continue on Rocky Butte Way as it loops up clockwise to the top of the butte. The views of the City of Roses and the surrounding mountains from the butte are exceptional.

POODLE PINNACLE
Poodle with a Mohawk 5.11a

Pro to 2½"

A neat climb located by itself along the eastern perimeter trail. Hike approximately 300' along the trail. Above the trail is a face with an easy start, a crack and an outside arête. Lead this to a tree and rappel.

TRIVIAL WALL

Hike east on the Rocky Butte Perimeter Trail to the tunnel under the roadway. Continue a few feet on the trail further and then angle north toward the cliff. There are belay anchors at the lip of the small outcrop. The base of Trivial Wall can be accessed on foot by a narrow steep path just to the east.

1. **Harlequin   5.10b**   ★
   Pro to 1½"
   Good climb. Commence up an easy slab and follow a curved crack up right (25') until it eases near the top.

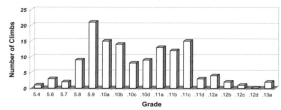

ROCKY BUTTE QUARRY

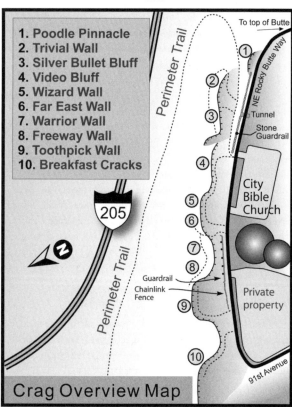

1. Poodle Pinnacle
2. Trivial Wall
3. Silver Bullet Bluff
4. Video Bluff
5. Wizard Wall
6. Far East Wall
7. Warrior Wall
8. Freeway Wall
9. Toothpick Wall
10. Breakfast Cracks

To top of Butte

NE Rocky Butte Way

Perimeter Trail

Tunnel

Stone Guardrail

City Bible Church

205

Private property

Guardrail
Chainlink Fence

91st Avenue

Crag Overview Map

2. Trivial Pursuit   5.10b
Pro to 1½"
A minor face climb.

3. The Joker   5.8

SILVER BULLET BLUFF

Aptly named because of all the bullet scars dotting the face of this crag. Approach by hiking east along the perimeter trail to the tunnel under the roadway. Aim north to the crag and step 20' down to a large ledge. Belay at the ledge for the routes on the main wall below. The height is approximately 40' (12m).

4. Captain She's Breaking Up   5.8 R
Pro to 2"

5. _____

6. Sundance Kid   5.10a
Neat shallow corner climb on upper left corner of Silver Bullet Bluff.

7. Panama Red   5.9+
Climb the smooth face broken with small ledges and cracks immediately right of Sundance Kid.

8. Miss Kitty   5.7

9. Gunsmoke   5.9 ★★
An excellent easy face climb just left of Bite the Bullet.

10. Bite the Bullet   5.11a R   ★★★
One of the best routes on Silver Bullet Bluff. Start up left of a tree and on a face with good but angled edges. From a good stance 15' up angle left onto a bullet-scarred face and climb desperately to a sloping ledge, then move up right to join with the last move on Jack of Hearts. Bite the Bullet has 5 bolts and gear to 1" if you are inclined to lead the route.

11. Jack of Heart   5.9+   ★★★
Pro to 1"
An exciting thin crack climb. Start up a short right facing corner to a stance, and then up a thin crack to a sloping ledge. Finish up a last vertical step to the belay ledge.

12. Silver Bullet   5.9 R
A good route that starts up the face, then enters a dihedral that is lacking a crack. Smear up the corner to join with Jack of Hearts.

13. Urban Cowboy   5.8 R

14. Last Tango   5.10a

15. Fandango   5.10c R   ★★★
A superb route of only moderate difficulty. Start up a crack on a slab left of a main corner. From an easy stance continue up the crack on the vertical face, follow the left crack and pull a mantle (crux). Move up further via a corner to a ledge. Belay from the large tree above.

16. Midnight Warrior   5.8
Pro to 2"
The main corner on this side of the wall.

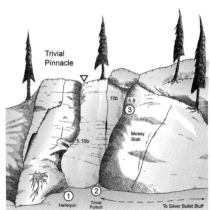

Central aspect of Silver Bullet Bluff, Rocky Butte Quarry

⑪ ⑫ ⑬ ⑭ ⑮ ⑯

Silver Bullet Bluff

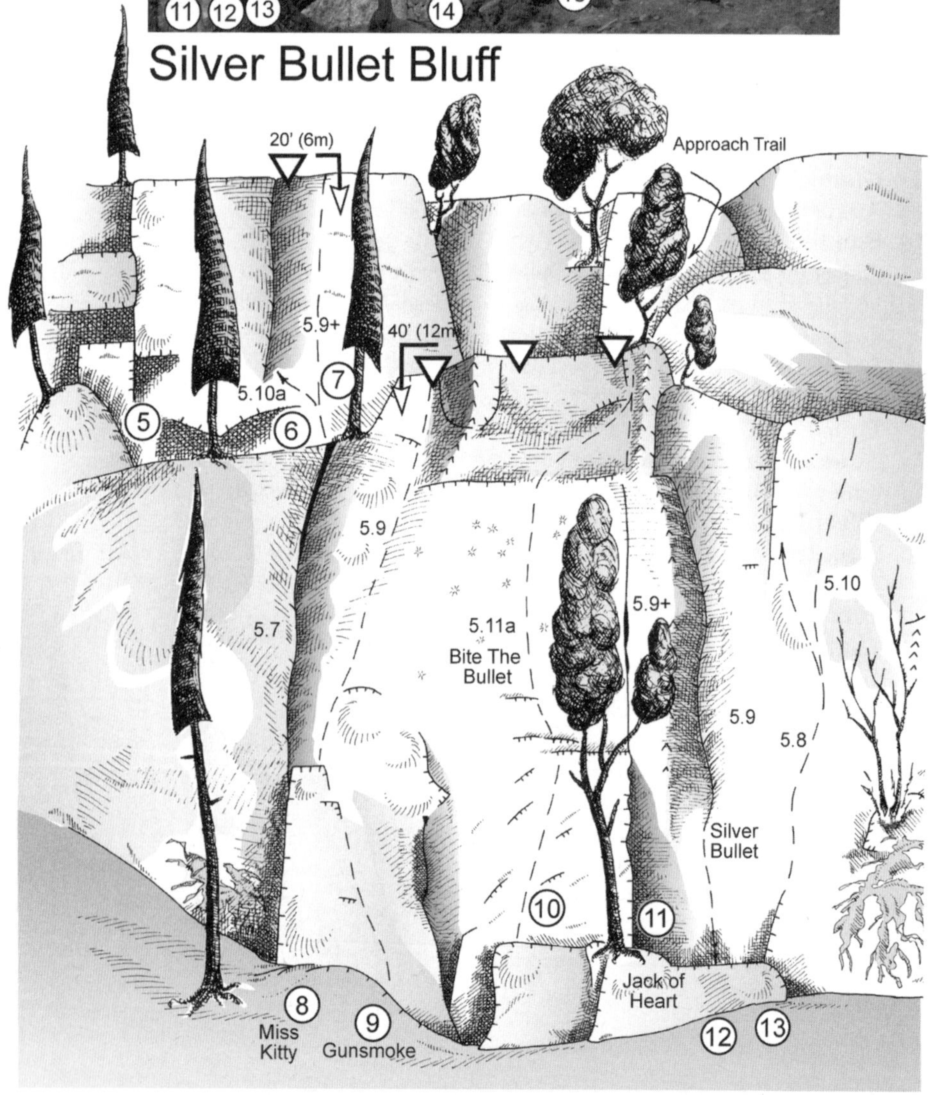

20' (6m)

Approach Trail

5.9+

40' (12m)

5.10a

⑤ ⑥ ⑦

5.9

5.7

5.11a
Bite The
Bullet

5.9+

5.10

5.9

5.8

Silver
Bullet

⑩ ⑪

Jack of
Heart

⑧ ⑨ ⑫ ⑬
Miss   Gunsmoke
Kitty

Climber on *Superman* 5.8, Silver Bullet Bluff.

Damaged Circuit 5.11a

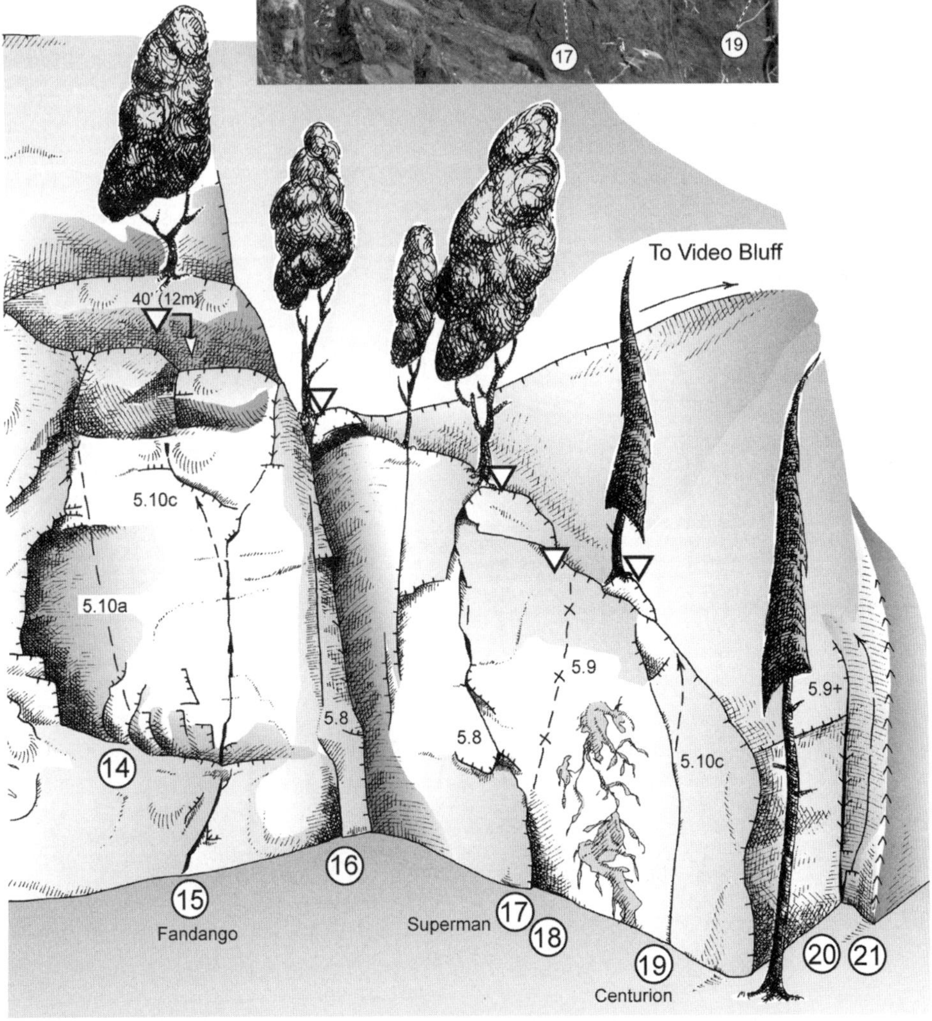

16

17

18

19

To Video Bluff

40' (12m)

5.10c

5.10a

5.8

5.8

5.9

5.10c

5.9+

14

15
Fandango

16

17
18
Superman

19
Centurion

20 21

17. Superman   5.8 R   ★★

Pro to 1"

A fun problem on good edges and sloping smears.

18. Glenn's Route   5.8

Pro is 3 QD's

Starts at the same crack as Superman but aim straight up the face to a bolt anchor at the edge of the cliff.

19. Centurion   5.10d   ★

A unique short vertical crack problem on the lower right corner of this wall. Climb the crack until you can reach over right (crux) and up to easy steps and tree belay.

20. Invisible Man   5.9+

21. Temporary Arête   5.10a

VIDEO BLUFF

One of the most popular walls at Rocky Butte. Excellent place to top-rope and learn technique. Approach Video Bluff by parking at the easternmost pullout just before the stone retaining wall and walk north a short distance to the crag. A well established trail meanders along the top of the precipice above Video Bluff. It loops along at the top of this crag and continues to the west to emerge onto the roadway at the guardrail descent trail. This trail gives excellent and quick access to setting up TR on virtually all the climbs from Video Bluff to the Warrior Wall. Cliff height is approx. 35' (10m).

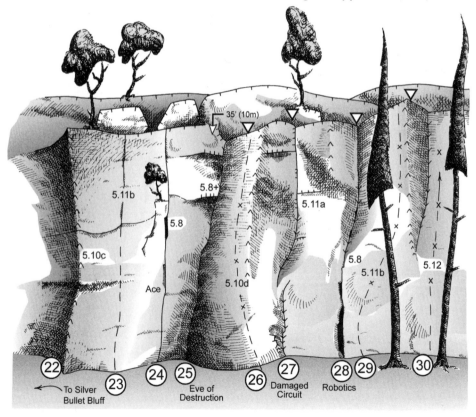

22. Body Language   5.10c R

The overhanging arête with a horizontal crack halfway up.

23. Body Bionics   5.11b R

24. Ace   5.8

25. Eve of Destruction   5.8+   ★★

A slabby dihedral problem. A good practice climb.

26. Live Wire   5.10d   ★

4 QD's

Difficult face climb on the round outside corner to the right of Eve of Destruction.

27. Damaged Circuit   5.11a   ★★

Challenging stem problem up a shallow scoop. Begin up a shattered start, pull a thin move to an awkward stance, then smear, stem up a face using strange finger holds in the seam.

28. Robotics   5.8

29. Edge of Might   5.11b   ★★

Fantastic climb. Begin up the face immediately right of Robotics and angle up onto the arête. Thin holds and pinches on the arête are the crux.

30. Hard Contact   5.12

31. Lever or Leaver   5.10c

4 QD's

Can be climbed using a difficult direct start.

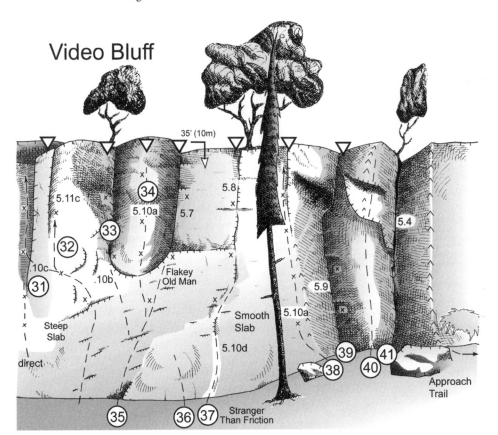

Video Bluff

32. Persistence of Time   5.11c

4 QD's

33. Zeeva   5.10b ★

3 QD's

An interesting steep corner climb with balancy moves.

34. Bikini   5.10a ★★

4 QD's

A popular face climb on a minor rounded buttress immediately left of Flakey Old Man.

35. Flakey Old Man   5.7 ★★★

4 QD's

The flake has long since fallen away but the popularity of this and other nearby routes continue to be a favorite for everyone to climb or top-rope.

36. MTV   5.10a

Minor boulder problem variation following the left seam at the ground.

37. Stranger Than Friction   5.10+ ★★★

In the center of the slab is a pocketed boulder start and slap move leading upward to a seam. The local classic on this wall and certainly worth it. The initial boulder move is a very long height dependent reach from a pocket to a small edge. Once you get past the initial bouldery crux start off the ground the remainder of the climb is a mere 5.8.

38. Panes of Reality   5.10a ★

4 QD's

Step left and up onto the face immediately left of Stained Glass. A neat problem on a rounded bulge.

39. Stained Glass   5.9 ★

QD's and pro to 2"

Obvious fun dihedral corner.

40. Toxic Waltz   5.11d

4 QD's

Vertical face to the right of the dihedral.

41. E-Z Corner   5.4

Bill's Buttress is a buttress-like formation about 70' to the west of Video Bluff that provides several rock climbs developed by Bill Coe. The climbs here are approximately 90' (27m) in length and have good anchors at the top of the crag for ease of access. A 60-meter rope is wise. There are presently five routes ranging from 5.8 to 5.10 and three possible variations in-between. Beware of the broken glass along the top and the base of this section of cliff.

DREAM WEAVER WALL

This is a narrow section of wall located between Video Bluff and Wizard Wall. These climbs are good though infrequently ascended. Height is approximately 65' (19m).

42. Dream Weaver 5.9 ★
Pro to 2"

43. Head Bangers Ball 5.10a
Pro to 1½"

44. Tiger's Pause 5.9 ★
Pro to 2"

45. Kleen Korner 5.9

WIZARD WALL

One of the finest long vertical sections of rock at the Butte. All of the routes are located on the upper half of the wall. Either set up a TR belay from the trees at the top of the cliff or rappel down approximately 70' (21m) to bolt anchors on the lower ledges and then lead climb back up. This wall is of superb quality, yielding some of the finest high angle face climbs at Rocky Butte.

46. Naked Savage 5.10a

47. Lord of the Jungle 5.9+ (variation)

48. Slavemaker 5.10b

49. Grub 5.10c
Pro to 3" Cams suggested

50. Eye in the Sky 5.10c R ★
Pro to 1"
Start at the Phylynx belay, but stay just to the left of the route on an outside corner after the bulge crux.

51. Phylynx 5.11b ★★★
Pro to 1½"
One of the finest routes at Rocky Butte. Rappel to a hidden anchor 80' down on the left, then lead up right (bolts), pull through bulge (crux) then directly up the crack on the face.

52. Walk on Water 5.11d ★
QD's and pro to 1"
An impressive and extreme face route to the right of Phylynx.

53. Mind Games 5.10a
Offwidth Chimney.

54. Wizard 5.11a ★★
QD's and pro to 1"
A dynamic and unusual climb.

FAR EAST WALL

This hidden corner of wall is the westerly extension of the Wizard Wall. Approach by rappeling in from the tree at the top of Seventh Moon or scramble up a 3rd class trail from the bottom. The height is 40' (12m) to the halfway terrace, and approximately 100' (30m) total cliff height.

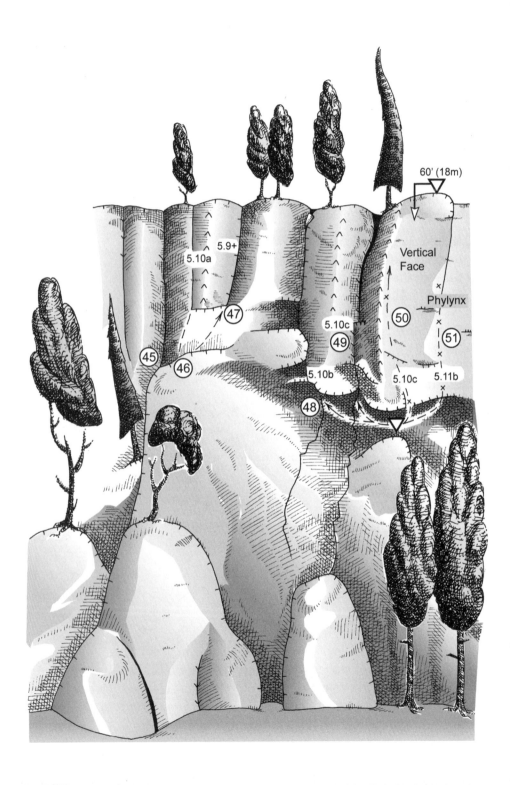

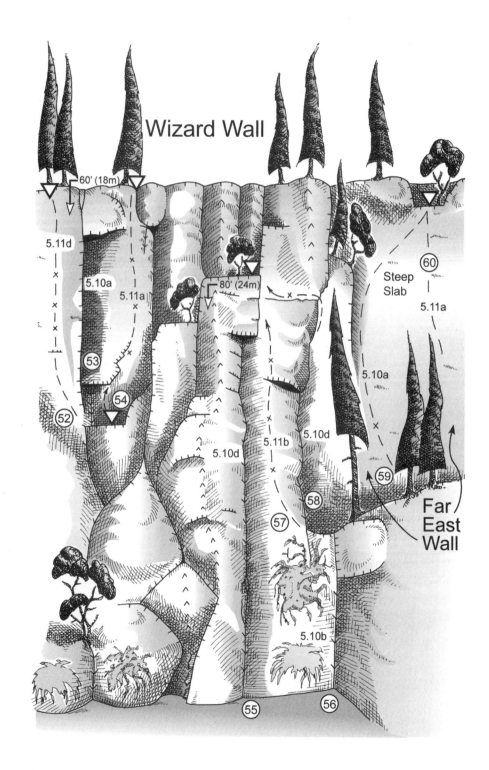

Wizard Wall

60' (18m)

5.11d

5.10a

5.11a

53

54

52

80' (24m)

5.10d

5.11b

5.10d

58

57

59

5.10b

55

56

Steep Slab

5.11a

60

5.10a

Far East Wall

55. The Wanderer 5.10d ★
56. Great Wall of China 5.10b ★
57. High Road to China 5.11b
58. Chinese Finger Torture 5.10d ★
59. Ghost Rider 5.10a
60. Flight of the Seventh Moon 5.11a ★ ★ ★

A neat, challenging face climb that goes up just left of the Orient Express dihedral and ends at the tree belay.

61. Orient Express 5.8 ★

Dihedral located at the center of the face.

62. Secret Maze 5.11b ★

A difficult face climb. Start to the right of the dihedral and climb up (crux) to a stance, then meander up the face using holds that seem to be in all the wrong places. Captain Granite said so.

63. Tigers Eye 5.10b

Fun direct start leading to the terraced ledges below Orient Express.

WARRIOR WALL

David Boekelheide on *Joy Ride 5.11a*

An extension of the Far East Wall it was coined because of the favorite difficult corner problem here. Also called the "Bug Wall". Access by a steep scramble descent via the standard guardrail descent trail next to the chain link fence. Approximate height ranges from 45′ (13m) on the left to 100′ (30m) on the right.

64. Smears for Fears 5.10a

Pro to 2"

A good crack climb further right of Secret Maze. Ends at the large fir tree on a ledge.

65. _____ 5.13a (TR)

The extreme face climb just left of Crack Warrior.

66. Crack Warrior 5.11b R ★ ★ ★

Pro to 1½"

A great climb with a nasty crux. Silverfish frequent here. Climb the corner stem problem up to a bulge (crux). Pull through and move up an easier right facing corner to the large fir tree.

67. You'll Dance to Anything 5.11c (TR) ★ ★

Beautiful face climb that makes use of a broken section of smooth rock. The exit is the crux due to numerous sloping finger edges.

Far East Wall

100' (30m)

45' (13m)

Orient
Express

5.8

5.11a

5.10d

5.11b

5.10d

5.10a

5.11b

61

60

Ledge

62

58

59

57

Steep
Slab

5.10b

55

56

63

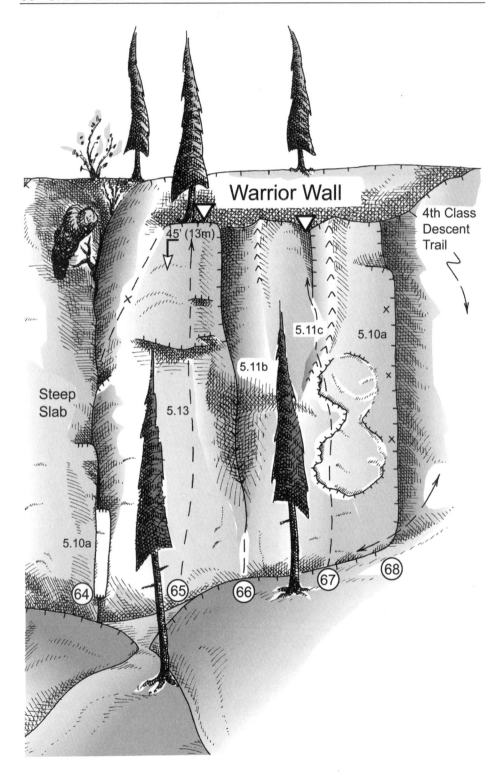

Warrior Wall

45' (13m)

4th Class
Descent
Trail

5.11c

5.10a

5.11b

Steep
Slab

5.13

5.10a

64

65

66

67

68

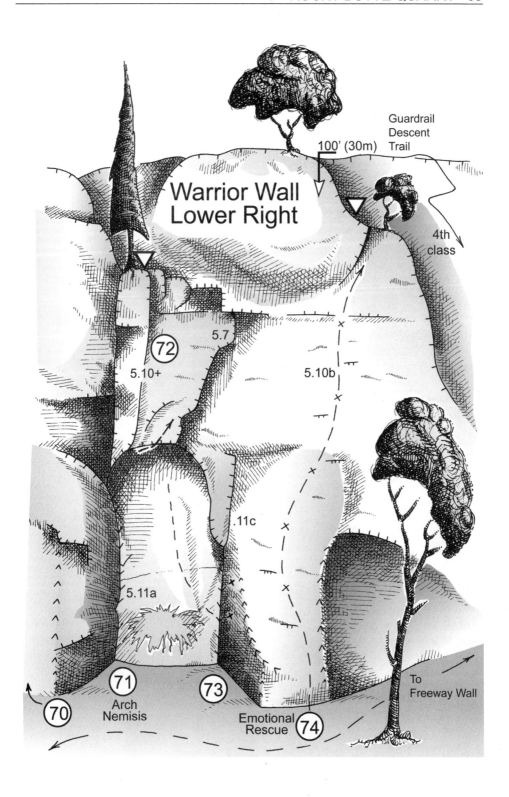

Warrior Wall
Lower Right

Guardrail
Descent
Trail

100' (30m)

4th
class

5.7

72

5.10+

5.10b

.11c

5.11a

71

Arch
Nemisis

73

Emotional
Rescue

74

70

To
Freeway Wall

68. Sheer Madness   5.10a
   3 QD's
69. Quarry Cracker   5.6
70. Lathe of heaven   5.11a
71. Arch Nemesis   5.11a ★
   Pro to 1½" including pitons
   A major dihedral on this face. Climb up the vertical corner until possible to step out right and
   up a flake that leads to a large fir tree.
72. Boy Sage   5.10+ (variation)
   Pro to 1½" including pitons
   Take the direct up a crack to the tree.

Lower right aspect of Warrior Wall, Rocky Butte Quarry

73. Jealous Rage   5.11c R
Pro to 1"
Leads up an indistinct face (bolts) left to join with Arch Nemesis.

74. Emotional Rescue   5.10b   ★ ★ ★
QD's and pro to 2"
One of the finest classics at the Butte. Very popular. Climb the steep bolt and pin protected face to exit up a crack and a bolt anchor hidden around corner.

FREEWAY WALL

Approximate height of this wall ranges from 20-40 ft (6m-12m).

75. Simple Twist   5.11
76. Hyper Twist   5.11
77. Passing Lane   5.6
78. Speeding Down South   5.8
79. Ranger Danger   5.9+
80. Telegraph Road   5.11a   (TR)
81. Highway Star   5.10c   ★
Pro to 1½"
A good crack climb with a strenuous exit move.

82. Dead Man's Curve   5.9

Mike on *Blackberry Jam 5.10b*

MEAN STREET

This steep wall is situated directly below the guardrail adjacent to the road. The routes are characterized by difficult, hard to protect and usually dust-covered rock. Height approximately 100' (30m).

83. Thunder Road   5.10a
84. Lethal Ethics   5.10d R
Poorly protected face climb intersected by a ledge halfway up.
85. Spiritual Journey   5.10d
Ascend the face just left of a minor arête and continue up an inside corner leading to the top.
86. Little Arête   5.9 R
87. Seamingly Endless   5.11b   ★
Pro to 1"
Start on right side of the arête and zig zag up discontinuous cracks and corners to the top.
88. Holy Bubbles   5.11b   ★
Start to right of the arête, ascend up and over a roof, then up an inside corner to a belay.
89. Pluto   5.12b
A bolted face left of the "nose". A bit runout, strenuous, a little dusty. Yet to see a free ascent.
90. Stump the Jock   5.11+
The crack and inside corner just left of the prominent "nose" of rock. Begin up and angle left up an overhang corner until it is possible to turn the crux and continue up a steep wall above.

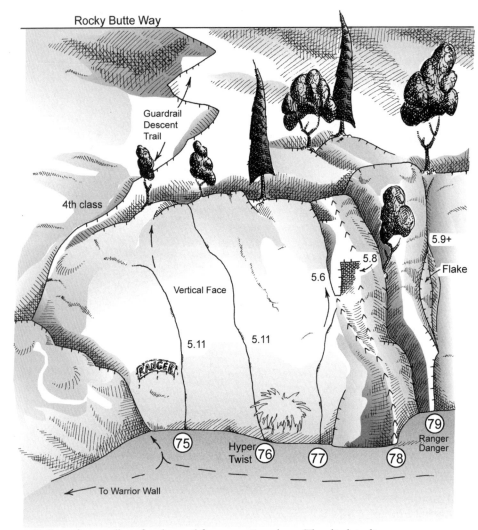

Rocky Butte Way

Guardrail
Descent
Trail

4th class

Vertical Face

5.11

5.11

5.6

5.8

5.9+

Flake

RANGER

75

Hyper
Twist 76

77

78

79

Ranger
Danger

To Warrior Wall

Pull another small roof and rappel from trees just above. The climb is dirty.

91. Packin' Heat 5.13a
QD's
The prominent bolted "nose" of rock.

92. No Leverage 5.11c
Could be a good climb, but the new drainage ditch pours down immediately to the right. Begin up a bolt and pin protected face to a corner and traverse directly left just below a large detached flake of rock to a bolt belay. Rappel.

93. Be Bold or Not To Be 5.11c
A true blue water course now.

94. Claymation 5.10c
A crack corner system to the right of the water course. May be dusty, but still feasible to climb.

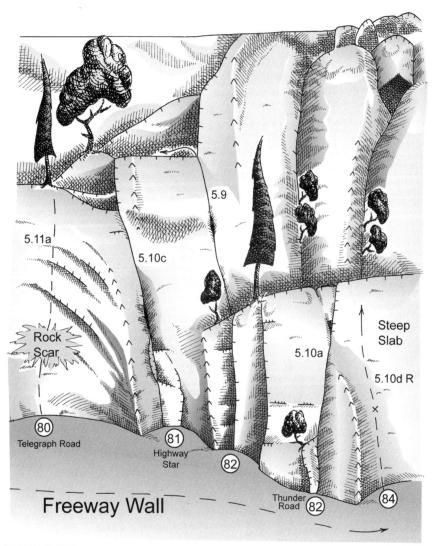

EASY STREET

A good practice wall to teach rappelling and top-roping; approximate height is 35′ (10m).

A.   Hand Crack 5.7
B.   Face 5th Class
C.   Chimney 5th Class
D.   Face / Finger 5.9
E.   Chimney 5.2

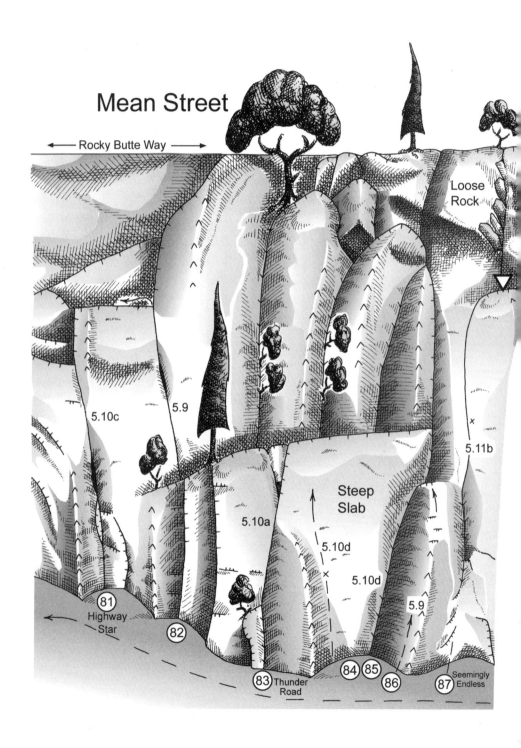

Mean Street

← Rocky Butte Way →

Loose
Rock

5.10c

5.9

5.11b

Steep
Slab

5.10a

5.10d

5.10d

5.9

81 Highway
Star

82

83 Thunder
Road

84 85

86

87 Seemingly
Endless

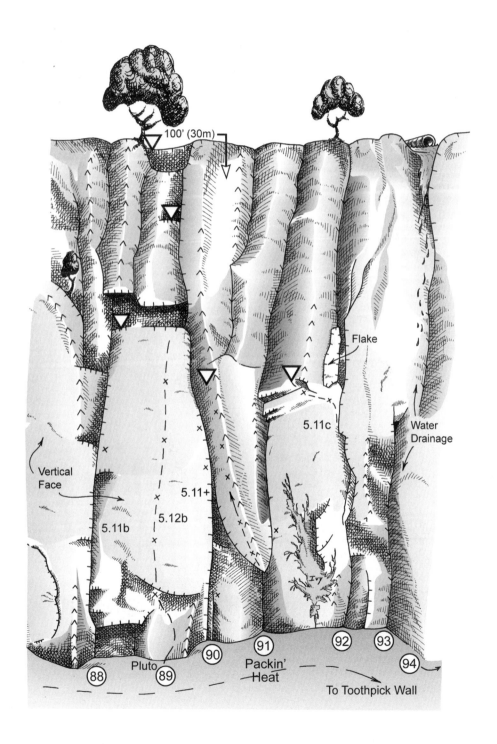

100' (30m)

Flake

Water
Drainage

5.11c

Vertical
Face

5.11+

5.12b

5.11b

88   Pluto   89   90   91   Packin'   92   93
Heat   94

To Toothpick Wall

TOOTHPICK WALL

A beautiful, colorful wall. Characterized by clean, steep rock and several incredible thin crack routes. Approximate height 50′ (15m).

95. Reach for the Sky   5.10a   ★

Pro to 2"

A fun climb. Ascend via a crack start then an outside corner until possible to move to the right side of the arête (1 pin - 1 bolt) and top out.

96. Zenith   5.12a   (TR)

97. Blueberry Jam   5.9 (5.10a   boulder start)   ★ ★ ★

Pro to 3"

A very popular practice climb. Start to the right or do the direct boulder start, then ascend to the top using a broken crack system and large holds.

98. Joy Ride   5.11a

Bolted face climb to the right of Blueberry Jam that has a large roof at the first bolt. Muscle over the overhang (crux) to a stance, then carefully balance up the remainder of the outside

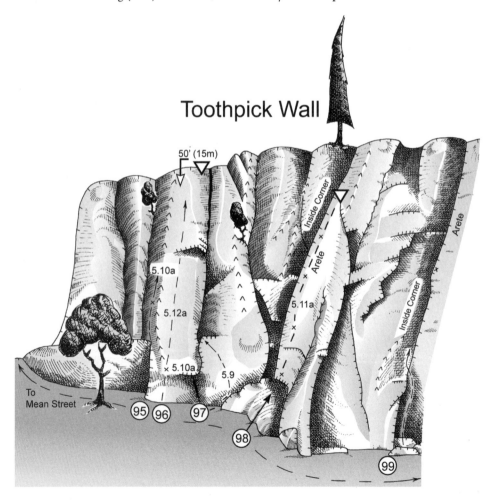

Toothpick Wall

arête to the anchor.

99.   Leading Edge   5.10d

A corner to face arête system to the left of Close to the Edge.

100.   Close to the Edge   5.11+   ★ ★ ★

Excellent climb on superb rock involving strenuous technique. Climb a thin crack that diagonals up rightward.

101.   Toothpick   5.11c   ★ ★ ★

The local classic, one of Rocky Butte's finest. Start on a ledge, step up left onto the vertical face via awkward holds. Either traverse left on a horizontal crack to finish up 'Close to the Edge' (the standard method) or climb straight up a crack-seam to the top (harder).

102.   Far from the Edge   5.11+   ★

103.   Rob's Ravine   5.9

Pro to 3"

A deep dihedral to the right of Toothpick.

104.   Competitive Edge   5.11a

Kind of interesting, not quite so easy to follow the arête.

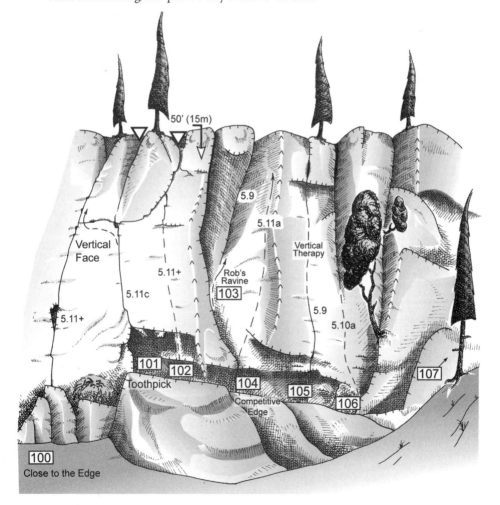

Breakfast Cracks

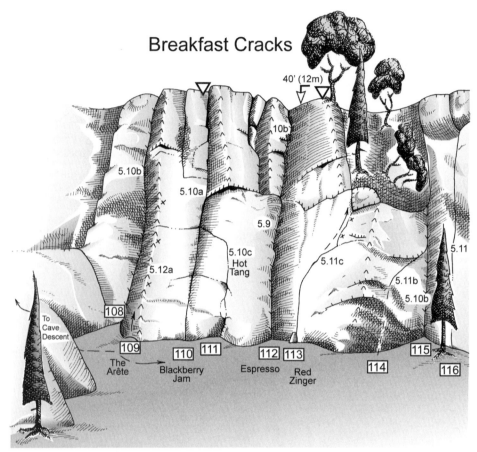

40' (12m)

10b

5.10b

5.10a

5.9

5.10c
Hot
Tang

5.11c

5.11

5.11b

5.10b

5.12a

108

To
Cave
Descent

109

110   111

112 113

115

The
Arête

Blackberry
Jam

Espresso

Red
Zinger

114

116

105. Vertical Therapy 5.9 ★★
Pro to 3"
Ascend up a crack leading to a face, then finish up a crack near the top. An excellent climb and a must for everyone.

106. Power Surge 5.10a

107. Stiff Fingers 5.9
Obscure route 30' right of the above climb.

BOULDERS IN THE WOODS
The T. Tube 5.9
Burgerville 5.10c
Kindergarten Snack 5.2

BREAKFAST CRACKS

This small historical amphitheatre offers several of the finest 5.10 cracks at the Butte.

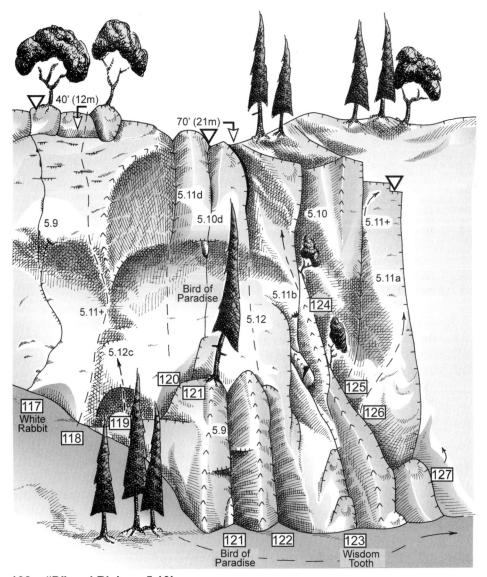

108. **"D" and Rising   5.10b**
109. **The Arête   5.12a**
    3 QD's and #2 Friend
    A bolted arête at the left corner of this little amphitheatre. Looks climbable but not easily clippable.
110. **Blackberry Jam   5.10b   ★ ★ ★**
    Pro to 2"
    Very popular local favorite at the Butte. A steep crack system ending with a stiff crux exit move.
111. **Hot Tang   5.10c (variation)**
    A quick fingertips start to Blackberry Jam. Interesting climb.

112. **Espresso 5.9 ★★**
Pro to 2"
An obvious dihedral corner with a dirty exit move. Fun and quite popular. Climb the right facing corner.

113. **Red Zinger 5.11c ★★**
Pro to 1"
An excellent and difficult undercling smear problem. Frequently top-roped and good for a quick pump. Start as per Espresso, but attack the seam that diagonals up right to a brushy slope.

114. **Orange Spice 5.11b ★**
A top-rope face problem that ascends vertical rock diagonally to join with Lemon Twist. A good but short climb.

115. **Lemon Twist (Direct Start) 5.10b**
Pro unknown
This is the brushy corner climb.

116. **Lunge and Plunge 5.11 (TR)**

117. **White Rabbit 5.10b ★★★**
Pro to 1"
One of the original all time favorites at Rocky Butte. Commence up right to a crack, then follow this up leftward then directly to the top of the cliff. Eases at about two-thirds height to sloping steps then a final vertical move.

118. **White Rabbit Buttress 5.11+ ★★**
An exciting climb ascending the outside face just to the right of White Rabbit. Start up thin holds just to the right of White Rabbit to several good large holds, then move up on side pulls and clings until possible to move up left onto the slabs above. Continue to the top.

119. **Unknown 5.12c (TR)**

120. **Harder Than Life 5.11d (TR)**

121. **Bird of Paradise 5.10d ★★★**
Pro to 2"
A very popular, well deserving classic at Rocky Butte. One of the best climbs at the Quarry. Start by angling up easy steps to a stance next to a fir tree (or by starting directly up a dihedral 20' below the tree and hidden from view), then climb the crack on the left of the tree. Undercling through the crux and jam upward to the top of the crag.

122. **_____ 5.12 (TR)**

123. **Wisdom Tooth 5.11b**

124. **_____ 5.10**
Prominent 100' long dihedral that diagonals up leftward to the summit.

125. **Trix are for Kids 5.11+ (TR)**
A beautiful, difficult overhang seam face climb partway up the same prominent dihedral. Step onto the right face at ½ height to ascend.

126. **Time of Your Life 5.11a (TR)**
An excellent arête problem that starts up the aforementioned dihedral. Traverse to the arête near a patch of bright yellow lichen. Ascend via the left then right side of the arête.

David climbing Orient Express 5.9

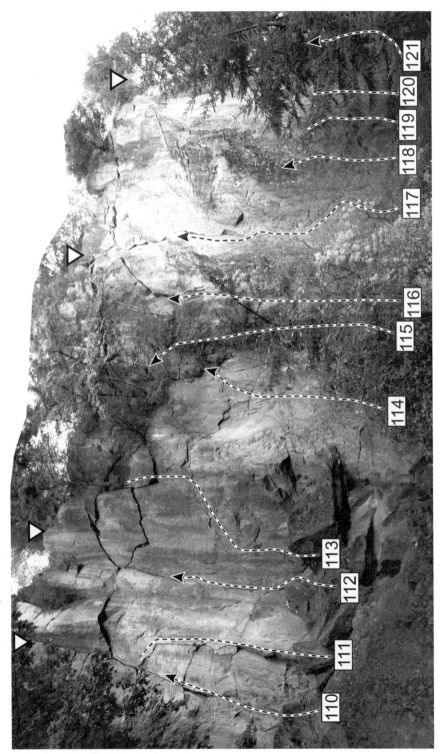

Breakfast Cracks Wall, Rocky Butte Quarry

127. Swiss Miss 5.10b

Pro to 2½" TCU's recommended

A crack that leads to the right side of the same arête. Use the natural pocket for protection. Crux is a minor bulge 25' up and may need pins.

WALL OF SHADOWS

As the cliff curves west from the Breakfast Cracks you will find the secluded Wall of Shadows, while beyond that is the Grotto. Housing development along the upper bluff places a limit on the continued use of the established climbs in this area.

128. **Shadows in Space 5.10b**
129. **Face Disgrace 5.11+ variation**
130. **Skywalker 5.10d**
131. **Mystic Traveler 5.11 (TR)**
132. **Spider Line 5.11+**
133. **Foot Loose 5.9**
134. **Joe's Garden 5.6**
135. **Hang Loose 5.11+ (TR)**
136. **Seventh Wave 5.12a**

Jacqueline climbing *Stranger Than Friction* at Video Bluff

LIVING ON THE EDGE
ALL FOR THE SPORT OF ROCK CLIMBING

ROCKY BUTTE QUARRY

CHAPTER 3

CARVER BRIDGE CLIFF

••

WELCOME TO THE FABULOUS Carver Bridge Cliff, a rare and unusual, private- ly owned sport crag that was unknown to rock climbers until 1987. The crag now features excellent climbs—as well as a series of superb bouldering problems in the forest below the crag.

Overlooking a beautiful Clackamas River near the community of Carver, this forested, private property continues to offer one of the region's best opportunities to experience the sport of rock climbing. Hopefully, this small Carver cliff will continue to be a valuable asset to Portland area rock climbers for many generations to come.

⛃ BRIEF HISTORY OF THE AREA

Though nearly unreachable, early "pioneers" did venture to Carver to climb on this hidden crag. The occasional fixed piton attested to this fact. Even on the Yellow Wall (on Angular Motion) there was an old fixed 10-foot rope hanging from a "bashie." A portion of this route on the Yellow Wall was ascended in 1975 by Jeff Alzner and Terry Jenkins.

Late in the summer of 1987, several climbers visited here and immediately realized its vast potential for free climbing routes. In a few short years these climbers transformed this place into a quality sport crag that now offers several fine classic climbs on excellent rock.

The Carver Bridge Cliff formation faces north and extends generally along an east-west axis for several hundred yards. A few minor outcrops exist beyond the main sections described herein, but these are not developed for climbing. The highest section of the cliff (Rockgarden Wall) is approximately 130 feet. The topographic maps have been separated into two sections. They are as follows: the Rockgarden Wall and the Yellow Wall. The majority of the routes are rated between 5.9 and 5.12. The lower-rated climbs tend to be mixed natural protection and bolts, while the higher-rated climbs (5.11 and above) tend to be more heavily bolted. The natural protection climbs

offer good equipment placements, so you may have to look hard to find an "R" rated climb at Carver.

Greg Lyon, Mike Pajunas, Robert McGown, Gary Rall, Wayne Wallace, Tim Olson, and many others were highly instrumental in the development of this crag.

Here are several astounding classics that will test your ability: Smerk (5.11a), Angular Motion (5.12a), Uncola (5.11c), Notorious (5.11b), Sea of Holes (5.12a), and Rites of Passage (5.10b). These and a host of other great climbs put Carver on many a rock climber's map.

There are also many classic bouldering prob- lems located in the woods below the main crag. A number of climbs have a rather healthy re-growth of moss and are generally not climbed anymore, in- cluding the small section of wall between the two main crags. Yet, all of the best climbs are very acces-

Ian Goss climbing *Angular Motion 5.12a*

Carver Bridge Cliff: A Cool Place to Climb

sible and always challenging.

ACCESS ISSUES

The following guidelines apply to all visitors who come to Carver Bridge Cliff to rock climb. This unique environment is privately owned, and access is granted only to members of the Carver Climbing Club.

Club members are expected to respect the property owner's privacy and to give due diligence to how the property is used. Do not litter, or vandalize, or cause excessive noise, and be vigilant when others trespass or cause problems that could jeopardize access privileges. Continued freedom to climb at this crag ultimately depends upon your willingness to obey the rules.

Limited provisional access is granted to each climber for a one-time membership fee. This membership requires signing a liability release waiver, obtainable at the website *carverclimbingclub. org.* Apply on this website for a number which will be emailed to you. Print the liability release form, complete it and take it to *either* **Climb Max Mountaineering** 928 NE 28th Avenue, Portland, Oregon 97232, or to **Portland Rock Gym** located at 21 NE 12th Avenue, Portland, Oregon 97232.

CARVER RULES AND OBLIGATIONS

Do your part to preserve our access by observing the following rules:
- You must be a signed member of the Carver Climbing Club to climb or boulder on Stone Cliff property and/or property owned by the Rosenbaum family.
- You may bring guests who are 18 years of age or older, but they may not boulder or climb. They may only observe, which does not include handling of any rope or other equipment.
- Only canned beverages are allowed. No glass of any kind.
- Dogs are not permitted.
- Each climber or boulderer is responsible for picking up their own garbage or garbage left by others. This is a joint effort.
- No new trails or paths or routes will be allowed. Use only those which are already in place.
- People must stay on the trails at all times. People walking off the trails can cause damage to the flora and fauna.
- Each person, whether a member or guest, must have picture ID on their person at all times and be able to present it to anyone acting on behalf of the Stone Cliff Inn to verify membership or identity.
- The Stone Cliff Inn parking lot may be used all days except holidays and Friday and Saturday evenings from 5pm on. During holidays or Friday and Saturday evenings, members may park at the intersection of Hattan and Gronlund Roads and come in through that trail starting on Stone Cliff Lane.
- Radios or other music players are not allowed.
- No rock wall climbing is allowed unless you are an experienced climber with skills suitable to the rock terrain.
- No removal of rock, moss, wood, or any other item from the site unless it has already been removed for climbing purposes.
- Be respectful of property and others. You are here at the discretion of the owners. Your right to boulder or climb here is subject to revocation at any time.

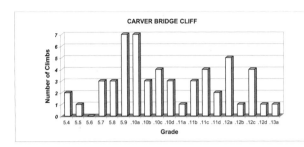

CARVER BRIDGE CLIFF

Greg climbing *Digital 5.12d*

Pay a membership fee of $8 cash to attain a numbered CCC card. The card should be visible on your harness or pack when you access the property to climb or boulder.

You must be 18 or older to rock climb or to practice on the rock boulders at this site. When visiting the crag you must carry photo ID. All bouldering activists are required to sign a liability release waver before entry onto the land. All persons under 18 are NOT allowed to rock climb at this site nor play on the rock boulders.

CARVER CLIMBING CLUB

The Carver Climbing Club (*www.carverclimbingclub.org*) was originally formed as a grassroots effort to keep a scarce and valuable resource available. The fact that this land is still being utilized as a climbing area is a testament to the efforts of many individuals, but mostly to the generosity of the owner. Signs are posted at the entrances to the Carver climbing areas.

The website *carverclimbingclub.org* allows an effective means of communication between the landowner and club members. Every member of the club must take an active role in making sure that the restaurant, the owners property in general, and their family and staff specifically, are treated with the respect and courtesy they deserve.

Everyone who climbs at Carver must treat the cliff, the boulders, and the property as they would their own, with the full knowledge that we are there only through the generosity of the owners family.

Work together as a community to help protect this valuable resource and allow climbing at Carver to continue. This can only be achieved through adherence to the following list of guidelines by all users of the property. Our presence at Carver Bridge Cliff as climbers is a privilege. Take an active role in maintaining the climbing at Carver, the property, and the privilege of access.

Continued access is by no means guaranteed, and depends wholly upon our ability as a community to police and maintain this area.

The Carver Climbing Club and the landowner have identified a number of guidelines that every user of this recreational resource will need to both personally follow, disseminate, and enforce if any of us are to continue to climb at Carver. Read the access guidelines. Attain the road directions, parking requirements and trail information when you sign the liability waver.

VISUAL BIO

6
Month 1 Min · N · Trees · Regs · Sport

These emblems represent all of Carver Bridge Cliff climbing site. Carver is generally a sport

climbing site, although there is some opportunity for gear leads.

ROCKGARDEN WALL

1. **Crack in the Mirror 5.9 ★★**
   30' (9m) in length, Pro to 1½"
   At the far left side of the wall and just uphill is a unique looking 'broken' flake start. Ascend this and exit right to an anchor at a ledge.

2. **Variation 5.10a**
   15' (4m) in length, Pro unknown

3. **Notorious 5.11c/d ★★★**
   35' (10m) in length, 5 QD's
   One of the great Carver classics. A very good climb! Climb the arête using large holds to a ledge and finish up left to an anchor.

4. **Marqueritaville 5.10d**
   40' (12m) in length, Pro to 2"
   The deep overhung dihedral. A stiff crux and joins with Uncola.

5. **Cherry Cola 5.11d ★★**
   45' (13m) in length, 4 QD's
   This difficult variation problem that begins off the top of a large boulder. Crimp thin holds up the face, then join Uncola as it cruises through it final ending difficult moves. Waltz up left on small holds and smears to a belay anchor.

6. **Uncola 5.11c ★★★**
   45' (13m) in length, 5 QD's
   One of the ten great Carver classics. Located just left of a large chimney. Start next to a large boulder and ascend up right onto a steep face. Bust up leftward through a crux section on a slightly overhung series of powerful moves. Waltz up left on small holds to a belay anchor.

7. **Neptune 5.9 ★★**
   40' (12m) in length, Pro to 1½"
   The obvious wide offwidth. A fun climb. Stem, jam and body climb up to a bolt belay. A minor crack on the right face of the chimney offers good small pro.

8. **Smooth Torquer 5.12d ★★**
   45' (13m) in length, 4 QD's
   An excellent, desperate, physical "tips" climb just to the left of Smerk. Eases to a smooth slab after the crux. Rap from anchor.

9. **Smerk 5.11a ★★★**
   120' (36m) in length, (40' 1ˢᵗ pitch) QD's
   One of the finest classic routes at Carver Cliff. Very popular! Route was coined from an old friends nickname. Ascend a bolted face left of New Generation past a crux (5.11a) exiting to the belay on the right. The second pitch (4 bolts) ascends directly up the head wall (5.10c) to another bolt anchor. The third pitch finishes straight up a smooth face (3 bolts) using a diagonal seam start. Rap from belay.

10. **New Generation 5.8 (1ˢᵗ pitch) ★★★**
    120' (36m) in length, (40' 1ˢᵗ pitch) Pro to 1½"
    A popular climb. Begin up an awkward start to a small corner and climb a sweet finger crack

(5.8) to a bolt belay. Angle up left via a low angle ramp to another bolted face. Continue up this (5.9) to a ledge, then finish up an arête (5.9) to a belay. Rappel.

11. Free Ride   5.12a
20' (6m) in length, 2 QD's
A bolted variation direct start to Scotch and Soda.

12. Scotch and Soda   5.10d   ★ ★ ★
40' (12m) in length, QD's and pro to 1½"
Fantastic crack and face climb. Start at a ledge beneath the Red Dihedral. Ascend a harsh finger crack until possible to maneuver left onto a small pedestal. Finish up a bolted face to an anchor.

13. Tequila Sunrise   5.10c
120' (36m) in length, Pro to 2"
Start as for Scotch and Soda, but traverse right to Red Dihedral, then up left around a minor corner to the New Generation anchor. Continue up easy ramps to the left then up and right (1 bolt) through a 5.10 A crux to a ledge. Move up a 5.8 crack and offwidth to the summit. Rap from belay anchor.

14. Red Dihedral   5.10a   ★ ★
60' (18m) in length, Pro to 1½" TCU's recommended
Interesting dihedral. Originally named due to the red lichen on the rock. Pull up a crux start into the corner and ascend this up and then right to a stubby maple tree. Move past this and up a tight crux corner to a large ledge and bolt anchor on the right.

15. _____   5.12+
60' (18m) in length (TR)

16. Jungle Safari   5.10a   ★ ★
120' (36m) in length, Pro to 3"
An excellent LONG dihedral climb. Begin just left of the offwidth (Combination Block) and stem, jam your way up an awkward corner. The crux is a narrow crack corner section about 80' up the climb. Finish up a steep but easy (5.8) fist crack to a tree belay.

17. Night Vision   5.11b   ★ ★
120' (36m) in length (65' 1ˢᵗ pitch), Pro to 1½"
Not often climbed because it requires some pro, but is a superb route nonetheless. Commence up the offwidth crack on the left side of Combination Block. Follow a minor corner up and over a wild bulge then up a stiff face (crux) to a bolt an-chor. The next pitch ascends a 5.9 crack up right to the top of the cliff.

18. Sanity Assassin   5.7 to 5.10
20' (6m) in length, 2 QD's

19. Sea of Holes   5.12a   ★ ★ ★
75' (22m) in length, 7 QD's
One of the best climbs at Carver. Begin from off the top of Combination Block and ascend the rounded buttress (crux) on unique pocketed face holds and edges. Enter a shallow dihedral where the route eases. Exit up right to a bolt belay anchor.

20. Sport Court 5.12c   ★ ★ ★
75' (22m) in length, 8 QD's
This exciting superior route exists by connecting the low-

Leading 1st pitch of *Smerk 5.11a*

Rockgarden Wall

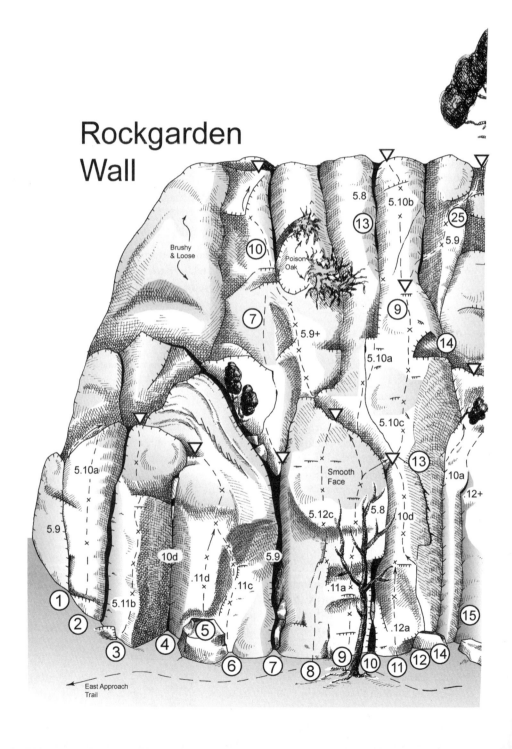

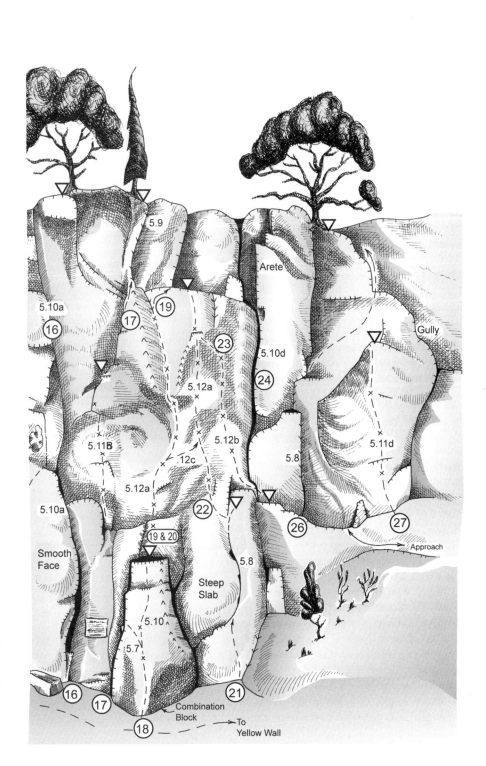

er half of Sea of Holes with the upper half of Wally Street.

21. Shadow Fox   5.8

25' (7m) in length, Pro to ¾"

A short crack climb on a smooth slab. A good approach to the upper face climbs.

22. Wally Street   5.12a   ★ ★ ★

70' (21m) in length, 5 QD's and minor pro to ¾"

Start as for Shadowfox but enter up left onto a stiff, vertical face climb of quality proportion.

23. Wally Wedding   5.12b

20' (6m) in length, 4 QD's

24. Sweat and the Flies 5.10d PG

20' (6m) in length, Pro to 3"

This bold flared offwidth is a surprising lead. Short and nasty.

25. Battleship Arête   5.9 (variation)

20' (6m) in length, 2 QD's

Bri Stekly on *Edges & Ledges*, **Broughton Bluff**

The next six routes are located on the In-Between Wall, but are inaccessible due to overgrowth of brush and vines on the routes and along the base of the wall. For exact locations of these routes refer to one of the older PRC guides.

26. Passport to Insanity   5.8

35' (10m) in length, Pro to 2"

Ascend a perfect corner, mantle to a ledge, then mantle again, continuing up right, then left to an oak tree belay.

27. Burning From the Inside   5.11d   ★ ★

20' (6m) in length, 3 QD's

This exhilarating problem dances up an overhung rounded face to a bolt belay. A great climb.

28. Hinge of Fate   5.10c

25' (7m) in length, 3 QD's and optional pro to ¾"

At the top of a dirt gully you will find a dark, water streaked face. Ascend this past a crux, then lay back and smear your way up a flared seam (the hinge).

29. Eyes of a Stranger   5.10a

40' (12m) in length, Pro to ¾"

30. Shady Personality   5.10b

65' (19m) in length, Pro to 1½" Cams recommended

A unique climb that can be done in two short pitches. Move up a smooth slab (5.9) and up easy steps to a belay on a ledge. Continue up a slightly overhung crack that begins as a mantle into an offwidth pea-pod. Bolt belay.

31. Rats in the Jungle   5.10a

20' (6m) in length, Wide pro to 6"

The large chimney problem immediately right of Shady Personality.

YELLOW WALL

32. Call to Greatness 5.10c ★★
60' (18m) in length, Pro to 2"

An impressive route. Classic thin hand jamming. Begin up a large brushing corner at the left edge of the Yellow Wall. Embark from a stance up the overhung crack system. Boldly climb around three small bulges, the toughest one being the last bulge.

33. Plastic Monkey 5.13a
60' (18m) in length, 7 QD's

A very difficult problem and one of the most difficult at Carver. Ascend the vertical bolted face on the left corner of the Yellow Wall.

34. Rites of Passage 5.10b ★★★
80' (24m) in length, 10 QD's

One of the best routes at the crag. Commence up a face (1 bolt) and move right (or start up a jam crack to this point), then up a bolted face (5.10b) until possible to move right to an anchor above Angular Motion. Move hard left and continue up via a shallow corner (5.10b) then up right to a flake that ends at a belay anchor just under an overhang. Rappel. The thin crack above (1 bolt and pro to 1") is seldom done (dirt/moss) and is 5.11c to the top of the bluff.

35. Digital 5.12d ★★ 🌂
20' (12m) in length, 4 QD's

A unique, yet difficult balance problem.

36. Angular Motion 5.12a ★★★ 🌂
40' (12m) in length, 5 QD's

One of the most popular climbs here. Super classic! To the left of Chemistry Slab is an overhung face. Power your way up this until you must make a long reach to a jug then up right on tenuous holds to a ledge and a bolt belay. An exciting route with dynamic moves.

37. Out on a Limb 5.10a ★ 🌂
60' (18m) in length, QD's and pro to 1½"

A good route. Start up the left side of Chemistry Slab alcove. Exit out left along a narrow ramp (crux) and up to a bolt anchor. Belay, then continue up a face (1 bolt) that leads to a dihedral above. Rappel from a bolt anchor under the final overhang.

The next six climbs are reasonably easy short slab climbs that are located on the Chemistry Slab. This section of rock is protected from the occasional rain shower during the summer months, making this a good practice slab for learning the basics of rope handling. There is an anchor on the upper right side, and the upper left side of the slab.

Tyler leading a Video Bluff favorite

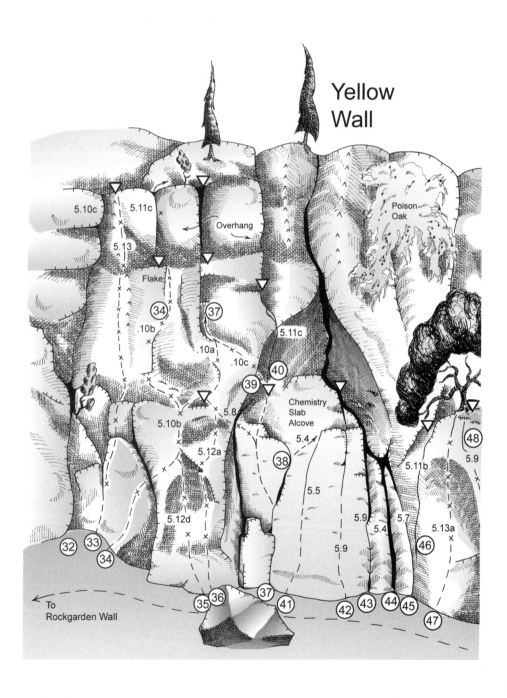

Yellow Wall

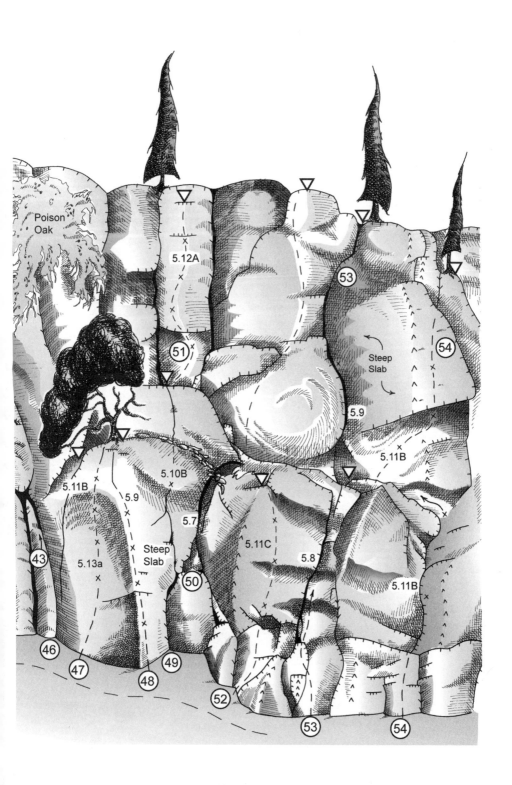

Poison
Oak

5.12A

51

53

54

Steep
Slab

5.9

5.11B

5.10B

5.11B

5.9

5.7

Steep
Slab

5.11C

5.8

5.11B

43

5.13a

50

46

47

48

49

52

53

54

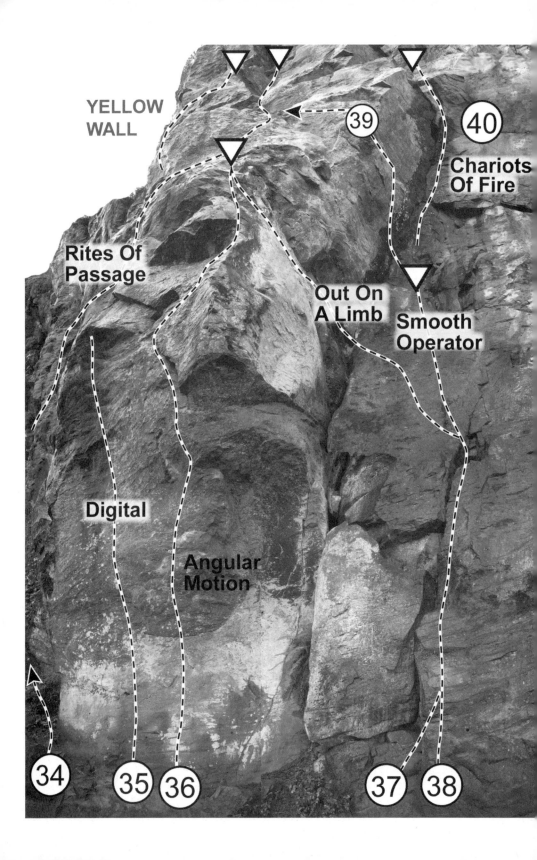

YELLOW WALL

Chariots Of Fire

Rites Of Passage

Out On A Limb

Smooth Operator

Digital

Angular Motion

34 35 36 37 38 39 40

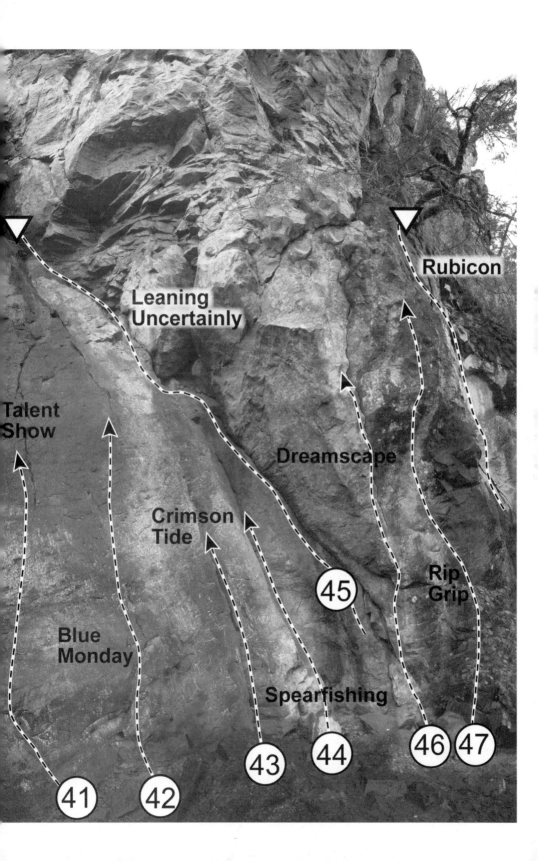

Bouldering Grades

Boulder problems use the well-known V-scale rating system. This effective grade comparison scale is designed to articulate a relational comparison involving short bursts of energy typical of concise boulder moves.

YDS	V-scale
5.9-	vB-
5.10a	v0
5.10c/d	v1
5.11a/b	v2
5.11c/d	v3
5.12-	v4
5.12	v5
5.12+	v6
5.13-	v7
5.13	v8
5.13+	v9
5.14-	v10
5.14	v11
5.14+	v12
5.15-	v13
5.15	v14
5.15+	v15

Barney leading *Jet Stream* at Bulo Point

38. Smooth Operator 5.4 ★
30' (9m) in length, Pro to 1 ½"

39. King Rat   5.10c
60' (9m) in length, Pro to 1½"

40. Chariots of Fire   5.11c ★★★
55' (16m) in length, Pro to 2"
An incredibly physical classic climb. Race up easy slabs passing a bolt anchor. Enter a hand jam crack leading directly up a desperately overhung wall. Exit past a block to a bolt anchor on a small ledge.

41. Talent Show 5.5
30' (9m) in length, Pro to ¾" TCU's and small wires
Left side of Chemistry Slab.

42. Blue Monday 5.9
30' (9m) in length (TR)
A steep face climb on Chemistry Slab.

43. Crimson Tide 5.9
30' (9m) in length, Pro to 2"
A steep face climb on Chemistry Slab.

44. Spear Fishing in Bermuda 5.4
30' (9m) in length, Large pro
Right side of Chemistry Slab.

45. Leaning Uncertainty 5.7
30' (9m) in length, Pro to 2"
Right side of Chemistry Slab.

46. Dreamscape 5.11b ★ ★
30' (9m) in length, Pro to 1½"
A difficult vertical tips crack that powers up the right outer face of Chemistry alcove. Rap from a fixed belay anchor left of the large maple tree.

47. Rip Grip 5.13a ★ ★
30' (9m) in length, 4 QD's
A difficult bolted face immediately right of Dreamscape.

48. Rubicon 5.9 ★ ★ ★
30' (9m) in length, 3 QD's and minor pro to ¾"
A very popular easy climb for everyone. Ascend the outside corner to easy edges, then up a steep face (crux) until you can grab the base edge of a thin crack. Rap from chains at a tree belay.

Brian leading *Gandalf's Grip 5.9*

49. Edge of the Reef 5.10b ★ ★
45' (13m) in length, Pro to 1" TCU's recommended
A really good climb. Challenging but not extreme. Move up the curved starting crack (numerous edges) then straight up a crack past a face crux with 1 bolt. Finish up a thin crack that rounds to a slab and bolt anchor.

50. Great Barrier Reef 5.7 R
30' (9m) in length, Pro unknown

51. Penguins in Heat 5.12a
30' (9m) in length, 4 QD's
A difficult problem located above the first pitch of Edge of the Reef.

52. Challenger 5.11b/c ★ ★
30' (9m) in length, 3 QD's TCU's optional
The name describes the route very well. This quality climb begins up easy steps until you must enter a smooth face broken with unusual edges. Finish up and left to exit to a small stance with a bolt anchor.

53. Last of the Mohicans 5.9 ★
40' (12m) in length, Pro to 2½"
A good, enjoyable climb to learn the basics. Ascend a broken crack system with a bulge on the right side just short of the anchor. The upper section of this

---

TEN GOOD SPORT ROUTES

UNDER 5.10

Every extreme climber started on reasonable ground somewhere, so here is our choice of local bolted sport routes.

1. Kung Fu, 5.9, Ozone
2. Dirty Jugs, 5.9, Ozone
3. Standing Ovation, 5.9, Ozone
4. Helm's Deep, 5.9, Ozone
5. Alpha, 5.8, French's Dome
6. Straw man, 5.8, French's Dome
7. Tin Tangle, 5.8, French's Dome
8. Orient Express, 5.8, RB Quarry
9. Flakey Old Man, 5.7, RB Quarry
10. Route Crafters, 5.8, Madrone Wall

A GREAT PLACE TO BE

far right section of wall is not available due to a luxurious growth of moss and dirt.

54. Riders of the Purple Sage 5.10b

40' (12m) in length, QD's and pro to 1"

Step up easy ground to a considerably overhung corner (1 bolt). Stem and lay back up right then left to the bolt anchor. The next pitch has moss and dirt and is not presently climbed. Rappel from bolt anchor.

..."we have ceased to be slaves and have really been men.
It is hard to return to servitude."
~Lionel Terray

CARVER BRIDGE CLIFF

WARNING!

MADRONE WALL BETA

ALL PURCHASERS OF THIS rock climber's guidebook should read the following regarding the information database provided in the following chapter on the Madrone Wall.

The Madrone Wall was a popular climbing venue until 1997 when the Clackamas County Commissioners closed it to all public access to prepare plans to quarry rock from the site. Due to a huge public outcry, the county commissioners agreed to take another in-depth look at the plan. Environmental and economic studies co-funded by the County and the Madrone Wall Preservation Committee along with the Clackamas River Basin Conservation Alliance, a local citizen group, determined that it would be uneconomical, even under the best conditions, to quarry this site. This site is now targeted to be preserved as a park or open space. The Commissioners unanimously responded to public pressure in 2006 by agreeing to not sell the site and to make it a priority in the parks master planning process. The Commissioners allocated funding for the park's planning process. The process will allow the area to reopen with adequate provision for managing use, such as parking facilities. Progress is encouraging and the community is hopeful that the park will be created soon.

Progress has come by working within the process. It is imperative that climbers continue to exhibit patience and persistence so that the Madrone Wall can reopen with climbers as a welcome group. You should check on the latest access status by viewing http://www.savemadrone.org or contacting the Access Fund's Regional Coordinator in the Portland area, http://www.accessfund. org/about/rc.php. Please do not jeopardize the future of Madrone Wall by ignoring the closure.

Progress on opening Madrone is so encouraging that these route descriptions are being included in this guidebook. This does not represent an endorsement to climb in a closed area. It is for your reference if and when the area is officially reopened.

The Access Fund

MADRONE WALL

WARNING!

MADRONE WALL BETA

ALL PURCHASERS OF THIS rock climber's guidebook should read the following regarding the information database provided in the following chapter on the Madrone Wall.

The Madrone Wall was a popular climbing venue until 1997 when the Clackamas County Commissioners closed it to all public access to prepare plans to quarry rock from the site. Due to a huge public outcry, the county commissioners agreed to take another in-depth look at the plan. Environmental and economic studies co-funded by the County and the Madrone Wall Preservation Committee along with the Clackamas River Basin Conservation Alliance, a local citizen group, determined that it would be uneconomical, even under the best conditions, to quarry this site. This site is now targeted to be preserved as a park or open space. The Commissioners unanimously responded to public pressure in 2006 by agreeing to not sell the site and to make it a priority in the parks master planning process. The Commissioners allocated funding for the park's planning process. The process will allow the area to reopen with adequate provision for managing use, such as parking facilities. Progress is encouraging and the community is hopeful that the park will be created soon.

Progress has come by working within the process. It is imperative that climbers continue to exhibit patience and persistence so that the Madrone Wall can reopen with climbers as a welcome group. You should check on the latest access status by viewing http://www.savemadrone.org or contacting the Access Fund's Regional Coordinator in the Portland area, http://www.accessfund.org/about/rc.php. Please do not jeopardize the future of Madrone Wall by ignoring the closure.

Progress on opening Madrone is so encouraging that these route descriptions are being included in this guidebook. This does not represent an endorsement to climb in a closed area. It is for your reference if and when the area is officially reopened.

The Access Fund

MADRONE WALL

MADRONE WALL

THIS BEAUTIFUL AND UNIQUE FOREST CRAG is considered by many local rock climbers to be the best year-round climbing site in the Portland metro area. The southwest facing cliff scarp of the Madrone Wall provides excellent sunny rock climbing opportunities for all seasons.

The crag is located a convenient 15 minutes from I-205, and sports an extensive list of over 100 rock climbs from 5.4 to 5.12.

Thanks to many years of special time intensive public and political action by the Madrone Wall Preservation Committee, during the early months of year 2006 the cliff was approved by Clackamas County for park status. Development under this status will certainly again allow climbers to enjoy one of the most rare climbing sites locally. Support for this group and for park development is one good step that you can do to assist in promoting wise use of this crag. The mailing address is listed in the back of this guide.

Until opening date the climbing information and the topographical maps provided in the next few pages are for historical reference only, and are not to be used for climbing purposes.

BRIEF HISTORY OF THE AREA

The crag received sparse attention by rock climbers as long ago as the mid 1970's. Yet the difficulty and overhung nature of the crag precluded extreme vertical development of the crag.

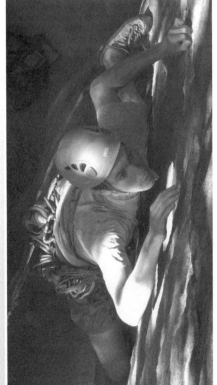

David on lead at Broughton Bluff

In the continual quest for the perfect climb, route exploration took hold of the Madrone Wall late in 1986. Through the special efforts of Chuck Buzzard, John Jackson, Scott Smith, and friends they pioneered numerous excellent super classics such as Beam Me Up Mr. Scott (5.11c), Mr. Noodle Arms (5.11b), Ant Abuse (5.10a), Catharsis (5.11c) and Sheesh (5.10c).

The area remained a well kept secret until October of 1988. In just two years nearly 100 routes were established. Chuck Buzzard, Wayne Wallace, Robert McGown, Greg Lyon, Dave Sowerby, and many others were instrumental in creating great classics like Where the Wild Things Roam (5.11d), Scott Free (5.12b), Full Spank Mode (5.12a), Shining Wall (5.12a), Nouveau Riche (5.10c) and Divine Wind (5.11c).

Geographically, the Madrone Wall complex is just one long crag, but out of necessity the cliff has been subdivided into six sections. They are as follows from left to right: Left Corner Wall, Orange Wall, Fourth Class Wall, the main section of the Madrone Wall, the Shining Wall and on the right side of the bluff Hardscrabble Wall.

VISUAL BIO

These emblems represent virtually all of Madrone Wall climbing site, except for the Shining Wall which receives a fair amount of direct sunshine in the afternoon hours.

🗷 HOW TO GET THERE

To reach this wonderland of rock, drive east on Highway 212 from the I-205 Clackamas exit #12. Drive east 3 miles to the Rock Creek Corner intersection. Turn south at the signal light onto Highway 224 that leads to Estacada. Drive one mile to the small community of Carver. Continue on Highway 224 for approximately 2¼ miles east of Carver. Entrance to the park is located on the east side of the road at a large white metal gate. Do not park on the access road in front of the gate.

🐾 APPROACH

Walk to the clearing below the Shining Wall. The left approach trail leads to the Madrone Wall proper, while the trail to the right leads directly to the Hardscrabble Wall.

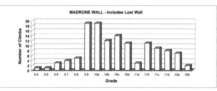

LEFT CORNER WALL

1. **Jackson's Daring Deeds   5.10a**
   45' (13m) in length, Pro to 2"
   This dihedral is located at the far left recesses of the wall.

2. **Patrick's Dihedral   5.9   ★★**
   35' (10m) in length, Pro to 1½"
   A large dihedral that begins as an offwidth and climbs up past a narrow crux section to a Madrone tree belay. Located to the right of a small rounded buttress.

3. **Sheesh   5.10c PG   ★★★**
   35' (10m) in length, Pro to 1" including RP's
   Excellent climb. Sheesh is the clean, smooth dihedral with a small half-moon imprint on the left face. Thin crux.

4. **Identity Crisis   5.10b R   ★★**
   35' (10m) in length, Pro to 1" including #4 Rock
   A great climb. Commence up the outside face to the right of Sheesh passing 2 bolts to an easy slab. Surmount a final bulge and move up left to a bolt belay.

5. **Mental Crisis   5.11d   ★**
   35' (10m) in length, QD's and minor pro to 1"
   A good, short, difficult problem. Face climb over a substantial bulge past 2 bolts to join with Identity Crisis.

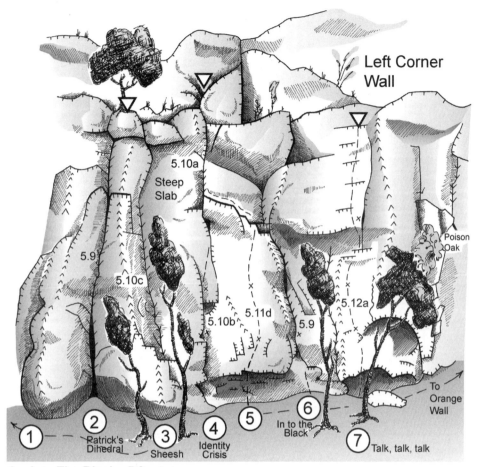

6. Into The Black 5.9 ★★

35' (10m) in length, Pro to 2"

A dark, contorted left-leaning crack system that joins with Identity Crisis.

7. Talk Talk Talk 5.12a ★★

30' (9m) in length, 3 QD's

A definite must on your list of climbs. This short, power packed line ascends up a rounded outside corner to a bolt belay. A harsh finger crux.

8. Verbal 5.11a ★

30' (9m) in length, 4 QD's

This climb starts 5' to the right of the main outside corner just to the right of the previous route.

9. Back in 'Nam 5.10b PG

50' (15m) in length, Pro to 1½"

This route is near the large tree at the left side of the Orange Wall. Follow a left leaning corner crack over a small roof about 30' up the cliff, then continue up left again. Angle up left to a madrone tree and rappel from there.

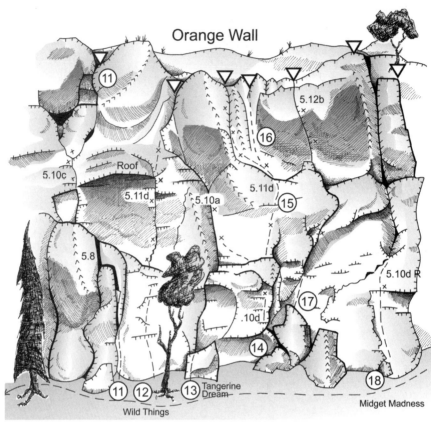

Orange Wall

Roof

5.12b

5.10c

5.11d

5.10a

5.11d

5.8

5.10d R

.10d

Tangerine
Dream

Wild Things

Midget Madness

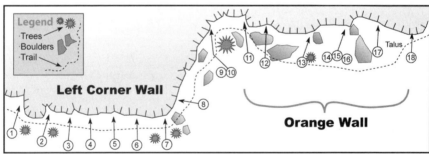

Legend

- Trees
- Boulders
- Trail

Left Corner Wall

Talus

Orange Wall

10. Feat of Clay   5.10-

30' (9m) in length, Pro to 3" including long slings

Starts the same at 'Back in 'Nam' but cut up right at 15' beneath the large roof until you reach a large ledge, then move back to the left to an anchor. Rappel. Several lead variations exist for this route.

ORANGE WALL

11. Wild Blue Yonder   5.10c   ★★   [Dry]

45' (13m) in length, Pro to 2"

An interesting route with plenty of variety. Start next to a large boulder. Begin up a sickle shaped offwidth crack to a small ramp. Step left, then proceed directly up the broken face (3

Orange Wall
Right Section

5.8+

5.10d

5.8

21

5.9

5.9

5.8

5.9

5.10d

19   20   22   23   24 Surfin'...

← Graduation   Route
                       Crafters

Cornick's
Corner

pitons) just left of the large roof. From an alcove pull over an awkward bulge to a bolt belay.

12. Where the Wild Things Roam (aka Wild Things)   5.11d   ★ ★ ★
45' (13m) in length, 5 QD's and minor pro to ¾"
One of the ten great classics at the Madrone Wall. Exhilarating problem ascending up a brilliant orange face. Begin up an easy slab to the first bolt, then up a continuously overhanging face using numerous in cut edges. Turn to the right side of the large roof and move up a reasonable dihedral to a bolt belay. This is an excellent rainy day climb.

13. Tangerine Dream   5.10a PG   ★
45' (13m) in length, Pro to 1"
A popular route. Start off a boulder and mantle over a crux bulge move, then continue up a dihedral (bolts) until able to angle up left to a bolt anchor.

14. Direct Start to Tangerine Dream   5.10d   ★
15' (4m) in length, QD's and pro to 1"

15. Agent Orange   5.11d   ★ ★
45' (13m) in length, Pro to ¾" including TCU's
A superb, demanding climb! Ascend TD Direct Start to a ledge then face climb up (1 bolt) past a horizontal crack, then up left to an overhung tight corner dihedral (3 bolts) to a bolt anchor.

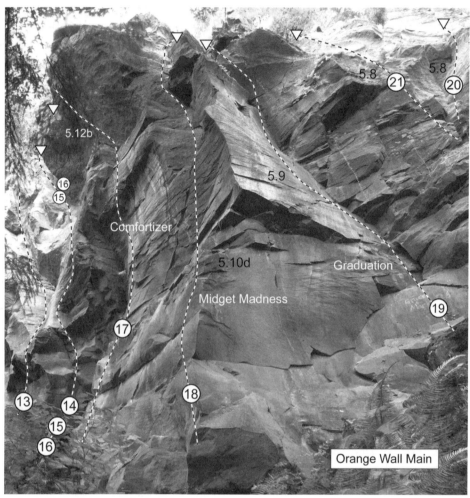

Orange Wall Main

16. O.J. 5.12a ★ ☂

50' (15m) in length, Bolts on Agent Orange, then small nuts and #0 TCU

Climb the lower portion of Agent Orange, except finish up the square cut flaring groove near the top.

17. Comfortizer 5.12b ☂

45' (13m) in length, QD's

A difficult line punching out a large overhang at the top. An upper left variation exists.

18. Midget Madness 5.10d R/X

45' (13m) in length, Pro to 2" including TCU's

A tantalizing problem, yet does not see much climber traffic. Move up easy ground just left of an outside corner. Follow a right-leaning seam and pull an awkward mantle (questionable pro!) into a dihedral. Climb straight up to the top of the pillar to a small tree belay.

19. Graduation 5.9

40' (12m) in length, Pro to 1½"

A left-leaning dihedral with one fixed pin. Step up on large holds then make a quick crux move to easier ground up left. A little dirty near the tree belay, but still a fun climb.

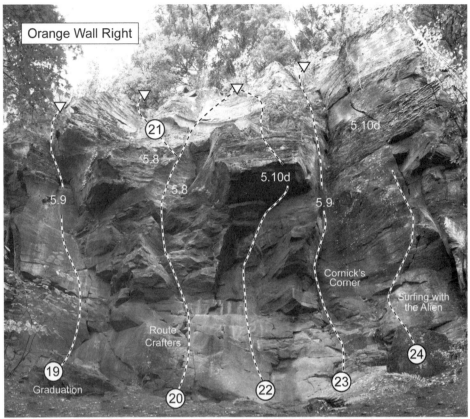

Orange Wall Right

5.10d

21

5.8

5.8

5.10d

5.9

5.9

Cornick's
Corner

Surfing with
the Alien

Route
Crafters

24

19

Graduation

20

22

23

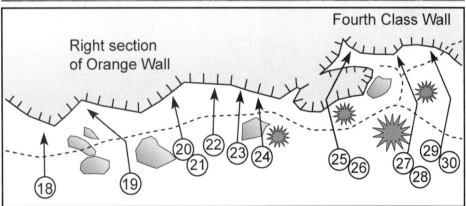

Fourth Class Wall

Right section
of Orange Wall

20 22 23 24

21

25 26

27 29

28 30

18

19

20. Route Crafters 5.8 ★ ★

40' (12m) in length, 5 QD's

A very popular and well-bolted route that wanders up steep ground via many ledges, then up a short dihedral to a bolt anchor.

21. Chop the Monkey 5.8+

20' (6m) in length, 5 QD's

A pin protected corner up left from the 3rd bolt on Route Crafters.

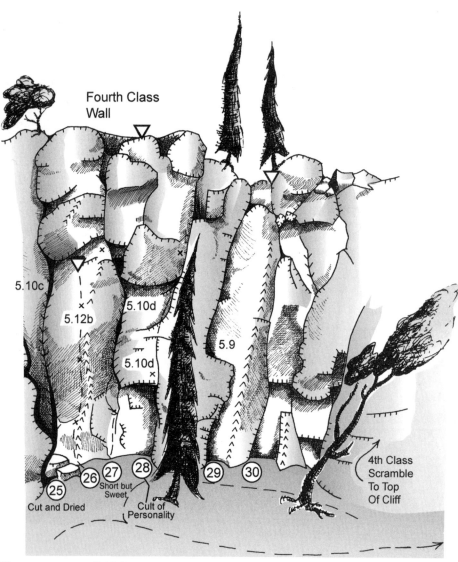

Fourth Class
Wall

5.10c

5.12b

5.10d

5.10d

5.9

4th Class
Scramble
To Top
Of Cliff

25
Cut and Dried

26

27
Short but
Sweet

28
Cult of
Personality

29

30

22. _____ **5.10d**

23. Cornick's Corner 5.9 ★★

40' (12m) in length, Pro to 1½"

An interesting route that ascends the obvious deep dihedral just to the right of a large roof. Bolt anchor.

24. Surfing with the Alien 5.10d R ★★

40' (12m) in length, Pro to 1" RP's, TCU's recommended

This technically demanding route is well worth the blast. Begin up the seam (immediately right of the large dihedral) that angles right to a vertical crack. Continue up a steep face and crack, then bail out left to the dihedral or proceed up through another crux via a thin seam to a bolt anchor.

FOURTH CLASS WALL

25. Cut and Dried   5.10c
40' (12m) in length, Pro to 2"
On the left side of this tiny section of cliff is a large dihedral. Climb up past a hard move until it eases. The quality deteriorates as the vegetation increases near the top.

26. Severed Heads   5.12b ★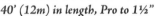
30' (9m) in length, 3 QD's
Difficult arête climb.

27. Short But Sweet   5.10d ★
40' (12m) in length, Pro to 1½"
An excellent climb. Proceed up the dihedral corner, moving past several small lips, step up left (1 bolt) and continue up easier vertical ground to a unique belay.

28. Cult of Personality   5.10d ★
40' (12m) in length, QD's
Step up and surmount a vicious move past a small bulge, then move up right and into a right-facing dirty corner. Rappel from belay anchor.

29. Wolf of the Steppes   5.9
35' (10m) in length, Pro unknown

30. Slippery Sage   5.8
30' (9m) in length, Pro unknown

MAIN WALL - SCOTT FREE AREA

31. Save the Whales   5.10a
30' (9m) in length, Pro to 3"

32. Hungry for Duress   5.10a
30' (9m) in length, Pro to 3"
Located 5' left of Beam Me Up, Mr. Scott. A quick pump.

33. Beam Me Up Mr. Scott   5.11c PG   ★★★
65' (19m) in length, Pro to 1½" including TCU's
One of the 10 super classics at the Madrone Wall. A fantastic, bold route of superior quality. Proceed up an overhanging face via in cut edges (2 bolts) to a small stance. Desperately continue straight up the crack above (bolt) to a small ledge, and bolt belay anchor.

34. Scott Free   5.12a /.12b   ★★★
60' (18m) in length, 5 QD's and minor pro to 3"
Another excellent super classic. This one involves a fierce lunge! Start at the inside corner and move up right to a stance. Step up and left onto the central face and climb straight up. Lunge to a jug, then finish up an easy right facing corner to a bolt anchor on the right.

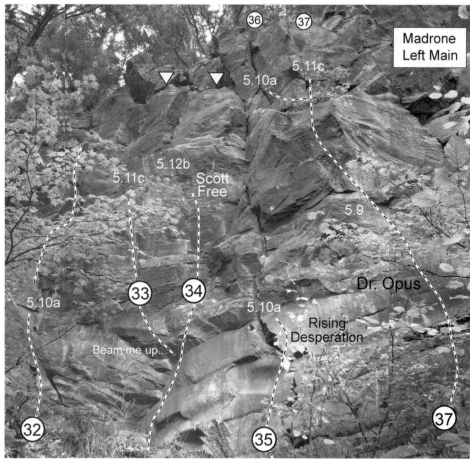

35. Rising Desperation 5.10a ★★ ☂

60' (18m) in length, Pro to 2"

Interesting, fun, jagged crack system that ascends the vertical blocky section immediately right of Scott Free.

36. Direct Finish 5.10a (variation)

15' (4m) in length, Pro to 2½"

37. Dr. Opus Goes Power Lunging 5.11c ★

60' (18m) in length, Pro to 1½"

An impressive climb with much variety. Begin up a smooth, clean 3 bolt face until possible to step out left onto a short (5.9) arête mantle move. From the upper ledge, power lunge your way up a very thin seam to the summit.

38. Spectrum 5.10b PG ★ ☂

20' (6m) in length, Pro to ¾" including TCU's

Excellent short problem. Start in a roof capped dihedral, then under cling out left and up the face (1 piton) to a fixed anchor on a ledge. A short 2 bolt 5.8 lead continues above Spectrum to another anchor.

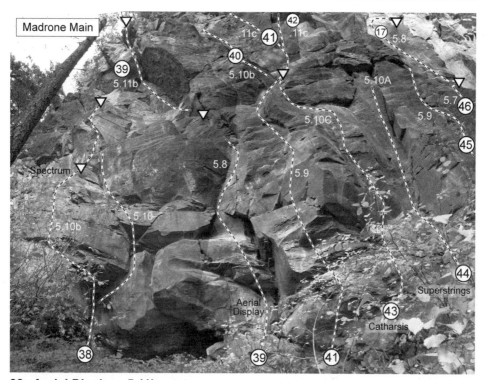

39. Aerial Display 5.11b ★★
100' (30m) in length, Pro to 1½"

One of the few exciting roof climbs at the Madrone Wall. Start to the right of the deep corner (Spectrum) and move up an odd but easy (5.8) groove to ledges. Step left and embark up easy ground to the huge slanting roof broken by an under cling crack. Cling desperately out (1 bolt) and up to the ramps above. Continue up left to a tree belay.

40. Mixing It Up 5.10b
100' (30m) in length, Pro to 2"

41. Catharsis (5.9+ 1ˢᵗ pitch) 5.11d R ★★★
100' (30m) in length, Pro to 1½" TCU's, RP's required

Mentally challenging and a serious lead. Begin up a vertical outside corner (5.9) that has numerous small edges (2 bolts) until you reach a ledge and belay. Step right and proceed onto desperate ground above, then angle up a difficult left seam (bolt) exiting to the top.

42. True Catharsis 5.11c PG
25' (7m) in length, Pro to 1½" TCU's, RP's required

Where Catharsis takes a left on the second pitch, this route goes straight up the crack system above. The rating is unconfirmed.

43. Superstrings 5.10c ★
30' (9m) in length, 3 QD's and optional pro to 1"

A frequently climbed shallow dihedral that ends on good ledges.

44. Lost in the Delta Neighborhood 5.10a
100' (30m) in length, Pro to 2"

Ascend a vertical corner crack system until you must pull over a semi-detached set of blocks split with a crack. Wander up another dihedral and vertical ground to the summit.

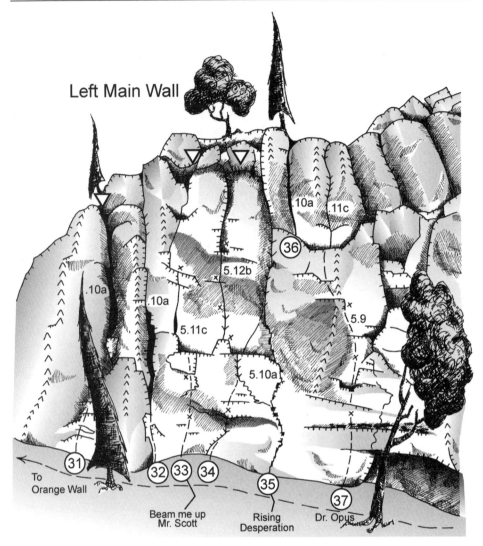

Left Main Wall

45. Sultans of Swing 5.9
30' (9m) in length, 3 QD's and minor pro to 1½''''

46. Double Dutch Left 5.7 ★★
25' (7m) in length, QD's and pro to 1"
Popular, easy dihedral with numerous ledges.

47. Scotty Hits the Warp Drive 5.10c
100' (30m) in length, Pro to 1½"
Start at the Double Dutch belay ledge, step left and ascend a short dihedral to another ledge, then up a slightly overhung crack to the top.

48. Subway to Venus 5.12a ★★
18' (5m) in length, 3 QD's
Just above the Double Dutch belay ledge is a unique but short arête problem. Bolt anchor.

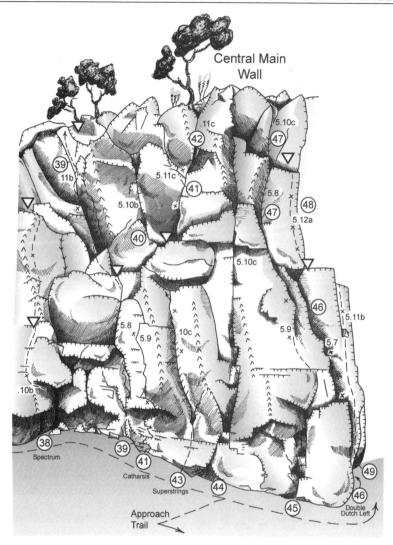

Central Main Wall

49. Trauma Center 5.11b ★★★
100' (30m) in length, Pro to 1½"
This route has an excellent second pitch. The first pitch (5.11a) climbs up a face (2 bolts) between the two Double Dutch routes. From the belay ledge, step right and finish up an orange dihedral (1 bolt) leading to (5.11b) the top. The second pitch is stellar!

50. Double Dutch Right 5.6 ★
20' (6m) in length, Pro to 4"
The obvious large offwidth corner.

51. Primary Gobbler 5.10c
20' (6m) in length, Pro to 6"
The second half of this large offwidth.

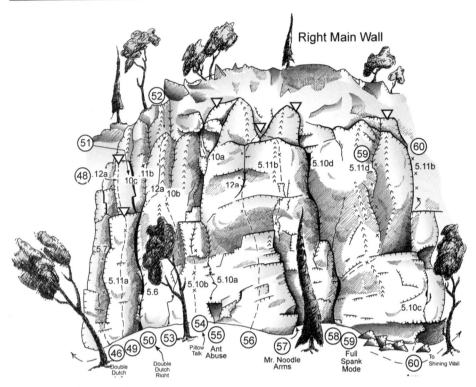

Right Main Wall

52. Never Mind   5.12a
25' (7m) in length, Pro is QD's
This line ascends up a short arête face to the right of the last portion of Trauma Center.

53. Whatever Blows Your Skirt Up   5.10b PG
65' (19m) in length, Pro to 1½"
Ascends up easy rock left of Pillow Talk to a smooth face (1 bolt), then up a shallow dihedral capped by a small bulge.

54. Pillow Talk   5.10b (variation)   ★★
20' (6m) in length, 3 QD's and pro to 1½"
A popular trade route, though it is much more interesting when combined with Ant Abuse.

55. Ant Abuse   5.10a PG   ★★★   🌂
60' (18m) in length, Pro to 1½" Cams recommended
This fun, clean route begins up the thin cracks immediately right of Pillow Talk. Pull up to the ledge, then move up a large open dihedral and step left to crank over an overhang (crux). Bolt belay.

56. Time To Kill 5.12a   ★★   🌂
50' (15m) in length, QD's
An enticing and quality face climb with a short but unusually difficult crux at a minor overhang. Rap from belay anchor.

57. Mr. Noodle Arm (Goes Limp)   5.11b PG   ★★★   🌂
50' (15m) in length, Mostly QD's, minor pro to 1" (TCU's or small nuts)
A route of stellar proportion. A very quality route and a must for everyone. Begin near a tall, thin fir tree. Climb a vertical broken arête (crux) to a stance, then move up left to a bolt

anchor.

58. Sisters of the Road 5.10d ★★ [Dry]

60' (18m) in length, Pro to 1½"

Highly recommended. Move up easy ground in a dihedral. The climb increases in difficulty with height until you encounter a deceiving crux in a pea-pod flare. From a small stance, pull through a mantle (piton) and finish up easy ground to a bolt anchor.

59. Full Spank Mode 5.11d ★★★ [Dry]

65' (19m) in length, 5 QD's and minor pro to ½"

One of the ten super classics. Start as for Sisters of the Road, but step right, lean out around on jug holds to a stance. Then embark up the difficult and slightly overhung face above. Eases to several ledges and a bolt belay. A variation (**Full Wank Mode** 5.12a) exists at the 4th bolt that powers up right (1 bolt) onto rounded feature to finish at same belay.

60. Arm Forces 5.11b R ★★★

65' (19m) in length, Pro to 1" including TCU's, RP's

A superior climb and one of the ten famous classics. This bold and demanding route begins up a thin (5.10d) vertical seam to a large ledge. Boldly march onto the sustained, overhung, rounded dihedral (bolts) leading to several ledges and a bolt belay.

SHINING WALL

61. Cold Hand of Technology 5.10c

70' (21m) in length, Pro to 1½"

Unique. Start at the large halfway ledge on Arm Forces. Step up right and ascend a dihedral until you can launch into a left leaning crack that turns a corner. Transverse left to the Arm Forces belay.

62. Red Scare 5.10c R

25' (7m) in length, Pro to ¾" RP's and thin wires

Step off a large boulder and ascend a thin seam (1 bolt) to the large ledge. Finish up one of several routes.

63. Domino Effect 5.9

25' (7m) in length, Pro to 1"

64. Dirty Dancing 5.9

80' (24m) in length, Pro to 2½"

Start at an overhang. Climb a corner up to the halfway ledges and step right to ascend a dirty meandering (5.7) corner system up a near vertical cliff. Bolt anchor at top.

65. Firing Line 5.11c R

40' (12m) in length, 2 QD's and minor pro to ¾"

An interesting bullet-scarred face. Run out and odd bolt locations. Pull through a flared over-

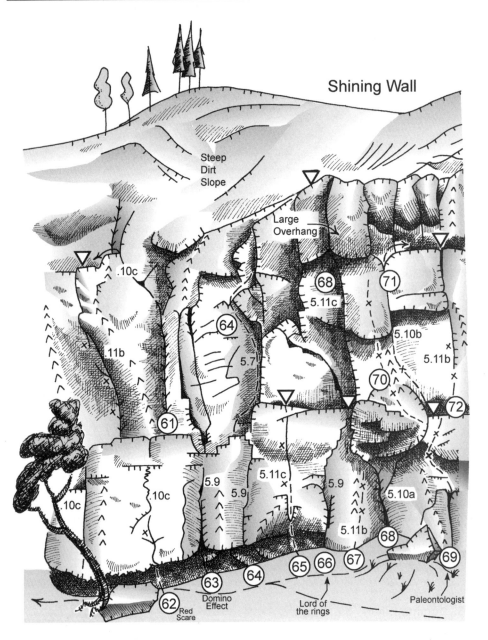

Shining Wall

Steep
Dirt
Slope

Large
Overhang

.10c

5.11c   71

64   68   5.10b

5.7   .11b   5.11b

70

.10c   61   72

5.9   5.11c   5.9   5.10a

.10c   .10c   5.9   5.9   5.11b   68

65 66 67   69

62   63   64   Lord of   Paleontologist
Red   Domino   the rings
Scare   Effect

hung slot, move up a smooth face, then up a short, vertical crux until you can mantle up to a bolt belay.

66. Lord of the Rings   5.9

25' (7m) in length, Pro to 3" Cams suggested

A short flare problem that angles up to join Dancing in the Lion's Jaw at the bolt anchor on a ledge.

67. The Gift of Time   5.11b (variation)

15' (4m) in length, 2 QD's and minor pro to 1"

68. Dancing in the Lion's Jaw   5.11c PG

80' (24m) in length, Pro to 1 1/2" including TCU's

A bold lead for the serious climber. Start up a central dihedral on the Shining Wall (5.10a) to a ledge and bolt belay. Commence up the prominent dihedral through two significant crux (5.11c) roofs. Pull wildly over the last bulge to the belay.

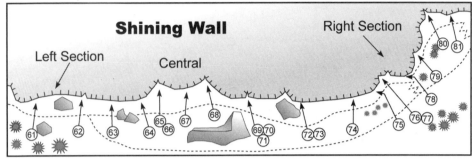

69. Paleontologist 5.10b ★★
60' (18m) in length, Pro to 2"
A popular climb, and rightly so. Start by stepping up onto a large rock platform. Move up left over a bulge (2 bolts) to a ledge and bolt anchor. Continue up left via a face then a crack to a large ledge with a bolt anchor on the right and above Rainman.

70. Extinction 5.10d PG
60' (18m) in length, Pro is QD's
This variation starts on Paleontologist using the first two bolts to the small ledge stance, then branches over left, and up to the roof, then moves right to the anchor ledge. Runout between the bolts and a risky fall.

71. Rainman 5.11b ★★
25' (7m) in length, Pro to 1"
Outrageous, gripping climb. From the first belay on Paleontologist, step up right and climb a

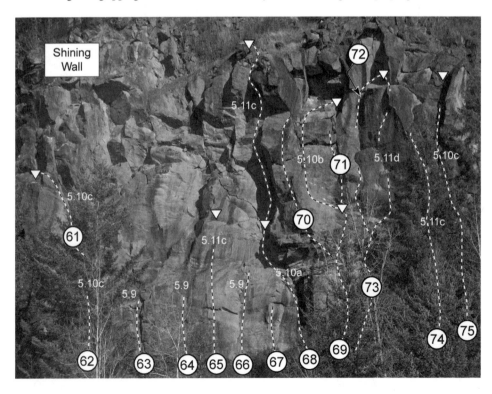

steep face to an easy vertical crack. Bolt anchor.

72. Playing with Fire   5.11b   ★
60' (18m) in length, Pro to 1"
Good route. From the large platform, move up a deep dihedral (1 bolt) to a ledge. Continue up a fun curving finger crack system (1 piton) ending at an upper ledge. Step right and belay at anchor above the Shining Wall route. It is a 5.10a if topping out above here.

73. Shining Wall   5.11d   ★★★
60' (18m) in length, 9 QD's
A super classic. Climbs the obvious bolted orange face. A physically difficult route using many sloping small edges that gets thinner near the exit move.

74. Cloudwalker   5.11c   ★
60' (18m) in length, Pro to 1" TCU's recommended
The first 15' is the crux. Start near a group of madrone trees on the right side of the wall. Surmount a difficult start, step up left to a steep but reasonable crack with one hard move (5.10b) at a bulge. Struggle over this to an easy dihedral and a bolt belay.

75. Banana Belt   5.10c R
60' (18m) in length, Pro to 1½" Needs bolts
An inconspicuous prow that would make a fine climb were it bolted. Climb an easy offwidth to a ledge, then up a vertical prow broken with numerous edges. Belay at Cloudwalker anchor.

76. Fits and Starts   5.10a
30' (9m) in length, Pro to 1 ½"

77. Beginner's Luck   5.5
60' (18m) in length, Pro to 1½"
You can't miss it. Obvious wide chimney corner behind several madrone trees.

78. Gym Rats From Hell   5.10c PG   ★★
40' (12m) in length, Pro to 2"
A unique climb. A great top-rope area because of its easy access from one anchor. This climb has two starts. The left start is a steep crack (PG), while the right is an easy approach via shattered flakes. From a halfway stance crank up a smooth face (bolts) and mantle using numerous sloping edges. Bolt belay.

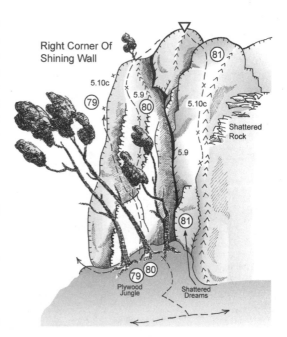

Right Corner Of Shining Wall

79. Plywood Jungle   5.9   ★★
40' (12m) in length, 3 QD's
Fun lead. Do it!

80. Dihedral of Despair   5.9 (TR)
40' (12m) in length
The large yet somewhat loose dihedral. Top-rope only!

81. Shattered Dreams   5.10c
40' (12m) in length, Pro to 1"
A bit dusty, but otherwise a fun

route. Start just to the right of Dihedral of Despair and ascend a short, jagged finger crack to a smooth face. A few tricky moves (bolts) and then traverse left to the bolt anchor.

HARDSCRABBLE - LEFT SECTION

82. Sacrifice   5.10a

40' (12m) in length, Pro to 1"

83. Inner Vision   5.11a

40' (12m) in length, Pro to 1" including TCU's

A bolted overhang left of Mind Games.

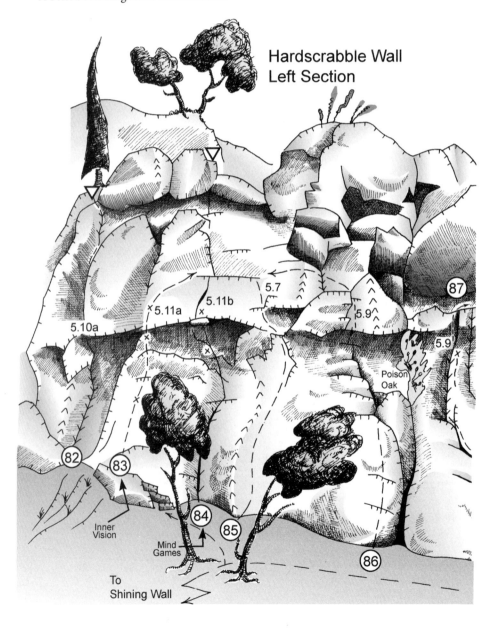

Hardscrabble Wall
Left Section

84. Mind Games 5.11b ★ ★ ★

40' (12m) in length, Pro to 1" including TCU's

One of the ten classics and a fun roof problem at that. Step up an easy slab, then ape your way out to the overhang (2 bolts) and straight up to easier ground. A final 5.8 move brings you to a bolt belay.

85. Chicken 5.7

25' (7m) in length, Pro to 1" including TCU's

A minor easy variation to get around Mind Games

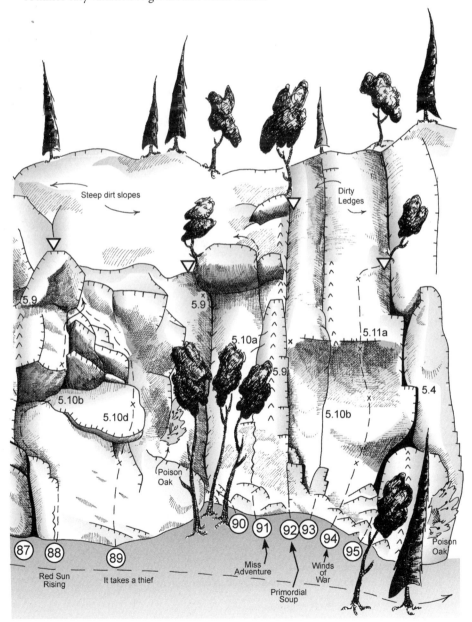

Steep dirt slopes

Dirty Ledges

5.9

5.9

5.10a

5.11a

5.9

5.10b

5.10b

5.4

5.10d

Poison Oak

87   88   89

90 91 92 93 94 95

Red Sun Rising

It takes a thief

Miss Adventure

Winds of War

Primordial Soup

Poison Oak

86. Gym Droids 5.9 (variation)
25' (7m) in length, Pro to 1"

87. Life As We Know It 5.8
30' (9m) in length, Pro to 1"
Thirty feet to the right of Mind Games is a beautiful red-orange face broken by an overhang halfway up. The left variation is the easiest.

88. Red Sun Rising 5.10b PG ★★★
30' (9m) in length, Pro to 1½"
A great climb and very popular. Begin up an unprotected seam immediately right of the offwidth. At the roof, under cling out and surmount the overhang (1 bolt) via large jugs. Continue up and left to a bolt belay.

89. It Takes a Thief 5.10d PG ★★
30' (9m) in length, QD's and pro to 1"
A tantalizing route. Ascend the steep red face (bolts) past a hard move, then angle up and left to the anchor.

90. American Girl 5.9
30' (9m) in length, Pro to 1"

91. Miss Adventure 5.10a
35' (10m) in length, Pro to 1½"
An interesting thin finger crack immediately right of the dihedral and behind several madrone trees.

92. Primordial Soup 5.9
40' (12m) in length, Pro to 1"
A nice climb that is actually better than it appears to be.

93. Crystal Hunters 5.10b
40' (12m) in length, Pro to 1"

94. Winds of War 5.10d ★★
30' (9m) in length, 4 QD's
Quality face climb. Begin up just left of the Mountaineer's Route. Ascend a steep face and pull through a thin crux, then step right to a tree belay. The cracks on both sides detract slightly from the aesthetics of the route.

95. Mountaineer's Route 5.4
30' (9m) in length, Pro unknown

HARDSCRABBLE - CENTRAL

96. Punters in Paradise 5.9+
50' (15m) in length, Pro to 2"
Proceed up the slightly overhung buttress via a crack just to the right of a poison oak bush. Angle up left and finish up an easy hand crack to a large fir tree near the summit.

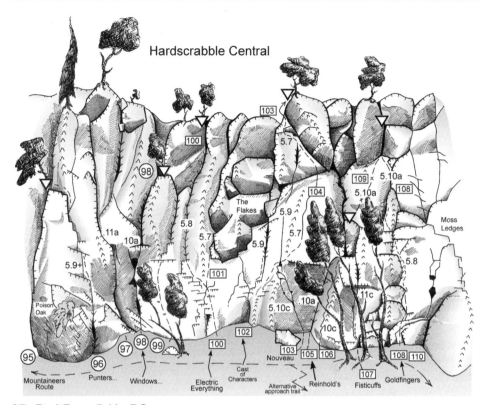

97. Red Fox 5.11a PG

50' (15m) in length, Pro to 1½"

An interesting climb with a nasty crux. Ascend a beautiful right-facing dihedral (has poison oak) and exit up left (crux) to easy slabs. Continue up a hand crack to the top.

98. Windows of Your Mind 5.10a ★★

40' (12m) in length, Pro to 1½" optional pro to 3"

This great climb starts up a vertical crack broken with several large triangular "windows." Pull through a thin crux and finish up an easy offwidth. Bolt belay.

99. PC 5.11b (TR)

40' (12m) in length

100. Screensaver 5.6

40' (12m) in length, Pro to 2 ½"

101. Electric Everything 5.7 ★

40' (12m) in length, Pro to 2½"

Climbs up around the left side of the Guillotine Flakes topping out via an offwidth.

102. Cast of Characters 5.9

20' (6m) in length, Pro to 1"

Start in a minor corner below Guillotine Flakes to a crux 5.9 move as you get near the flakes. Then continue up steep ground to where the flakes overhang, and angle over right to join Nouveau Riche for the last steep but easy bulge section that leads to an easier slab just under a left-sloping roof. Move around a block then up to a tree belay.

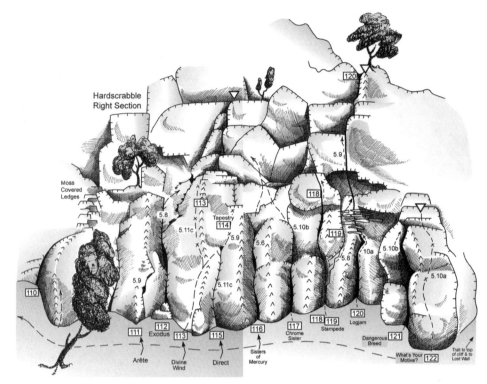

Hardscrabble
Right Section

Moss
Covered
Ledges

5.8
5.11c
5.9

113
Tapestry
114
5.9
5.6
5.10b
119
5.8
5.10a
10a
5.10b
5.10a
5.11c

110

111   112   113   115   116   117   118 119   120
Arête   Exodus   Direct   Sisters   Chrome   Stampede   Logjam
Divine   of   Sister   Dangerous   121
Wind   Mercury   Breed
What's Your   122
Motive?
Trail to top
of cliff & to
Lost Wall

103. Nouveau Riche (New Wealth) 5.10c ★★★

70' (21m) in length, Pro to 1½" TCU's suggested

A super classic and well worth it. Superb, fun climbing. Begin at a large boulder near the head of the approach trail. Dance up a steep left-leaning crack (5.10c) to a stance, then up a 5.9 crack splitting a smooth face. Step right, surmount an easy bulge. Wander up easy slabs just under a left-sloping roof, and move around a block then up to a tree belay.

104. Stamina 5.7 R (variation)

20' (6m) in length, Pro to 3" Cams recommended

Starts same as for Cast of Characters, but angles across Nouveau Riche up rightward following a minor crack. A bit runout for a lead, and should have a fixed bolt.

105. Reinhold's Dihedral 5.10a

30' (9m) in length, Pro to 1½"

A short right leaning dihedral, followed by several ledges leading to a bolt belay.

106. Eye of the Tiger 5.10c PG ★

15' (4m) in length, Pro to ¾"

The dull arête just to the right of 'Reinhold's.' A thin seam protects the moves.

107. Fisticuffs 5.11c ★

20' (6m) in length

A short but physically demanding top-rope problem that ascends a smooth overhang split by a flared crux move.

108. Goldfingers 5.10a ★★★

60' (18m) in length, Pro to 1½" TCU's recommended

A fabulous and popular route. A must for all. Begin up an odd corner near four madrone trees. Move past a thinly protected seam (5.7) to a series of ledges. Proceed up a clean flared crack until able to step left to an offwidth. Pull up to a ledge and bolt belay.

109. Girl Crazy   5.10a (variation)
15' (4m) in length, 2 QD's and minor pro to 1"
An interesting variation that joins Reinhold's Dihedral with the Goldfingers offwidth section.

110. _____   5.10
20' (6m) in length, Pro unknown

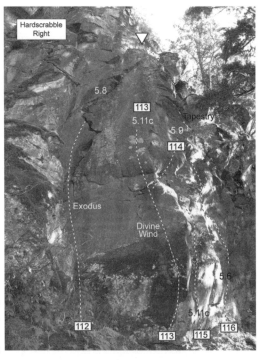

HARDSCRABBLE - RIGHT
111. The Arête   5.9 (TR)
25' (7m) in length

112. Exodus   5.8 ★
40' (12m) in length, Pro to 1½"
A deep dihedral with a unique large jagged crack on the right face. Climb the dihedral until possible to exit up right to easy ledges. Step up to a bolt belay above Divine Wind.

113. Divine Wind   5.11c ★★★
40' (12m) in length, QD's and minor pro to ¾"
One of the ten super classics. Begin on the left side of a minor outside corner. Move up to and ascend the bolted smooth arête, past a crux move to easier ledges. A very popular route. Bolt anchor.

114. Tapestry   5.9 ★
40' (12m) in length, QD's and minor pro to ¾"
Start up Divine Wind but step right and venture up a separate line of bolts passing a bulge to easy ledges. Bolt belay.

115. Direct Start to Divine Wind   5.11c
15' (4m) in length, Pro to ¾" TCU's and RP's
An odd but demanding problem. Originally led on-sight.

116. Sisters of Mercury   5.6 ★★★
40' (12m) in length, Pro to 1"
A good quality climb for beginners. Ascend the obvious corner to the right of Tapestry.

117. Chromesister   5.10b
40' (12m) in length, Pro to 1"
Starts as an offwidth but involves a slightly overhung thin crack crux move.

118. _____

119. Stampede   5.9
40' (12m) in length, Pro to 1½" Cams suggested

120. Logjam   5.10a
40' (12m) in length, Pro to 3" Cams suggested
This fun, wide crack is located immediately left of a dirty gully. Ascend this and angle up left

to a stance below a steep upper section. Several quick jam moves lead to good ledges and a madrone tree belay.

121. Dangerous Breed   5.10b ★

30' (12m) in length, Pro to 4"

The next two climbs are located on the last climbable buttress at the southern end of the Hardscrabble Wall. Dangerous Breed is the 'enjoyable' offwidth. Rap from belay.

122. What's Your Motive?   5.10a PG ★★

30' (9m) in length, 2 QD's and optional pro to ½"

The last climb at the bluff, but a great one at that! Climb up the outside face of the buttress to a belay anchor.

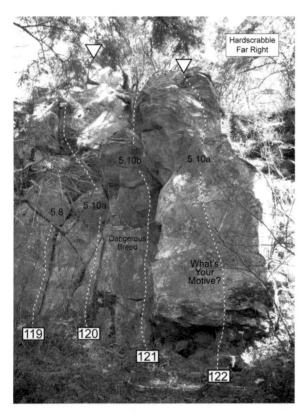

"Even if a person has spent just a single day out of a lifetime in the mountains, they will have been given something that will sustain them through any and everything they have to face for the rest of their life."
-Heinrich Harrer

MADRONE WALL

CHAPTER 5

OZONE

Ozone introduction written by Jon Bell
Route beta provided courtesy of Kevin Evansen and associates
This Ozone chapter is dedicated to the memory of Kevin Rauch

I t's not often that an outstanding climbing crag just outside a major metropolitan area sits undeveloped for very long. But Ozone, an 800-foot-long andesitic-basalt cliff full of classic cracks and heavenly jugs less than 20 miles from Portland, managed to remain relatively hidden — and essentially untouched — for nearly 25 years after it was originally stumbled upon and climbed back in 1984.

Today, thanks to the efforts of a handful of dedicated and hardworking climbers, Ozone has been transformed from an illegal roadside dump into not only a splendid mass of top-notch climbs, but a valuable recreational resource as well. The more than 75 routes that have been put up primarily since 2004 range in difficulty from 5.6 to 5.12c, with the majority falling somewhere between 5.8 and 5.10. There are single and multi-pitch climbs, pure trad routes that only take gear, fully-bolted sport climbs, and routes that employ both gear and bolts.

Hidden among the evergreens just north of the Columbia River in Washington, Ozone also affords sweeping and unique views of the Columbia River Gorge. And the cliff, which is now fully developed, provides an alternative venue for climbers during Beacon Rock's seasonal closure.

HISTORY AND DEVELOPMENT

Heading east on I-84 toward the Eagle Creek trailhead back in 1984, Jim Opdycke caught a glimpse of something across the Columbia River that intrigued him.

Contrasted against the darkened evergreens that blanket the steep walls of the Washington side of the Columbia River Gorge was a narrow band of gray rock. He saw it only briefly, but Opdycke, a veteran climber who by then had been climbing at Beacon Rock, Yosemite, and elsewhere for almost a decade, knew it was something worth seeing again.

Soon after this first sighting, Opdycke paid a visit to that narrow band of rock. He found it just a few miles east of Washougal despite the absence of a trail or any other sign that someone had been there before. Opdycke bushwhacked through the trees, dropped down a steep hillside, and found himself at the base of an imposing andesite-basalt cliff that looked out to the Columbia River through an evergreen thicket. The wall, about 800 feet long and 200 feet tall at its highest point, was overgrown with moss and trees and thick shrubs of poison oak. There were a couple dead

Misako on *The Humbling 5.12a*

deer and the scattered remnants of illegal trash dumping. But all that wasn't enough to hide the snaking cracks, the textured faces, the clean lines running up the face.

Opdycke and his friend Mike Jackson returned to the unknown cliff that same year and worked their way up a few of the more natural cracks on the face. Those first few routes are now known as the Opdycke Crack (5.9+) and Eight is Enough (5.8).

They also decided to name the wall Ozone because, like the invisible layer of stratosphere miles above the earth, so too was this Ozone invisible.

At the time, however, Opdycke and his friends were more into climbing and developing new routes at Beacon Rock than they were in taking on Ozone. So they focused their attention on the 850-foot monolith up the road and left Ozone for another day.

Over the ensuing years, Ozone sat relatively untouched and unknown, though a few local climbers like Dave Dick spent some time at the wall climbing and putting up a handful of routes. Then, around 2003, Opdycke clued several folks in on Ozone, including Bryan Smith, Kevin Evansen, Glen Hartman, and Mark Deffenbaugh. Though various parties paid various visits to the wall — eyeballing prospective routes among the tangle of trees, moss, loose rocks, and massive growths of poison oak —it would be another year before serious development began at Ozone.

In late December 2004, Kevin Rauch, having heard about Ozone from Deffenbaugh, ventured out to Ozone with Smith and a borrowed drill for a little reconnaissance. In a meticulously-kept climbing journal, Rauch mentions Ozone for the first time on Dec. 18, 2004: "Fixed 2 lines; installed 1 anchor bolt prior to darkness . . ." A new wave of development had begun at Ozone.

By very early 2005, full-on development of new routes, as well as work on cleaning up the area and establishing a better trail system, had set in at the crag, driven primarily by climbers like Rauch, Jon Stewart, Kevin Evansen, Deffenbaugh, Smith, and Glen Hartman.

Though the intent of some of the original developers — many of whom had never done any route development before— was to put up all trad climbs, or at least to utilize natural protection wherever possible, and though the first few routes put up were done without the use of bolts, differing development styles and approaches emerged.

Some routes were put in from the ground up without any bolts; some were established by rappelling from above and installing bolts the entire length of the climb; some ended up being protected by a mix of gear and bolts. Whatever the style, all routes along the overgrown wall had to be painstakingly cleaned of moss, dirt, grass, trees, loose rocks and boulders, and poison oak.

Throughout this early develop-

Steve Wolford on Carrots For Everyone

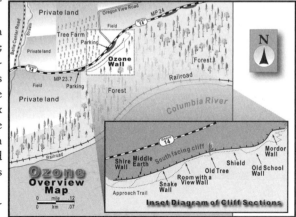

ment phase, Ozone remained unknown to all but the handful of tight-lipped climbers focused on cleaning up the wall and putting up routes. But, as can happen within the climbing community, grist began grinding through the rumor mill, and within a year, more and more cars started to make their way to a random pullout just off Washington State Route 14. This led not only to more people climbing at Ozone, but to further development of the wall until the final few routes were established in an area on the east end of the crag known as Mordor in May 2008.

GEOLOGY

Ozone lies within the Grande Ronde Basalt, a formation of basaltic andesite within the Columbia River Basalt Group. The CRBG comprises immense outpourings of lava that erupted from vents in central and northeast Oregon during the Miocene period of 6 million to 17.5 million years ago. These eruptions created one of the largest flood ba-

Map 1: Shire Wall - right section

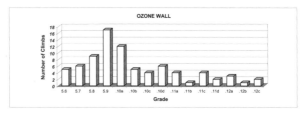

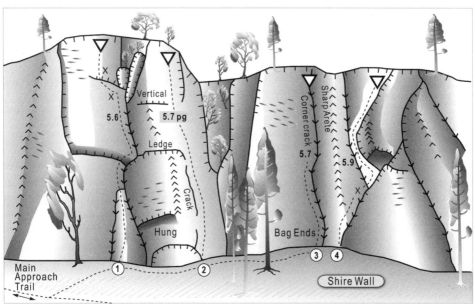

Topo A: Shire Wall

salt provinces in the world, with an outpouring of lava that would have been immense enough to construct a wall one mile wide and two miles high around the earth.

The ancestral Columbia River provided a natural conduit for these lavas as they made their way to the Pacific Ocean, and the river successively moved north as it cut new channels through the hardened lavas. The basalt cliffs of Ozone were likely exposed during the Missoula Floods, cataclysmic floods of the last Ice Age 13,000 to 15,000 years ago. The floods were the result of periodic ice dam failures of Glacial Lake Missoula in what is now northwestern Montana. Floodwaters racing through the Columbia River Gorge at speeds of up to 80 miles per hour carried away debris and steepened the walls of the Gorge, exposing the more resistant basalt cliffs and paving the way for modern-day climbing enjoyment.

OZONE BETA

Ratings: All the climbs at Ozone are rated based on the Yosemite Decimal System, e.g. (5.10a/b = 10-) (5.10b/c = 10) (5.10c/d = 10+). The crux of each climb is identified by its rating on the corresponding topo maps.

Gear: Fixed protection should always be considered suspect and when possible backed up with protection you place yourself. Many routes are mixed sport and traditional.

Do not assume that there is adequate protection available higher up. Make use of all available protection until you become familiar with the route. An extensive gear rack allows you to take advantage of all climbs listed below.

It should be noted that as of July 2008, the USDA Forest Service, Columbia River Gorge National Scenic Area, has proposed a recreation and management plan for the Cape Horn planning area in Skamania County, which covers the land where Ozone sits. The purpose of this planning effort is to identify and locate preferred recreational assets, such as hiking trails and scenic overlooks, on the contiguous federal land parcels near Cape Horn. Again, it is not clear how or if Ozone will be affected by this planning effort, but because the crag falls within the planning area's boundaries, it will be important to remain informed of this process.

For more information, visit www.fs.fed.us/r6/columbia/projects/ and look under "Current Projects" for "Cape Horn Recreation Management Plan."

Ownership: Ozone sits on public land owned by the federal government as part of the Columbia River Gorge National Scenic Area. People were climbing at Ozone before the establishment of the CRGNSA in 1986, though the land does fall within the boundaries of the scenic area, which is managed under the auspices of the Columbia River

Gorge Commission: In order to preserve and maintain unfettered access to Ozone, please respect and take care of the land and the crag.

VISUAL BIO

8
Month 5 Mins   (S)   Shade   All Day   Sport   Trad

These emblems represent virtually all of Ozone. The entire wall can be accessed by either the *Westside Trail* or the *Eastside Trail* in five minutes or less. The upper portion of many climbing routes are in the full sunshine, especially from about 70'-120' and just when you are getting pumped a few moves short of the belay anchor. The Mordor Wall, which is heavily shaded receives a very limited mid-afternoon sunlight, and it is so steep it can be climbed for 12-months of the year. The cold windy Gorge temperatures tend to dissuade most climbers from using this site during the heart of Winter. The site offers considerable sport route opportunities, but also a variety of partly bolted gear leads. Ozone offers some less-traveled quality crack climbs.

DIRECTIONS FROM PORTLAND

The Ozone crag is in southwest Washington, roughly 7½ miles east of the town of Washougal on State Route 14. From Interstate 205 in Portland or Vancouver, head east on SR 14 for approximately 18¼ miles to a small pullout on the south side of the highway, just about three-tenths of a mile east of Belle Center Road in between mile markers 23 and 24. (See note about parking below.) Hop on the rugged trail hidden in the trees and walk to the base of the crag in just a few minutes. There is also a second pullout a few hundred feet east of the first pullout on the south side of the road. The east end of the trail is accessible from this pullout as well.

Parking: As of this publication, only the two pullouts mentioned above are available for parking. As those areas are extremely limited in capacity, it is absolutely imperative that climbers carpool to the crag. And please, park at an angle, not parallel to the road.

Andrew Blake leading *Snake Face*

The west side climbers path descends from the roadside down eastward to the base of the wall. The initial cliff section is short, but quickly lengthens as you continue to descend to the base near Masterpiece Theater.

The Shire Wall (Map 1, Topo A) encompasses a selection of four short/moderate rock climbs at the first side trail as you descend the main trail.

1. **Bearded Lady 5.6**
   40' (12m) in length, Pro to 2" and QD's
   Ascends a broken corner system that heads up left past two bolts to an anchor.

2. **Old Toby 5.7 PG**
   40' (12m) in length, Pro to 2", cams and wires

3. **Bag Ends 5.7 ★**
   40' (12m) in length, Pro to 1", cams
   From the level belay platform ascend straight up to a left facing open corner by stemming or face climbing. Has a tough move to get to the anchor.

4. **Brandywine 5.9 ★**
   40' (12m) in length, Pro to 3½"
   From the ground aim up right into a deep corner system past one bolt to a small roof (crux). Pull up right over the roof to a short slab that leads to the anchor.

Map #2: Middle Earth

Middle Earth (Map 2, Map 3 and Topo B): A short side trail angles up to this section onto the top of a small rock tower with a large flat ledge on it. These next six climbs are on the wall left and above the small rock tower.

Map #3: Middle Earth

Small Rock Tower

5.   Rude Boy   5.8

80' (24m) in length, Pro to 4"

Ascends moss covered ledges up left to a crack system. Follow it over a bulge (crux) to a wider crack and boulders leading to an anchor. Loose rock near the top of the climb.

6.   Why Must I Cry   5.10a   ★

80' (24m) in length, Pro to 1" and QD's

Ascend up the face, and aim left under a small fir tree in the wall, and up to a ledge. Continue up left to the Rude Boys anchor.

7.   Night Owl   5.6

80' (24m) in length, Pro to 5"

Climbs the gully to the right of the previous route.

8.   Leisure Time   5.9

90' (27m) in length, Pro to 1"

Ascends a shallow corner system past a small roof. Use slings to rap from a tree on the upper right near the top of the bluff.

9.   Variety   5.10

100' (30m) in length, Pro to 5"

Long steep hands-to-offwidth crack corner system that takes lot of pro. Rap from same tree on Leisure Time.

10.   House of Pain   5.11a   ★★

50' (15m) in length, QD's

From the large belay ledge on top of the rock tower head up a corner, then right and over the roof (crux), then continue up an arête to an anchor.

11.   Redhorn Gate   5.9   ★

50' (15m) in length, Pro to 4"

Ascend up the smooth face to the flake, then follow crack system up to the left (crux). Use larger gear in the upper part of the crack.

12.   Helm's Deep   5.9   ★★★

80' (24m) in length, Pro to 2" and QD's

From the very lip of the small tower step across the gap onto the face to the first bolt. Continue up the bolted route powering up incut holds. Gear protects a runout in between the 4th and 5th bolt.

Snake Wall (Map 4 and Topo B): Just past a prominent rock tower another short trail heads up to the cliff. Two

Kevin Evansen on *Chain Mail*

large roofs identify this section of wall. These climbs start below and right of the small rock tower.

Map #4: Snake Crack

13. Before the Storm   5.9

95' (28m) in length, Pro to 2" including small cams & wires

Ascends a steep corner crack immediately left of Snake Face route. Good rest stances with an optional early exit off right to attain the Snake Face anchor. A 60-meter rope is needed for the rappel from the cliff top anchor.

14. Snake Face   5.9   ★ ★ ★

70' (21m) in length, Pro to 1" and QD's

Just to the east of the rock tower ascend a bolted route up the face. Small gear protects between the 2nd and 3rd bolt. A slight crux bulge in the upper crack system quickly eases to a gear crack. Angle up right to bolt anchor. A top-rope problem (5.11+) exists by aiming up right through the roof after the last bolt. TR only; detached blocks.

15. Snake Roof   5.10a   ★ ★

70' (21m) in length, Pro to 2½" including cams and wires

This route climbs through the large double large roof. Ascend the deep corner crack system to the first large roof. Move left on small edges around the first roof, then up right to the second roof (bolt). Surmount this section and angle up easy steps left to the same anchor as the previous route.

The next 4 climbs can be accessed by a short 4th class scramble up to a large ledge immediately right of Snake Face. Reference Map 4 and Topo B for clarity.

16. Vicious   5.11a   ★

70' (21m) in length, Pro to 3" and QD's

From a belay ledge ascend up left and follow the bolts on an arête. Pull a difficult boulder problem then use gear (small cams) to continue up left onto the Snake Roof route. Or angle up right into the Opdyke Crack route using large gear to finish on that line.

17. Opdycke Crack   5.9+

70' (21m) in length, Pro to 3"

Ascends a large crack corner system, traversing under a detached block, then up right in a wide corner system to an anchor.

18. Party at the Moon Tower 5.10a ★★

65' (19m) in length, QD's

Start up the previous route, then aim up right onto the arête. Follow this directly up to an anchor.

19. Eight is Enough 5.8 ★★★

65' (19m) in length, Pro to 2"

From a ledge aim up right, and stem past a sustained corner that gets steeper. A series of runout jugs lead to an anchor.

Room With a View / Gold Wall (Map 5 and Topo B): The access trail lands at a wide stance immediately below this tall vertical section of the wall at the Masterpiece Theater route.

Map #5: Masterpiece

20. Chaos 5.8 ★★★

80' (24m) in length, Pro to 1" and cams

This partially bolted climb begins where the trail initially meets the main wall. Follow up the right facing corner, and pull up left under the roof and up to a stance. The climb continues by ascending up a steep arête to the anchor.

21. Siddartha 5.8

40' (12m) in length, Pro to 3" and long slings

Starts same as for Chaos up the right facing corner, past the roof, and then traverses up right along the obvious ledge to the broken crack system. Ascend up the nice left facing open book corner system. When the crack ends pull up right to the anchor.

22. Masterpiece Theater 5.11c ★★★

95' (28m) in length, QD's and a ¾" to 1" cam

This line is certainly one of the testpiece classics at Ozone! Ascend up an initial short slab clipping several bolts as the climb steepens into an overhang. The cam protects a critical moves between the 3rd and 4th bolt immediately above the crux. Continue to climb the long vertical sustained arête up to an anchor.

23. Beyond the Glory 5.11d ★★★

90' (27m) in length, QD's

Ascends a thin seam through an overhang using large underclings and thin edges to a no hands stance, then continue up a steep face on runout but good edges to join

Bennett Kornbrath powers up
Masterpiece Theater 5.11c

with the last bolt on Masterpiece Theater.

24. Screaming For Change 5.10c ★
90' (27m) in length, Pro to ¾" including cams

Ascend past a bolt to a chimney move that leads to a block stance. From the top of the block lean out left and then climb up left using face edges. Sustained climbing leads up a cliff section of mixed bolts and gear to an anchor.

Kung Fu (Map #6): A consistently steep non-descript section of cliff with several popular climbs.

25. Afternoon Delight 5.7 - 5.10 ★★
100' (30m) in length, Gear to 2", Small cams and optional 3½" cam

Start as for Kung Fu, but move up left into the obvious vertical crack in a shallow dihedral corner system. At approximately 80', exit left to the Sreaming For Change (5.7) belay anchor. Or...continue up one of three crack options to the top which involves climbing over a block and past a deep overhung section. Reach around to the left to surmount the gaping maw overhang (use the large cam here).

26. Kung Fu 5.9 ★★
80' (24m) in length, QD's, and 1" cams

Start up vertical terrain on positive holds. Clip the first bolt (avoid the crack system on the left) and aim up right onto a minor steep arête. The quality of the rock and the climbing improve considerably as you climb further up onto this quality arête.

27. Whine and Cheese 5.10d PG
80' (24m) in length, Pro to 3" and QD's

Ascend up past two bolts to a ledge. Aim up the corner system past a face climbing section (crux) to the next ledge. Traverse left using gear around a large boulder, then aim up the face past one bolt (involves some serious runout) using small gear until you reach the anchor. Not a casual stroll.

28. Ganesh 5.9 R
90' (27m) in length, Pro to 3"

A dirty left facing corner system which currently shares the same start as for Dirty Jugs. Runout sections. Beware of the large chockstone on the route.

29. Dirty Jugs 5.9 ★★★
90' (27m) in length, QD's

Look for a huge suspended boulder about 30' up the cliff face. This route ascends a face on the left side past some awkward moves to a 'Room with a View' ledge. Continue directly up following dirty jug holds that are protected with bolts.

Tim Pitz leading *Carrots for Everyone*

30. Sweeping Beauty   5.10b
★★★

*100' (30m) in length, Pro to 3"
and QD's*

Begin by climbing up steep terrain on the right side of the huge
suspended boulder that is situated 30' above the ground. **Room
With A View** ledge is the top of
this masive block. Belay here or
continue up and right, following a
crack system to a steep headwall.
A 60-meter rope will marginally
get you back down from the top
anchor.

Old Tree Area (Map #7 & Topo B): A
crooked old tree grows next to the
base of this section of cliff. See cliff
photo map for clarification.

31. Carrots   For   Everyone
5.10a   ★★★

*60' (18m) in length, QD's (op-
tional ¾" cam for start)*

A very popular first class Ozone
route! From the belay anchor on
Room With A View ledge climb
up the left face, and then pull past
nice jug hand holds up to the chain anchor.

Map #7: Old Tree

32. Trinity Crack 5.9   ★★★
100' (30m) in length, Pro to 3" and QD's

Immediately to the left of the 'old tree', ascend steep terrain
up to the top of the large suspended block. Climb numerous
steep steps and hand edges (inobvious pro) till you are even
with Room With A View ledge. Aim for a short corner crack
system up on the right, then climb up the broken corner system (protected with some bolts) passing a fir tree. Continue
up a hand crack to a fascinating finish to the anchor.

33. Kamikaze 5.10a ★★
90' (27m) in length, QD's and optional small cams

A stellar climb. From the 'old tree' aim up the slab into a
squeeze chimney. From the ledge above the chimney move,
aim up left into the corner system, and then back onto the
arête. This route has a difficult crux getting established onto
the arête, but a nice finish near the anchor.

34. SOS (variation) 5.11+
Top-rope only. Do not bolt.

Matt leading *MD Route*

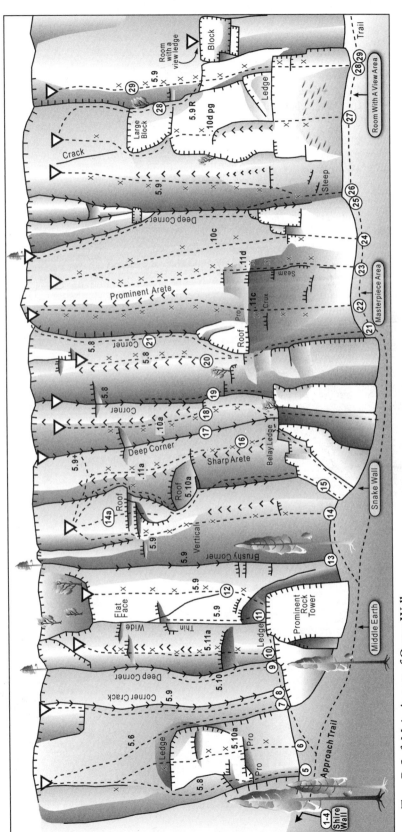

Topo B: Left Main Aspect of Ozone Wall

35. May Day   5.10b   ★ ★ ★

*80' (24m) in length, Pro is QD's (can also merge with
Trinity Crack but will need 3" pro and 60-meter rope*
To the right of the 'old tree' is a corner. Stem up this
past solid flakes and pull up left onto a ledge. Aim up
right, then past several sustained moves at a bulge, and
then climb up left to the arête to merge with Kamikaze. Shares belay anchors with Kamikaze, but can be
extended by traversing left to climb the last portion of
Trinity Crack (3" gear).

36. There and Back Again   5.10+   ★ ★

90' (27m) in length, Pro to 3" including cams
Climb up the outer face of a pyramid shaped pedestal
of tock past one bolt, and then move over to the right.
The climb quickly becomes steep below the obvious
large roof. Pull this roof to a ledge and step up left onto

Brad Jarrett leading *Chain Mail*

Map #8:
The Shield

.10+

.10c

.11b

.11+

36

39
Rauch
Factor

37
Chain Mail

38
MD Route

a face climbing section as you get nearer to the anchor.

The Shield (Map #8 & Topo C): A very steep, slightly overhung section of cliff with a popular selection of very difficult routes.

37. Chain Mail   5.11b   ★★★   [Dry]
50' (15m) in length, Pro is mixed, including QD's and #3 BD Camelot.
This is certainly one of the Ozone classics! Ascend the left bolt line using the path of least resistence, and then step up right into a crux section. Gear protects the obvious wide crack. After you pull through the roof the rock climbing will ease up.
Chopped Suey is a top-rope between Chain Mail and MD Route that goes free at 5.11. TR only; please do not bolt.

38. MD Route   5.11+   ★★   [Dry]
45' (13m) in length, QD's and minor cams to 2" (TCU)
A difficult free climb on the central portion of this clean wall.

39. Rauch Factor   5.10c   ★★★
50' (15m) in length, Pro to 1" and QD's
A great Ozone climb on steep pumpy edges. Ascend up a deep right-facing corner system (bolts). Cut out left for several moves, then up right onto a steep face climbing with mixed gear. Continue up a slightly overhung sustained crack using positive hand holds.

40. Back in the Saddle   5.9   ★   [Dry]
50' (15m) in length, Pro to 1"
Begin up route Rauch Factor, then traverse up left to the anchor for Chain Mail. Move up onto the face climb section then up to a crack system on the right past a small roof.

41. Short Straw   5.11a   ★★★

100' (30m) in length, Pro to 1½" and QD's, cams suggested

Climb the 3-bolt start on a slightly overhung smooth face to a rest stance on a small ledge. From the small stance continue climbing up a very sustained steep crack through small bulges to an anchor.

42. Meat Grinder   5.10c   ★★

100' (30m) in length, Pro to 4" and long slings

From the top of the 'razorblade flake' place gear, and then free climb up to the next ledge (runout or clip a bolt). Aim up left in a right-facing corner system, then jam your way up the crack (crux) past a belay anchor and continue to the top of the cliff.

43. High Plains Drifter   5.10c   ★★★

80' (24m) in length, QD's

An Ozone classic and very popular to lead! From the 'razorblade flake' climb up past a bolt to a large stance. Pull past a rounded buldge to another small stance, then embarkc onto an overhaning power climb usin large incut edges. The crux is the smooth face using small edges just before the anchor.

Marcus D. on *Carrots*

Heaven's Wall (Map #9, Map #10 and Topo C): This section of cliff is open to the sunlight since most of the trees are not next to the base of the cliff.

44. Rolling Thunder   5.10d   ★

70' (21m) in length, QD's

Begin on top of the Lion's Head large boulder. Ascend a steep face to a minor prow (bolts). Balance up a delicate slightly overhung section to a stance. Then up balancy thin face move on a smooth face, then exit up right to a belay anchor on a large ledge.

To lengthen the climb merge into the Tip Top route [bring gear] and continue to the next anchor.

45. Jacob's Ladder   5.9   ★★★

70' (21m) in length, Pro to 2" and QD's

Begin on the right side of the Lion's Head large boulder, and ascend up good edges (two bolts) to a large ledge at the base of a scooped out overhang. Carefully move up into the scoop and place some pro, then surmount the hang (crux). Continue up easier edges to the Heaven's Ledge belay anchor.

46. For Heaven Sake   5.10   ★

70' (21m) in length, Pro to 1"

Map #10: Stairway

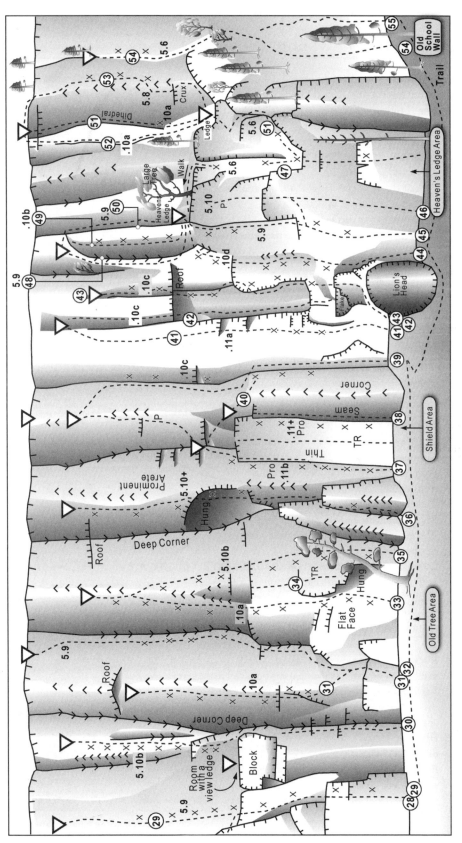

Topo C: Right Main Aspect of Ozone Wall

and cams

Ascend good edges (gear placements are inobvious and small) till you encounter a thin crack (fixed piton) splitting a minor overhang. Surmount the overhang using face edges and continue to the main ledge above to belay.

47. Stairway to Heaven 5.6 ★
70' (21m) in length, Pro to 1" and QD's

A basic climb on easy ledges. Ascend a series of large ledges (bolts) and angle up left in a corner (bolts), then past some bushes to a dirt ledge. Continue up a few moves then traverse hard left to the Heaven's Ledge (belay anchor) with a big fir tree growing on it.

The next three rock climbs begin at the roomy Heaven's Ledge. All three routes end at the upper belay anchor on a slab.

Andrew Blake on *Rauch Factor*

48. Tip Top 5.9 ★★
25' (7m) in length, Pro to 2½"

From the Heaven's Ledge belay anchor step directly left past the Burrito Killa arête into a crack corner. Stem up this corner past a crux move onto the slab and belay anchor. Anticipate rope drag on this climb.

49. Burrito Killa 5.10b ★★
25' (7m) in length, QD's

This terrific climb ascends directly up the arête immediately left of the bolt anchor from the Heaven's Ledge. A good line to connect with Jacob's Ladder which ascends up to this route from below.

50. There Yare 5.9
25' (7m) in length, Pro to 3

This is the obvious steep hand crack corner system immediately right of the bolt anchor on the this large ledge. The belay anchor for this route is on a slab above the crack.

51. Love Supreme 5.6 1st pitch (5.10a on 2nd pitch) ★★
150' (45m) in length, Pro to 2", cams and QD's

Pitch 1: This first pitch is quite popular. Begin as you would for the route Stairway to Heaven, but at the second bolt angle up right past a bolt (5.6), then directly up a minor corner to a bolt belay anchor at Cloud 9 ledge.

Pitch 2: This section is 5.10a and ascends up a steep slab using small gear in a seam. Clip the bolt, and make several face moves to the right and gain a ledge at the bottom of the corner system. Continue up the corner past the roof and follow more ledges to an anchor.

52. Bitches Brew 5.10a ★★
60' (18m) in length, Pro to 1"

From the Cloud 9 belay anchor climb up the same steep slab up left (gear), place a long sling on the bolt around the corner, and then continue up to the top of the large

Nick leading *Chain Mail*

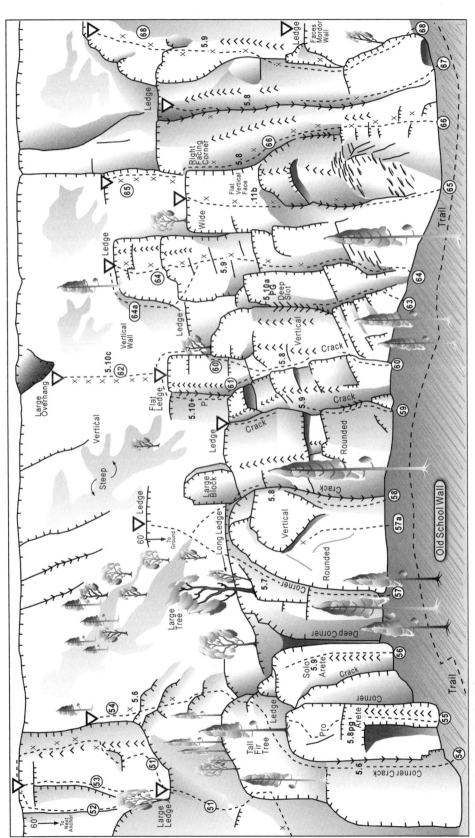

Topo D: Old School Wall

boulder. Continue up the face (gear) and climb up over a fascinating roof, then finish climbing up some ledges to the bolt anchor.

53. Hang Up Your Hang Ups   5.8   ★★★
60' (18m) in length, Pro to 1" and QD's
From the Cloud 9 belay traverse around a corner to another small ledge. Directly above is a slightly overhung face with a crack in it. Place pro in the crack and surmount the bulge using large holds. At a tiny stance clip the bolt, then move up right on tiny holds to easier terrain. March up good large edges another 30' to a fir tree. Traverse left about 20' to a bolt anchor above Love Supreme and rappel.

Old School Wall (Topo D): Follow the trail as it gradually ascends up into the dense forest again. This section has some older climbs established during the late '80s and '90s, but now sports some newer rock climbs, as well.

54. Mountaineer's Route   5.6   ★★
190' (57m) in length, Pro to 2" and QD's
Ascend a deep corner system to the top of a crack, past a block and continue to climb up and to the right. Continue up 30' to a tree, and then proceed up onto a nice section of face climbing (2 bolts) to a small tree and an anchor just beyond. Rappel from here, or continue up past a minor bulge to the top of the Ozone cliff. Walk off to descend.

55. Ivans Arête   5.8 PG
30' (9m) in length, Pro to 1" and QD's
This is a direct start for the Mountaineer's Route which climbs a short clean arête. Place pro in a small crack 15' above the ground. Merge with the previous route on the large ledge system.

56. Rasta Arete   5.9
30' (9m) in length, No pro
Uphill and to the right of Ivan's is another short steep arête. Solo.

57. Flayel Bop   5.7
80' (24m) in length, Pro to 3"
A short corner system which can be climbed to a ledge system. Rappel from a nearby tree, or continue up and right to join with the route Stigmata.

58. Stigmata   5.8   ★★
80' (24m) in length, Pro to 3"
This good route ascends an obvious clean crack to a slight overhang, then up the crack to a large ledge system. Continue another 40' to a chain bolt anchor. Two rappels will take you to the ground with one 60m rope.

59. Ripper   5.9   ★★★
35' (10m) in length, Pro to 2"
Ascend a very nice finger crack through a slight overhang then up to a chain bolt anchor.

60. Little Dipper   5.8   ★★
60' (18m) in length, Pro to 3"
Ascend a left leaning crack corner system to a ledge, then aim up right into a crack system

which will lead to an anchor on the left at Flat Ledge belay.

A top-rope climb called **Star Gazer** is located on the arete immediately right of Little Dipper. The first half is .12a and the upper half is .11b.

61. Piton Variation   5.10+   ★

60' (18m) in length, Pro to 2"

Climb either Little Dipper or Ripper to the ledge, then traverse left to a corner crack system with one piton fixed in it. Climb the corner crack to the Flat Ledge belay.

62. Orion   5.10c   ★★

35' (10m) in length, QD's

Use any of the previous two climbs and climb up to the Flat Ledge belay. From that ledge climb up the bolted face past a bulge to the anchor and rappel.

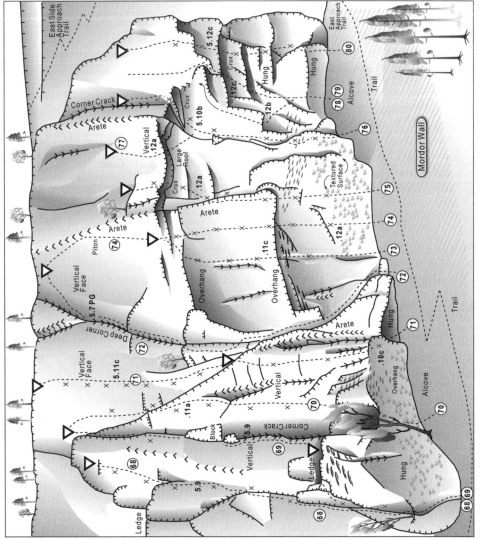

Topo E: Mordor Wall

Map #11: Mordor Wall

63.   Big Dipper   5.10a PG
40' (18m) in length, Pro to 4"

Start as you would for Standing Ovation, but aim up into an off-width slot. After you exit the peapod slot, continue up and left to the Flat Ledge belay.

64.   Standing Ovation   5.9
★ ★ ★

80' (24m) in length, Optional cam pro to 3" or 4" but mostly QD's

A stellar Ozone climb with small leftward-sloping edges that will surely keep you on edge! Start by climbing up next to a large flake which can be protected with a very large cam. Step up over right and ascend a vertical face (5 bolts) using small left slanting edges. From a nice stance move up and surmount the small roof overhang (2 bolts) then march up to a tree ledge and bolt belay anchor. Rappel.

Standing Variation: An alternate variation exists which follows the original ascentionists line. Instead of using the last three bolts step left to a large ledge, then climb up right using a short crack corner. Ends at the same belay anchor.

Mordor Wall (Map #11, Map #12 and Topo E): At the far right end of the Ozone Wall is a dark cliff section capped by large overhangs on the right and a long steep slice of vertical wall on the left.

65. Gophers Gone Wild   5.11b
80' (24m) in length, 7 QD's

Ascend a corner to a steep vertical face that commits you to crux move up right to a flat stance. Dance up a short face to a belay anchor on a large ledge. Rap or continue up Numb Nuts.

66. Numb Nuts   5.8   ★ ★
80' (24m) in length, 14 QD's

On a prominent clean buttress of rock just prior to the main Mordor alcove are two long climbs. This is the left bolted line which ascends a steep corner system with ample good edges and steps. The last several moves short of the belay anchor are pumpy. It is possible to climb portions of this route on natural gear.

67. Small Nuts   5.8
60' (18m) in length, Pro to 1½" and QD's

At the lowest point on the foot trail are two climbs on a long steep section of cliff buttress. This is the crack corner system on the right that sports one bolt near the top and one near the bottom of the climb. Beware of the sparse protection near the central crux section of the

Matt leading *The Crumbling 5.12a*

climb.

68.   No Nuts 5.9 ★★
80' (24m) in length, QD's

Begin on the right side of a prominent mossy buttress. Ascend knobby rock and a corner to a ledge. Climb a steep corner till it is possible to move up right onto a section of face climbing. Continue up this nice section to a bolt anchor.

69.   Dad's Nuts 5.9 ★★★
80' (24m) in length, Pro to 3½"

A superb crack climb on a slightly overhung wall. Begin as you would for No Nuts, but step up right on a large ledge to a bolt belay anchor. Climb the very steep but quality crack corner system past several blocks. Surprisingly sustained lead but the difficulties ease near the top.

70. Getting Your Kicks 5.11a ★★
100' (30m) in length, QD's and optional pro to 1"

A stellar long face climb immediately right of a steep corner crack. Start at a thin tree where the bluff leans out. Clip the bolt and balance over the bulge to easier terrain. Move up right the climb a fun series of continuously overhanging positve holds and balancy moves to the top. There are two crux sections between the third and sixth bolt.

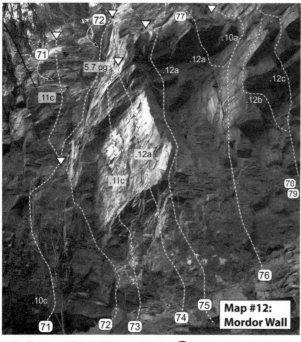

Matt climbing *Dark Lord* on the Mordor Wall

71. Route 66   5.11c   ★ ★ ★

100' (30m) in length, QD's

A classic long sport route on the left side of the Mordor alcove.
Pitch 1: Clip the first bolt to protect your moves (5.10c) off the deck. Scamper up to a small ledge and bolt anchor. **Pitch 2:** Launch onto the fabulous slightly overhung long face climb above (7 bolts). Climbs the steep face to a sequential move to attain a ledge, then more sustained climbing to a bolt anchor.

72. Meth Rage   5.7 PG

80' (24m) in length, Pro to 4"

From the midway belay anchor on Route 66 launch up right into an obvious challenging and loose corner system. Rappel from bolt anchor at the top of the cliff above The Crumbling.

The following climbs ascend consistantly steep terrain through a series of unusually difficult roof sections.

73. Mrs. Norris   5.11c

60' (18m) in length, QD's and optional small wire or RP pro to ½"

Climb a slightly overhung face, then power through the roof using positive holds to a sit-down rest above the first roof. Place optional pro at the top of the shield (8' above the rest spot), then ascend sustained ground through another overhanging roof section and move up right to the same anchor as The Crumbling.

74. The Crumbling   5.12a   ★ ★ ★

60' (18m) in length, QD's

A stellar route! Stick-clip the first bolt, then boulder through a series of difficult pumpy moves all the way to the rappel anchor.

75. The Humbling 5.12a ★ ★ ★
60' (18m) in length, A superb climb! This line powers through a large roof that makes you feel as if you are wrestling upside-down with huge overhanging blocks, and then culminates with several sloper moves to finish.

76. Stepchild 5.10a ★ ★ ★
50' (15m) in length, QD's and optional pro to 2"
An excellent route! Ascend up moderately steep terrain on good edges to a stance, then up a short crack. Angle up to the right under the great ceiling, then pull around the roof on balancy holds to a bolt anchor.

77. Hell Boy 5.12a
60' (18m) in length, 3 QD's
A difficult variation that branches up left from Stepchild at the large roof.

78. Grace 5.12b ★ ★ ★
40' (12m) in length, 7 QD's
Ascends the prominent overhang by traversing up left through a series of tight moves to a thin face section. Continue up the face rightward to merge with Dark Lord to the belay anchor. A powerful link-up variation called **Slackface** (.12d) connects the first two bolts of Grace, then merges with the upside-down foot jam slot crux on Dark Lord. Like Dave said, "It ain't over till it's over".

79. Dark Lord 5.12c ★
40' (12m) in length, 8 QD's
Power up through a prominent overhang past a very difficult foot lock reach problem. From a tiny stance continue up the 5.11 face to the belay anchor.

80. Angle of the Dangle 5.12c ★
40' (12m) in length, QD's
Last climb on the Ozone Wall. Begin from the right side of a small cave to a large roof crack. Power your way out past this crux lip move, then ascend more difficult overhung moves to the anchor.

> **TEN GREAT 5.12 SPORT ROUTES (NO GEAR)**
> For the extreme climber already firm with the upper numbers, here is a cool list of select 5.12 sport routes (no gear-just QD's) .
>   1. Road Face, 5.12a, French's Dome
>   2. Jackie Chan, 5.12b, French's Dome
>   3. Angular Motion, 5.12a, Carver
>   4. Dracula, 5.12a, Broughton Bluff
>   5. Bad Omen, 5.12b, Broughton Bluff
>   6. Bloodline, 5.12b, Broughton Bluff
>   7. Kashmir, 5.12a, Broughton Bluff
>   8. Closet Nazi, 5.12a, Broughton Bluff
>   9. Grace, 5.12b, Ozone
>   10. Scott Free, 5.12b, Madrone
>
> FOR THE EXTREME CLIMBER

Grace 5.12b

Dave on lead at Mordor

Tymun on lead at Mordor

"*Going to the mountains is going home.*"
-John Muir

OZONE WALL

CHAPTER 6
THE FAR SIDE

The Far Side introduction written by Jon Bell

Like Ozone, its neighbor about a quarter-mile to the west, the Far Side is a hidden wall of andesitic basalt high above the Columbia River in southwest Washington. Also like Ozone, the Far Side was discovered by local climber Jim Opdycke in the early 1980s, then left relatively untouched for more than twenty years. The Far Side later became a unique climbing area much the way Ozone did as well, when dedicated climbers took the time and energy to explore the area, establish routes, and otherwise transform an abandoned roadside dump into a one-of-a-kind crag just an hour outside of downtown Portland.

But that's where most of the similarities between the Far Side and Ozone end. Tucked into a forest with more maples than firs, the Far Side enjoys much more sunlight during the winter months than its neighbor, and Doug fir trees at the top of the cliff help shield the wall during light showers. At about a hundred feet tall, the Far Side is shorter than Ozone, and where Ozone's eighty-plus routes include more than thirty bolted ones, the Far Side has close to sixty-five routes, only a handful of which include a few bolts.

The routes at the Far Side tend toward more traditional adventure routes with natural protection, and though many of them are more moderate than those at Ozone, they can mentally challenge even the most solid on-sight climber. Moves span the spectrum and placing gear can be tricky and requires real thought. The wall also includes a wide variety of routes, from the 5.11b Tunnel Vision to the 5.7 Silverdycke. There are purely trad routes, one trad-sport route, several top ropes, a couple multi-pitches, and even an area near the wall's western base that's poised to become popular with little climbers known as Kiddie Litter.

HOW TO GET THERE

The Far Side crag is in southwest Washington, about 8 miles east of the town of Washougal on State Route 14 near milepost 24. From Portland or Vancouver, head east on SR 14 for roughly 18.5 miles. Beyond the two pullouts for Ozone, look for two long pullouts on the south side of the road that are just barely separated. Park at the second pullout. Trails to either the east or west end of the crag begin at opposite ends of the pullout.

Gear: Though there are a few bolts, pitons, and bolted anchors at the Far Side, traditional gear and knowledge of its placement is required for climbs here. Most of the routes have anchors, though if an anchor is not visible from the ground, bring gear to set one up. Some of the cracks used for protection are thin seams ideally suited for micro nuts, Lowe Balls, or micro cams.

Special Considerations: The Far Side sits on public land within the Columbia River Gorge National Scenic Area. Please respect the area and keep it clean to help preserve access.

VISUAL BIO

8
Month 5 Mins S Shade Trad

These emblems represent the Far Side, a gorge climbing site with southern exposure, shaded with deciduous trees and a quick five-minute approach.

East End Formation: A small rocky formation at the utter east most end of the bluff.

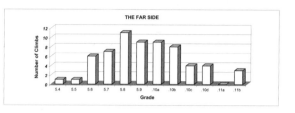

1.   Silverdyke   5.7

Pro: several nuts & small cams

Start on the 3'x 6' flat ledge and ascend past a bulge to an interesting 25' short thin crack. Uttermost east end of cliff formation.

2.   Monkey Moves   5.9+

Pro: nuts and cams to 3"

Start in an alcove at the east end of the cliff. Monkey pull through two mini roofs up discontinuous cracks. Getting off the ground and out of the alcove over the first roof is the crux.

3.   The Pin   5.10

Pro: several nuts and cams

Immediately to the left of Silverdyke is this good, but short route that starts off the Silverdyke platform. A one-move 5.10 crux. Located at the eastmost end of the cliff formation.

4.   The Trembling   5.9

Pro: wired nuts, one optional 3" cam

Climb a steep lumpy rock formation past a fixed pin and a bolt to where the rock radically changes character, then up a broken dihedral to the top to the fixed anchor.

5.   Introductory Offer   5.8 to 5.9

Pro: small nuts and cams to 1½"

A nice route at the east most edge of the cliff formation. Step on the Lizard Locks starting blocks, move straight up veering right, then climb the dihedral (harder) or wander to the right and up to easier ground then up left to the Lizard Locks rappel tree.

6.   The Arête   5.11 TR

This squeeze job between 'Lizard Locks' and 'Introductory Offer' was intentionally left as a top-rope. It is an excellent top-rope route.

7.   Lizard Locks   5.10b

Pro: nuts and cams to 1½", including large cams to 3½"

The obvious crack near the far eastern end of the wall shared by Introductory Offer has three stacked blocks between two shallow caves. Attack the highball moves direct from the ground to the crack placing 3½" cams. Opt #2: Or boulder through the lumpy blocks for 12' and step left 7' and up until 20' off the deck and place first pro at the base of the obvious crack with a 3" cam. Continue up a thin crack utilizing small cams to 1". Say "Hi" to the Northern Alligator Lizard if he hasn't moved on yet. Climb past a small tree growing in the crack; finish up slightly to the right of the buttress on easy moves to a huge fir with the rappel sling.

Indian Head: A minor rock formation with a steep broken flat face on its west aspect.

8.   MJ08   5.6

Pro: small cams to 1½"

Climb the buttress following one of several lines (the line of least resistance) to the top.

9.   Birthday Surprise   5.6

Pro: small to medium cams

Climb the face to the right of Wounded Knee using pro in marginal horizontal cracks. J.O.

turned 65 today, but missed out on this ascent.

10. Wounded Knee 5.6
Pro: small nuts, including a 3" cam
Climb the shallow chimney using face holds, and rappel off the tree. Expect creative pro.

11. Dulcinea 5.5
Pro: large nuts, medium sized chocks and cams
On the east aspect of Indian Head buttress climb a short 12" wide crack to a capstone (near a dihedral). Rappel from a rock horn.

12. Sheep Skinners Delight 5.10
Pro: several small nuts and small cams to 1½"
Climb the obvious varicose cracks on the west side aspect of the Indian Head buttress and rappel from a rock horn.

Giant Fir Tree: The landmark Bare Buttress section is immediately to the right of White Lightning. A huge fir tree with large blocks of rock located next to the base of this part of the wall provides shade as well as protection from the wind and occasional sprinkle of rain. The bluff forms a wide open ravine offering several climbing alternatives at a nice fat landing platform. Several routes on it were inspired and named due to the clothes-free style of the first ascent.

13. Scary As... 5.7 🌲
Pro to 3" including a large cam, long slings
Start in the offwidth under a big tree and climb the easy edges (no pro) to a sloping dirt ledge above. At this point the climb crosses lines with Sweet Surprise. Continue up into a small gully immediately to the left of the open book. Once through the gully look right for the hand-to-fist sized cracks described in Sweet Surprise. Expect some loose rock in the gully.

14. Sweet Surprise 5.7*ish* 🌲
Pro to 3" including a large cam, long slings
Begin at the shared start of the Right Cheek; ascend till you are above the lower face, then traverse right ten feet and climb up good edges to an easy open book with nice hand and fist jam moves, and then exit this to a fir tree. Rappel or walk off.

15. Right Cheek 5.8 🌲
Pro: small nuts and cams to 1½", small cams & nuts are crucial
The right cheek sits directly to the right of Adam's crack and shares the start with Sweet Surprise and Scary. Climb the crack 9' to the left of the large fir tree growing out of the cliff. Rappel from the same tree anchor as Adam's crack.

16. Adams Crack 5.8 🌲
Pro: small nuts and cams to 1½"
Ascend the crack and large face holds to a small obvious maple tree where the route eases. Aim up to a large Douglas fir and rappel off. Good gear route for aspiring leader.

17. Left Cheek 5.7 🌲
Pro: small nuts and cams to 2"
This fun route is situated directly to the left of Adam's crack and stays closer to the left side of the buttress and uses the same belay anchor at the top.

18. Bill's Thrill 5.7 🌲
Pro: small cams up to 2", small to medium wires, long slings
Shares same start as White Lightning but at the ½ way point stay slightly right and up the obvious crack past a small tree to the shared belay anchor.

19. White Lightning   5.8
Pro: nuts and cams to 3"
Next to the giant fir tree is a flat roomy platform surrounded by a wide low angle bluff. Ascend up a wide finger crack or thin hand crack that eases to the right and leads to some large face holds to an obvious move left. Pull over a bulge then race straight up to a belay anchor.

20. Snake   5.8
Pro: small rack and a 3" cam for the top
Start up the White lighting gully and follow the Snake like crack that wanders up and right. Finish at the fir tree 20' from the top, or finish off on Happy Crack.

21. Snake Buttress   5.8 to 5.11 Top-rope
Several starting points of varying degrees of hardness. Start on the left in Happy Crack, or start on the right, or higher up on the right in the Snake route. Finish up Snake or Happy Crack. Nice climb with nice ledges to work laps on.

22. Happy Crack   5.8
Pro: Medium and large wired nuts, several small cams to 1½"
A five star classic climb like a well designed staircase. Ascend easy shallow dihedral straight up to the top using face holds interspersed along a crack. A nice left-hand variation uses under clings and face moves. The easier right-hand variation aims right about ½ way up the route by dancing up small ledges before rejoining the route. Sling a small fir tree en route, and then finish straight up 20' to a rappel point at a large fir tree.

23. 2Trad4U   5.9
Pro: Quick Draws
A 'non-sport' sport climb that starts at a flat landing site near two tall Maple trees. A fun little route that dances up moderate terrain using ample edges to a slight bulge crux power move.

24. Ur Baby's Daddy   5.10a
Pro to 3" and Lowe Ball Nuts
Start up the moderate dihedral to a seam in the face to the anchor.

25. Freak Freely   5.10b/c
Pro to 1"
Right of the above route is an interesting line ascending natural cracks and features using small gear. A boulder start traverses 5' right into the obvious crack, then follows up through various features to a dihedral groove crux with a thin crack. It bypasses the belay anchor of TLW by aiming to the top of the bluff via three possible endings. Rap from a tree or walk off.

26. The Lonesome Winner   5.10a/b
Pro: Thin nuts and cams to 2"
Has three fixed bolts and a piton on lower portion of face. Begin up steep terrain (bolts & piton) using small cams aiming up rightward to a stance under a large roof. Move up a thin crack on the right side of the roof, and power up the sustained tricky thin crack moves to an anchor. The alternative is to follow the crack above the roof up leftward to the Oracle anchor.

27. Wushu Roof   5.10+ / .11-
Pro to 5" cams mandatory
Start on Lonesome Winner and then head slightly left and up using features interspersed with small cracks. Turn the lower feature to the left to gain the Bombay roof visible from the ground, and high step up right through the chimney/wide crack to the anchor.

28. Oracle   5.10c
Pro to 6"
Moderate face/crack climbing leads to rest below first roof. Long reaches over the roof will get

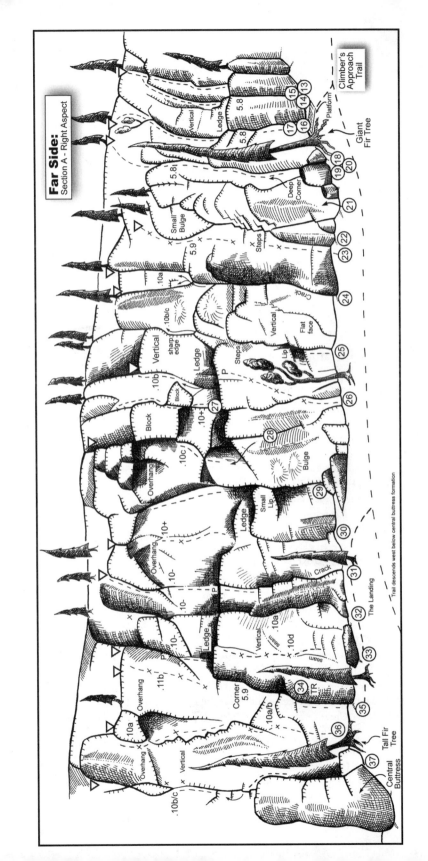

Far Side:
Section A - Right Aspect

Climber's Approach Trail

Platform

(13)(14)(15)

5.8

Ledge

(16)(17)

Vertical

5.8

5.8

(18)(19)

(20)

Giant
Fir Tree

Deep
Corner

(21)

Small
Bulge

5.8

Steps

(22)

5.9

(23)

.10a

(24)

Crack

Vertical

.10b/c

Flat
face

(25)

sharp
edge

Ledge

Steps

P

Lip

(26)

Vertical

.10b

Block

.10+

(27)

(28)

Overhang

.10c

Bulge

(29)

.10+

Overhang

.10-

Ledge

Small
Lip

(30)

.10-

P

.10-

Crack

(31)

.10-

Ledge

Vertical

.10a

(32)

The Landing

.10-

P

.10d

seam

(33)

seam

.11b

P

Corner
5.9

TR

(34)

.10a/b

(35)

Overhang

.10a

(36)

Vertical

.10b/c

Overhang

Tall Fir
Tree

(37)

Central
Buttress

Trail descends west below central buttress formation

you to a stance. From the stance expect sustained and steep climbing to the anchor.

29. Solid Gold 5.10-
Pro: Nuts to 1", and an optional 3" cam, extra small cams

To the right of Hollow Victory is an obvious long slightly golden corner that angles up toward the left. Start below the Sword of Damocles feature on a shallow crack and aim right up a corner avoiding the hanging block. Continue up the corner where it eases to a steep face. Power up several moves (small cams helpful) and tuck back into the corner before you finish to the top to the Hollow Victories belay anchor.

30. Hollow Victories 5.10+/5.11-
Pro: Nuts and cams to 2", mostly very small cams

In the center of a tall flat section of bluff, ascend a very thin crack below and slightly left of a wedged block hanging like the Sword of Damocles. Climb the thin crack to a small ledge till you are standing on the wedged hanging block. Then cruise up interesting and challenging features past a single bolt using strangely hollow but secure holds on the face.

The Landing: A common roomy meeting area where climbers will usually first arrive to socialize and become oriented at the site.

31. Day of Atonement 5.10a 🌂
Pro to 3" including Lowe Ball Nuts, small TCU's or other cams

The first official route established at the crag. Climb a steep short hand crack to a series of edges to the base of a smooth vertical face split by a thin crack. Opt #1: Power up the spicy moves on thin holds (small nuts, Ball nuts, or tiny cams), and balance carefully directly up a minor corner till it eases near an anchor. **Opt #2:** at the smooth face traverse left to Lion of Judah finish. **Opt #3:** or move further left to a small stance [above Naughty and Nice] then balance up an awkward steep short dihedral crux to a belay anchor.

32. Lion of Judah 5.10a PG13 🌂
Pro to 3" including small cams

Start just left of Day of Atonement and head up a shattered left-facing shallow corner crack. Continue directly up a minor corner/chimney feature until you can traverse left under an overhanging block to gain the anchor on top. The second official route established here.

33. Naughty and Nice 5.10d 🌂
Pro: 3 QD's and gear to 3"

A great climb involving a series of steep technical face moves. Start up the shattered left-facing corner, then traverse left to the first bolt. Pass two more bolts to gain a flat ledge, step up left, and then climb the overhanging right-facing dihedral and exit left to a belay anchor.

34. Squeeze Play 5.10C 🌂
A top-rope that utilizes the entire arête immediately right of Tunnel Vision.

35. Tunnel Vision 5.11b 🌂
Pro to 1" (optional 3" cam) and bolts

Start up dark left-facing dihedral, then continue up the nice corner above to reach first of three bolts. Commit to steep face climbing by pulling over a stout overhang to an anchor.

Fir Tree Ledge: The next three routes start at a flat landing next to a very large fir tree.

36. The Darkhorse 5.10a 🌂
Pro: Minor cams and nuts to 2"

A quality route that begins at a large fir tree. Boulder up a steep hung face (just left of a corner crack) to a small stance and continue straight up (natural pro) on small ledges and blocks using

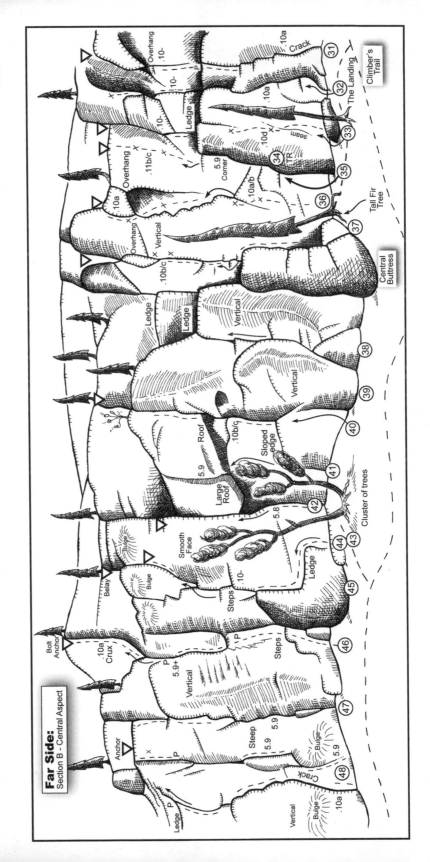

Far Side:
Section B - Central Aspect

in-cut holds and a thin seam past a bolt. Clip another bolt at a small overhang, and then power over the roof on the left angling up right to the anchor.

37. Center Squeeze 5.10b/c 🌂

Pro: Small gear rack, small cams, Lowe Ball Nuts, optional cam to 4"

Start next to a large fir tree on a rock stance, make a boulder move start up to a stem past the outside of the obvious 40' squeeze chimney that you face climb to avoid the 'squeeze', then up easy climbing to a couple of small staggered ledges mid-pitch. Clip two bolts and climb over a detached pillar and aim up an easier 20' finish to a rap anchor on top.

Central Buttress Formation

38. Boo Coup 5.10- PG

Pro: Nuts and (offset) cams to 2"

Start on a small pedestal of broken square blocks, place an offset cam for the initial flaring crack semi-mantle at the ground. Use face holds and intermittent cracks moving up left, then up right along the walls natural features to gain the upper ledges just below the very top. Traverse left a short distance to the Good Vibrations belay anchor.

39. Sharpen your Teeth 5.10+

Pro to 2" has two fixed bolts

This is the mixed gear route on the face to the right of an obvious corner 12' left of Boo Coup. Climb up to the obvious ledge with the chain belay shared with Good Vibrations.

40. Good vibrations 5.10b/c

Pro to 2"

Head up the right side of the large roof to same anchor as Boo Coup

41. Closeout 5.9

Pro to 2"

Same start as Good Vibrations. Traverse left under the roof, then clip the bolt and pull over and up a seam to the anchor.

42. The Martyr 5.8

Pro to 1.5"

Follow the crack up left side of large roof to a two bolt anchor and rappel.

43. Step and Fetch It TR

Starts same as the Head Wall, but instead of traversing left, go directly up via a hard step move, then up the middle of the upper slab tending right and over the top of the buttress and then left. Can exit left early to Head Wall route.

Maple Tree Cluster

44. The Head Wall 5.10-

Pro to 2" especially ¾" to 1" nuts for crux

Start by the Maple tree cluster, and make a few face moves up to a small ledge, then traverse to the left a few feet. Ascend the broken buttress with a crack in parts of it up to a stance 20' below the top to a fixed belay anchor.

45. Shoulder Hop TR

Located right of the above route on the outer scarp.

46. Sweet _____ 5.10a

Pro: Small nuts and cams (TCU's) to 2", Lowe Ball Nuts, slings

One of the better routes here in terms of mental and physical focus. This route is located at the right section of the short Hummingbird Wall just before the path descends down around

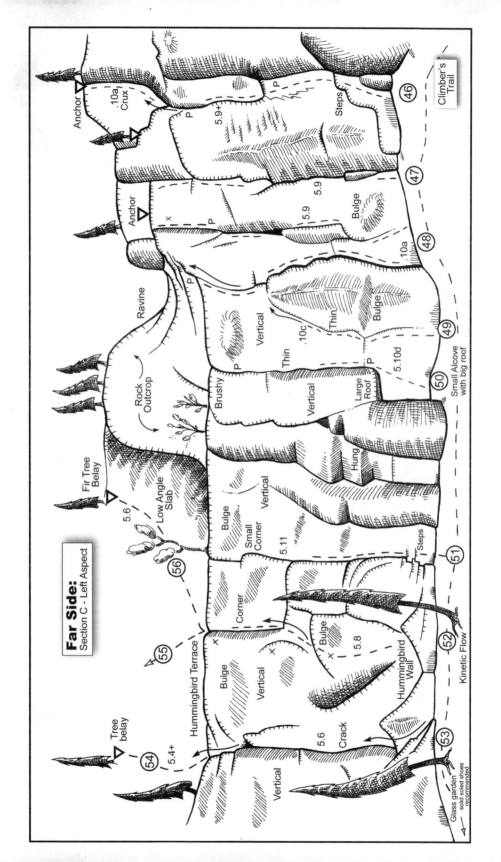

Far Side:
Section C - Left Aspect

Climber's Trail

Anchor
.10a Crux
Anchor
Anchor

5.9+
P
P

Ravine

Rock Outcrop

Fir Tree Belay

5.6

Low Angle Slab

Brushy

P

P

Vertical

Thin

.10c

Thin

5.9

5.9

Bulge

Bulge

.10a

Steps

5.10d

P

Large Roof

Small Alcove with big roof

Hung

Vertical

Small Corner

Bulge

Vertical

5.11

Corner

Tree belay

5.4+

Hummingbird Terrace

Bulge

Vertical

Bulge

5.8

Hummingbird Wall

Steps

Vertical

5.6

Crack

Kinetic Flow

Glass garden
solid soled shoes recommended

46
47
48
49
50
51
52
53
54
55
56

the central formation. To start the climb: Ascend up several initial steps to a steep corner like face with some pods and small intermittent cracks (two pitons) requiring some small TCU placements between the pins. Once you move up beyond the tricky section at the pitons, you will pass a small fir tree that is located on your left. Aim up right over a tree root to a steep headwall crack, and then power up this crack to a fixed anchor.

47. 'Je' Mapel Jon Phillip   5.9
Pro: Nuts and cams to 3"
An initial muscular boulder move ascends quickly up past the bulge, and then continues up an offwidth and face climbing (piton & bolt) to an anchor.

48. French Intern   5.9 to 5.10a
Pro: Nuts and cams to 2"
A minor crack weakness in the wall located between Exchange Student and 'Je Mapel'.

49. Exchange Student   5.10c
Pro: Thin nuts and cams to 2"
A powerful quality climb that shares the same start as Stewart's Ladder and then immediately moves right on a right arching seam.

50. Stewart's Ladder   5.10d
Pro: Small wires and cams to 1"
Start at an obvious right facing large roof next to the ground. Power up thin holds past the roof to the steep shallow corner (pitons) passing a midpoint crux, then finish via Well Hung in a single pitch lead or aim for another rap anchor at the top.

Hummingbird Wall: Located towards the west end of the main cliff, just east of the broken glass debris drop zone. Various local residents scavenge for glass bottles here. Refrain from placing bolts or fixed pitons on this section. The ledge area has no fixed belay anchors so ascend to the top and walk off. A single 60-meter rope is sufficient to rappel from the trees at the bluff top. The lower routes are described first, then the upper routes on the Hummingbird Terrace.

51. The Warm Up   5.11
Pro: small cams, nuts and Lowe Balls
Still dirty but with additional cleaning would be easier. Climb some relatively easy steps using gear for 35' to a crux directly below a rotting old Maple tree at the edge of a ledge. Continue up Northern Passage or Well Hung to the top or rappel from trees.

52. Kinetic Flow   5.8
Pro to 2½" including cams
Ascend three bolts to the left of the Warm Up route, sling a tree root and aim up left. Finish to the top by one of the upper routes. Bring gear for upper route.

53. Northern Passage Lower   5.7
Pro: Minor nuts and cams to 1¼", including Lowe Ball Nuts
West of the Maple tree cluster 15' is an obvious crack. Ascend this to Hummingbird Ledge, and then follow the steep rocky steps left to the large fir tree.

The Upper Routes on Hummingbird Terrace

54. Northern Passage Upper   5.4+
Pro: small nuts and cams to 1" (6" optional), slings
Northern Passage Upper starts from the left side of the Hummingbird terrace. A large short 6" crack at top can be climbed or bypassed by heading left to the large fir tree and up the short

face above to top out. Tread gingerly across the dirt ledges.

55. Senior Moment

Thrash through the 4th class brush off Hummingbird Ledge ascending dirt slopes in the center-right of the upper area to get to the top; dirty and no protection.

56. Well Hung   5.6

Pro: Nuts and Cams to 1½"

Starts from the right hand side of the terrace off Hummingbird Ledge. A nice climb with subtle gear placements on nice stances, and an easy upper portion.

57. _____   5.7

Pro: Small nuts and cams to 1"

Limited gear options protect this line between Tribal Therapy and Northern Passage. Bring long slings for the large tree. Traverse in from easy ledges that go to the left or climb the poorly protected difficult direct start straight up to it. Pass the fir tree on Hummingbird Ledge on the left side and finish up Northern Passage upper or via the top of Tribal Therapy.

Dropzone area: Just west of the glass garden the bluff provides a tall sweep of broken corners and cracks. The following climbs start jus a few feet west of the Maple Tree Cluster on the trail.

58. Tribal Therapy   5.9

Pro: small nuts to 1", small cams to 2½"

A good route that starts at 20' left of a four Maple tree cluster on the trail. Scramble up a broken pillar section to the obvious perfect finger crack. Climb up to an obvious traverse left gains a horizontal ledge below a thin hand crack that widens near the top into the Far Side perfect hand jams and an anchor at the top.

59. Dwarf Toss   5.8 PG

Pro: Minor set of small nuts, cams to 2½"

Located 30'+ west of the four Maple trees cluster, it passes Hummingbird Ledge on the far left side about 20' left of a large fir tree. Start to the right of the Far Side or 13' to the left of Tribal Therapy. Climb ledges straight up past a fixed horizontal pin just below the right facing dihedral at the ½ way point. Finish on the Far Side hand crack.

60. The Far Side   5.8 PG

Pro to 2½"

Start up to the left of Dwarf Toss. Traverse right at the ½ way point and finish up a dihedral, traverse right onto the face slab at the ¾ mark to the obvious sweet hand crack below the top. The PG encompasses moves from the dihedral to the hand crack on easy terrain.

61. Gas Station Fashion   A1

Unfinished aid line up the center of the face.

62. Fall From Grace   5.10b R or A2

An initial roped solo attempt in February '09, but finally went free a year later.

63. Fool's Rush In   5.9

Pro: Gear to 3"

Start up the thin seam located to the right of the large off width. At the crux climb around the detached block then onto easier rock. Step left below a slab and finish up the low angled ramp to the right.

64. Mark it Eight Dude   5.9+

Pro: Variable gear to large cams

Start with some bold boulder moves on thin gear to gain a very wide crack which slightly diagonals to the right to two bolts. Pitch two extension is called 'Smokey' at 5.10- and continues up and right and up past a single bolt up a crack to the top.

65. Child Abuse 5.8
Pro: need ¾" to 1" cams, small-med Nuts, 5" or 6" cam on last 10'
Ascend a short finger crack up and slightly left, then up right slightly to a gully of easy broken flakes to a ledge with a fixed rap anchor. Utilize all various placement options.

66. Happy Ending 5.10
Pro to 1"
Stem up the dihedral just left of 'Child Abuse' using small and funky gear then transition onto a uniquely featured but cryptic face past two bolts. Mantle onto a ledge, then battle through a steep crack section before escaping right to the anchor.

Arena of Pleasure area: A minor outcrop located to the west of the main cliff.

67. Kiddy Litter 5.2+
Ascend an easy ramp 50' and rap off a large fir tree. Second ascent was followed by Wes' 4 year old daughter.

68. Wet and Dirty 5.7
Pro: minor nut and cams to 2"
Climb up to a left slanting ramp just right of the preceding route to a shared anchor at 30'.

69. 31 Feet of Pleasure 5.6
Pro: Minor small gear, minimal large gear
Start in the middle of the arena and head up to a wide crack that slants slightly to the left. Duck under the horizontal fir tree to get to the sling on the tree anchor.

70. 41 Feet of Pain 5.6
Pro: Mixed gear rack
Start to the right of Thirty-one feet of Pleasure.

Shane leading *Excalibur*

...*"Remember that courage and strength are naught without prudence." Edward Whymper*

BEACON ROCK

T HIS MAGNIFICENT GEOLOGIC MONOLITH of the Columbia River Gorge is the centerpiece to an extensive Washington State Park system. The park provides a multitude of activities including camping, boating, hiking, horseback riding, as well as fabulous rock climbing.

Captivating scenic views of the very heart of the Columbia River Gorge are part of the unique experience you will find when climbing here!

Portland area climbers could not have asked for a finer big wall crag than Beacon Rock. Technically sustained and demanding rock climbing of the finest degree can be found here on the huge 400-foot vertical south face aspect.

📚 BRIEF HISTORY OF THE AREA

Beacon has enchanted and hauntingly enticed generations of adventurers even before the first ascent of the SE Face in April of 1952 by John Ohrenschall and Gene Todd. This historical monument was named Beacon Rock by Lewis and Clark while on their expedition of 1805–1806 to

Southwest face of Beacon Rock

the Pacific Ocean. Later, in 1811, it attained the name "Inshoack Castle" but was generally known as "Castle Rock" until 1916 when the U.S. Board of Geographic Names reestablished the original name. The rock's first ascent was recorded on August 24, 1901 by Frank Smith, George Purcell, and Charles Church. They ascended a series of brush covered ledges on the west side. Several old fixed 1" thick by 12" long metal bars can still be seen on the 3rd pitch of the "spike" route.

In 1915 Henry J. Biddle initiated the building of the present-day trail leading to the summit of the rock. In 1935 Beacon Rock became part of the Washington State Parks system so that all could enjoy the beauty and wonder of this majestic monolith.

In 1961 the early roots of rock climbing at Beacon had begun. The spectacular efforts of Eugene Dod, Bob Martin, and Earl Levin came to fruition when they succeeded in ascending a prominent crack and offwidth system to Big

Ledge. To this day, Dod's Jam (5.10c) stands as a remarkable and classic example of early route pioneering achievement.

Throughout the latter half of the 1960s a core of climbers broke major barriers via mixed free and aid climbing technique. They developed excellent climbs like Flying Swallow (5.10d), Right and Left Gull (5.10a), Jensen's Ridge (5.11b), culminating with an ascent of Blownout (5.10a) in January 1969 by Steve Strauch and Danny Gates. Dean Caldwell, Dave Jensen, Steve Strauch, Kim Schmitz, Bob Martin, and others involved in the climbing scene will long be admired and remembered for their efforts.

The next decade provided an even wider variety of mixed free and aid ascents. Two such notable feats certainly would have to be Les Nugent's ascent of Steppenwolf (5.10d) and Free For All (5.8) in 1973 by Dean Fry and Steve Lyford. The mid-1970s brought a new group of climbers to the crag as they ascended superb routes

Jim Toon, Dod's Jam (5.8 first pitch)

like Flight Time (5.11c); Pipeline (5.11a); Blood, Sweat, and Smears (5.10c); and Free For Some (5.11a). Jeff Thomas, Mark Cartier, Ted Johnson, Avery Tichner, Alan Kearney, Jim Olson, Mike Smelsar, Robert McGown, and others frequently turned toward the countless old aid lines, discovering that these routes produced excellent free climbs. Free climbing was now in vogue.

Subsequent decades brought an even wider spectrum of climbers to Beacon. From this new generation came quality routes like Cruisin' (5.7), Fear of Flying (5.10b), Bladerunner (5.10c), Winter Delight (5.10b), Borderline (5.11b), Excalibur (5.12b), Flying Dutchman (5.10b), and Windsurfer (5.10b). Those who continued to test the edge in the 1980s and 1990s were mainly Ron Allen, Scott Tracy, Mark Cartier, Darryl Nakahira, Robert McGown, Wayne Wallace, Nathan Charleton, Jim Opdyke, and Jim Yoder. Uncountable tales will be told in the years to come, as time will attest. So stay tuned to Beacon Rock.

REGULATIONS

Beacon Rock is a part of the Washington State Park system. This state park has a Climbing Management Plan in effect, which regulates all rock climbing activity at Beacon Rock. The following Washington State Park rules are to be respectfully observed while climbing here.

+ Climbing is presently limited to the south face and to the northwest face. The south face is closed from February 1 until approximately July 15 in order to facilitate and encourage the nesting habitat of the resident peregrine falcon. The south face occasionally opens early each year, but this is dependant upon the falcon chicks having fledged and the Park Rangers' approval to open the south face.

+ The east face is closed to all climbing. Portions of the east face had been considered for potential open-

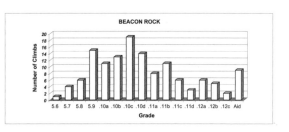

ing, but at the present time that section of the monolith will remain as a species habitat zone.

♦ The <u>northwest</u> section of Beacon Rock is open year-round and presently offers about twelve rock climbs. These routes are seldom climbed and are generally technically difficult to lead. This area is located in the forest to the right of the north side water spigot and ends just before reaching the west side hiking trail as it zigzags back left to meet the cliff. This portion is adequately marked with signs.

♦ Rock climbers must use the east side approach trail only. Do not park at the boat ramp and camping area west of Beacon Rock to approach the cliff. (The amount of space for automobiles is limited and the railroad company does not appreciate seeing people walk along the tracks.)

♦ Use dark-colored slings or webbing for the belay anchors. Chalk use is allowed. Bolting is allowed as specified in the climbing management plan, but any climber who wants to develop a new route must file a route development application form with the Park Manager and attain approval.

♦ Contain all waste and dispose appropriately at the parking lot restroom facility.

♦ Organized group climbs of 6 or more persons must obtain a day use permit.

Please review all the rules and safety regulations posted on the bulletin board at the parking lot before climbing at Beacon Rock. Any violation of the rules would jeopardize the privilege of climbing on Beacon Rock. Review the State Park Internet Web site, the bulletin board near the climbers trail, or check with the park manager if you are seeking more detailed information concerning the State Park rules. In keeping with these regulations, climb safely and enjoy your adventure while visiting Beacon Rock.

PRECAUTIONS

There are some distinct dangers at the south face of Beacon Rock: poison oak and rockfall. The rockfall is often generated near the west side hiking trail at a point above the third tunnel where sightseers gather. Another point of rockfall concern is above the Southeast Face route where rock climbers occasionally stir up trouble when dragging the rope through loose rocks on the Grassy Ledges route.

Numerous incidents due to stone fall have occurred. Because there is a risk of encountering rockfall while at the base of the cliff, climbing helmets are highly recommended. If others are known to be climbing above you on the Southeast Face or Right Gull, take extra precaution when moving about on the lower sections of the cliff and while standing around at the base of the wall.

The other problem, poison oak, is seasonal. Long pants may suffice in protecting most climbers who visit Beacon, but persons whose skin is more susceptible to poison oak need to take greater precautions. Learn to recognize the shiny green three-leaf shape, the season, and the habitat where poison oak flourishes to limit your risk

Mark Retzlaff leading the 5.7 crux slab pitch on the *SE Face* route.

of infection. Some climbing routes up left of the Arena of Terror on the West Face are virtually unclimbable because of the poison oak.

In addition, excellent rock climbing, knowledge-based skills are highly recommended when climbing at Beacon Rock! The activity of rock climbing here is neither for beginners nor for learning basic skills. Many of the routes are multi-pitch, bold leads that offer many difficult variables from steep, thin crack climbs to overhung offwidth corner systems.

To most rock climbers, visiting Beacon Rock simply means to experience the nature of the climb. Do take some time to relax on a ledge with a snack and a drink of water where you will surely develop a deeper appreciation for the vast beauty of the tremendously scenic Columbia River Gorge.

VISUAL BIO - SOUTH FACE

South Face: **Month** **6** · **5 Mins** · **S** · **All Day** · **Regs** · **Trad**

These emblems represent most of the south face of Beacon Rock. The south face offers some limited shade for the belayer, but not for the climber. You can escape some of the heat on a summer day by climbing on any southeasterly facing routes #1 to #26 after 3pm. Beacon is a traditional climbing site with plenty of gear leading up virtually endless steep crack systems.

🡵 HOW TO GET THERE

From I-205 (in Washington) drive east on State

Kyle Lehman leading *YW* (5.8, P4)

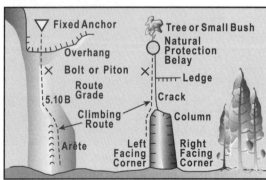

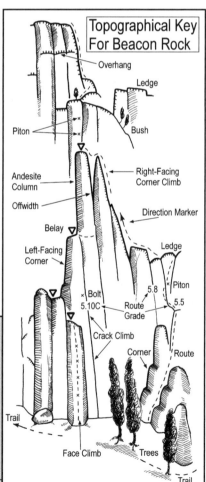

Topographical Key For Beacon Rock

Route 14 for 28.8 miles to Beacon Rock. Or (in Oregon) drive east on I-84 to Cascade Locks. Cross the Bridge of the Gods, then drive 7 miles west on SR 14 past Bonneville Dam to this famous andesitic monolith of the Columbia River Gorge. Park at the east end of the parking lot near the rest facility.

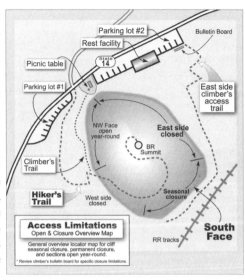

🥾🥾 APPROACH

The east side climber's trail gently zig-zags downhill beneath the great east face overhangs and on toward the south face until the main southeasterly cliff face meets the trail. The trail continues west along the entire base of the scarp, passing routes like Stone Rodeo and Cruisin' to a prominent buttress, which is very close to the railroad tracks. Along the base of the south face are three man-made tunnels; once there, you can pinpoint your location using the topographical maps herein to find your next climb.

Parking & Trail overview map: *Beacon Rock*

The climbing routes at Beacon Rock are described from right to left, beginning with the first climb near where the east side hiking trail meets the base of the southeast buttress. The first section details climbs from Pacific Rim to the SE Corner and is immediately followed by details about all of the upper routes on or near the Grassy Ledges. The next section details climbs from just left of the SE Corner and ends with Jensen's Ridge. The last section details the climbs on the upper southwest face of Beacon that are accessed by way of Jensen's Ridge.

1. Pacific Rim II 5.10c ★
60' (18m) in length, QD's and minor pro to 1"
A route that keeps you on the edge all the way. Begin below an overhang thirty feet downhill and left of an alcove. Commence up a shallow corner then face climb (bolts) up right along the virtual edge of the abyss directly below. Belay at anchor, then rappel 60'.

2. Rhythm Method 5.7 ★★
80' (24m) in length, Pro is 6 QD'
This is the bolted line immediately to the right of Boardwalk. A nice clean face climb that is definitely worth doing! An 80' (24m) rappel from the belay. This route has another very bold pitch above the anchor, which angles up right slightly to a near vertical right facing corner ramp system at 5.10a/b R. It is a ground-up route that ascends through several small roofs to a belay. Rappel with two ropes (55-meter rappel).

3. Boardwalk 5.6
120' (36m) in length, Two rope rappel, Pro to 2"
A long, obvious right facing corner system approximately 40' uphill from the trail. Climb the corner up to a roof, step right then up to a bolt anchor.

Pete G. on *YW* (5.8, P3)

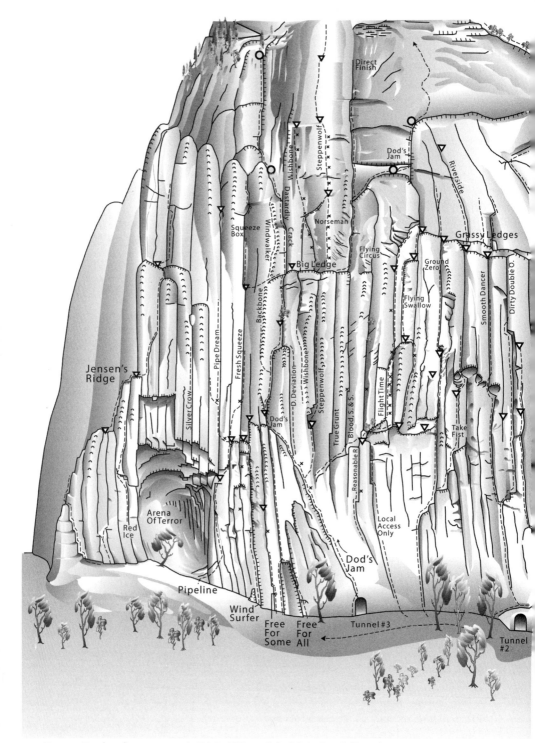

Beacon Rock reference map 1: *Digital View of the Main South Face Aspect*

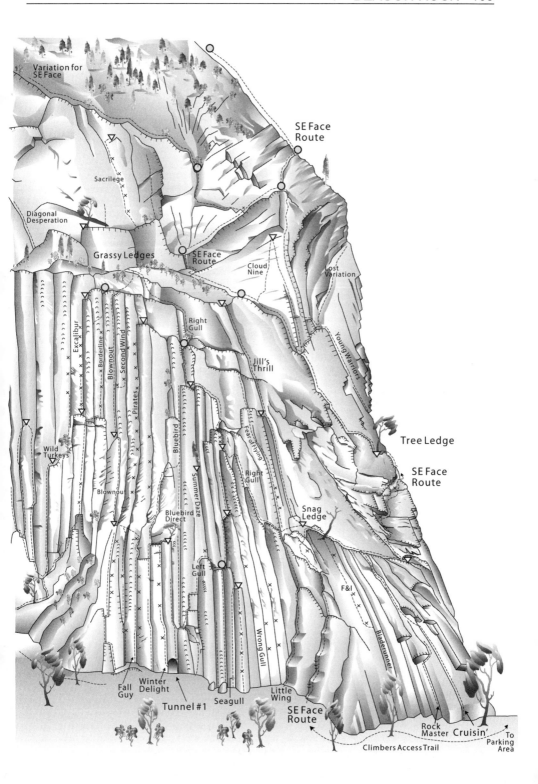

Variation for
SE Face

SE Face
Route

Sacrilege

Diagonal
Desperation

Grassy Ledges

SE Face
Route

Cloud
Nine

Lost
Variation

Excalibur

Borderline

Blownout

Second Wind

Right
Gull

Jill's
Thrill

Young Warriors

Pirates

Bluebird

Fear of Flying

Tree Ledge

SE Face
Route

Wild
Turkeys

Right
Gull

Blownout

Summer Daze

Bluebird
Direct

Snag
Ledge

Left
Gull

F & I

Fall
Guy

Winter
Delight

Wrong Gull

Bladerunner

Tunnel #1

Seagull

Little
Wing

SE Face
Route

Rock
Master Cruisin'

To
Parking
Area

Climbers Access Trail

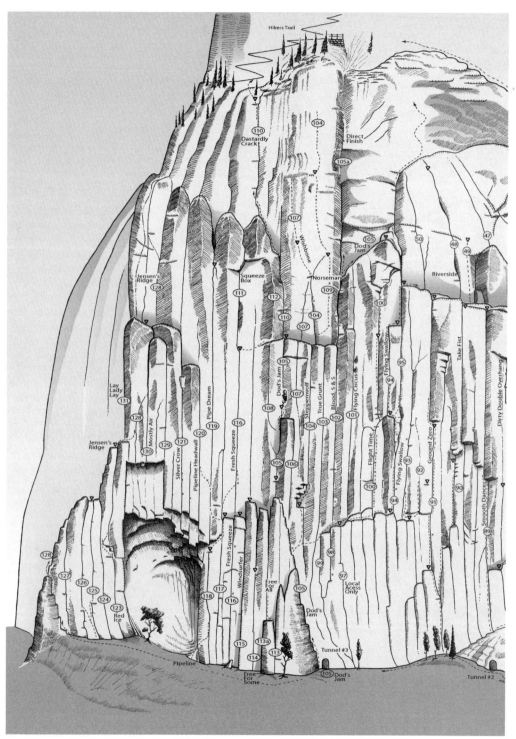

Beacon Rock reference map 2: *Ink Illustrated View of the Main South Face Aspect*

Beacon Rock 15"x20" map available at the source: PortlandRockClimbs.com

Beacon Rock reference map 3: *Photographic View of the Main South Face Aspect*

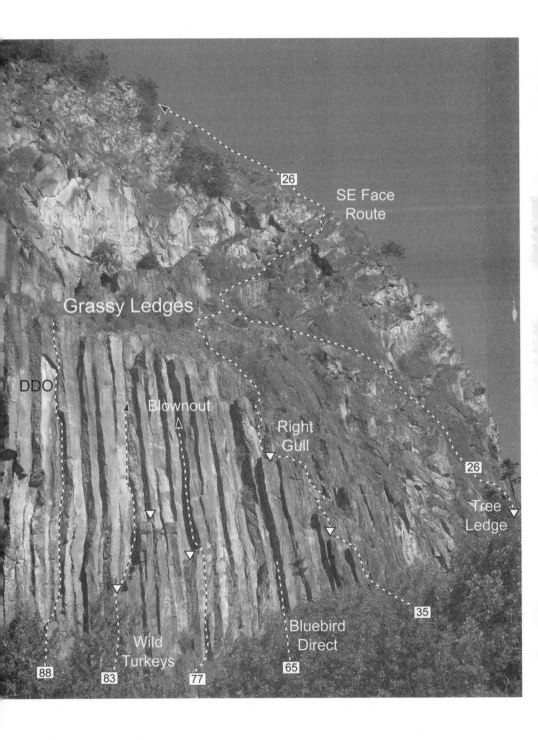

SE Face
Route

Grassy Ledges

DDO

Blownout

Right
Gull

26

Tree
Ledge

35

Wild
Turkeys

Bluebird
Direct

88

83

77

65

4. Young Warriors III 5.9 ★★

Multi-pitch, Pro to 2½" including cams

This 6-pitch route begins left of Boardwalk a short distance, and ascends in a fairly direct line via crack corner systems passing Tree Ledge on the right.

Pitch 1 (5.8) : Climb a nice long face with mixed bolts and pro to a bolt anchor at 110'.

Pitch 2 (5.9): Move left and climb up through an overhanging 'A' shaped feature (5.9) to merge into SE Face route. Step to the right to a stance at a bolt anchor just short of Tree Ledge.

Pitch 3 (5.9): Continue straight up a minor but long corner system to a large slab and ledge. Angle up left into a small alcove with some old fixed gear nearby.

Pitch 4 (5.9): Move up out to the left onto the obvious arête. Stay on this rounded arête, then go up a short slab and a shallow corner system to an airy belay stance. The upper SE Face route also uses this airy belay stance. You can finish up the regular last upper portion of the SE Face route, or you can move up right via a short ramp and corners for short 5.10ish move.

5. Stone Rodeo 5.12a ★★★

65' (19m) in length, QD's and minor pro to 3" and cams recommended

A powerful punch of physical endurance. As the trail meets the cliff beneath Cruisin', look to the right 25' past an oak tree. Beyond is a bolted overhung face that leads up through a roof split with a crack. Excellent climb. Protection will be needed for the roof move.

6. Rock Police II 5.10c

Multi-pitch, QD's and pro to 1" and TCU's required, Poor hangers

To the right of the same oak tree 15' is a bolted face that follows a right leaning arête. An unusual climb that is still fun, but presently has poor hangers. Climb up a short face (immediately right of Return To The Sky) to a bulge crux move (bolt). Angle up right on a steep slab while staying near the outer right edge (crux) till the climbing eases to a ledge and bolt anchor. Rappel 65' or angle up left to the second belay on the SE Face route. From there step up right (5.9) onto the outer edge of a steep slab, until it rejoins with the SE Face route near the top of this slab.

Jim Meyer, 1ˢᵗ pitch of SE Face

Jim Toon on Cruisin'

CRUISIN'

The route *Cruisin'* is an excellent high quality and challenging 5.7 alternative start to getting onto the *Southeast Face* route. This route merges with the traverse pitch to belay at the 2nd anchor of the *Southeast Face*. Be sure to bring some thin pro.

7. Return to the Sky   5.10a

65' (19m) in length, Pro to 1½"
A seldom climbed route that angles over several dihedrals then up a corner. Start behind the oak tree and climb up right past a bolt (crux) then upward to a bolt belay. Rappel.

8. Sky Pilot   5.11a

95' (28m) in length, Pro to 2"
Start as for Return To The Sky except storm through a weakness in the overhang above. Obscure climb.

9. Couch Master   5.9

100' (30m) in length, Pro to 1½"
Start up slab behind oak tree, step left and turn corner stemming up (crux) to join with Cruisin'.

10. Jingus Jam   5.9 (variation)

35' (10m) in length, Pro to 2"

11. Cruisin' Direct Finish   5.11c (variation)

25' (7m) in length, Pro to ¾" and pitons

12. Cosmic Dust   5.10b (variation)

25' (7m) in length, Pro to 1"

13. Cruisin' (aka Cruise Master)   5.7 ★★★

100' (30m) in length, Pro to 2"
An excellent local favorite, and rightly so. Start up a fun slab 15' left of the large oak tree. Follow a thin crack (crux) to an overhang. Move left to sidestep the roof, the continue up a dihedral to easy ledges. Belay at the established anchors on the SE Face. Reference Topo Diagram A.

14. Stardust   5.8 ★

100' (30m) in length, Pro to 1½"
Start up a left facing corner to a small roof. Turn this by sidestepping around to the right and continue up until it joins Cruisin'.

15. Rock Master   5.11c PG ★★

100' (30m) in length, Pro to 2" TCU's required
Technically very bold. Stem up a left facing corner (crux) using very unorthodox maneuvers to succeed (#0 TCU). Pull through a difficult roof move and continue up a crack system that eases and joins with the SE Face route.

16. Rookie Nookie   5.10c PG ★★

100' (30m) in length, Pro to 2"
Slightly uphill and left of Rock Master is a prominent left-facing dihedral with one fixed piton.

Topo A: *Cruise Master*

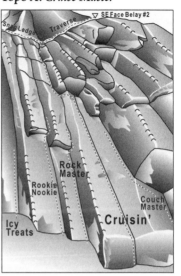

SE FACE ROUTE

The *Southeast Face Route* is the premier climb at Beacon Rock and rightly so. The SE Face route (5.7) is the most frequently climbed technical route on the river face at Beacon. This favorite climb is certainly worth sending on your first visit here. It offers 600' of multi-pitch rock climbing on variable terrain ranging from long ramps, a tour across the *Grassy Ledges*, to the famous high angle crux pitch face climb, all with good cracks. A great climb for skilled crack protection climbers.

A great climb. Joins with the SE Face route.

17. Icy Treats (aka Frozen Treats) 5.10d R
100' (30m) in length, Pro to 1½"

Look for a shallow corner with two bolts near the start. A difficult stem problem with hard to place pro and a little run out in places. Climb up past the bolts to a halfway stance. More awkward, desperate smears lead to the top where it joins the SE Face route.

18. Switchblade 5.11a PG
110' (33m) in length, Pro unknown

19. Bladerunner 5.10c ★★
110' (33m) in length, Pro to 2"

An incredible route and an excellent prize. Begin up and pull through (1 bolt) a loose section of rock to a stance. Angle up left then straight up a seam (2 bolts and crux) until the crack widens and eases in difficulty. Belay at bolts just below Snag Ledge tree.

20. Fire and Ice 5.11b ★★
110' (33m) in length, QD's, small wires, and TCU's to 1"

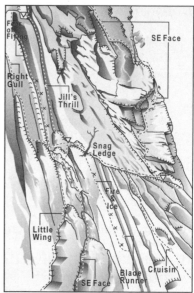

Topo B: *Southeast Face*

A high quality route. Ascends a smooth, rounded arête slab left of Bladerunner. Climb up Bladerunner to the second bolt, traverse left onto the face and go straight up the bolt line. From a stance above the halfway crux, step left to finish up a thin seam (pitons) which ends at the snag Ledge tree.

21. M B T N 5.11b R
50' (15m) in length, Thin pro to 1"

22. N B N F 5.11a
50' (15m) in length, QD's and pro to "

23. Levitation Blues 5.10d
50' (15m) in length, QD's and pro to 1"

24. Repo Man 5.10c
40' (12m) in length, Pro to 1"

25. Lethal Ejection 5.9
60' (18m) in length, Pro to 2"

26. SOUTHEAST FACE III 5.7 ★★★
Multi-pitch, Pro to 2"

Crux P3 move of *Southeast Face*

This is THE Beacon Rock classic route, and was the first established rock climb here. It is

---

EXIT OPTIONS FOR UPPER SE FACE

Two possible exits are available from the 'good stance' at the top of pitch 5; you can climb the *Upper West Ramp* or the *Standard SE Exit* to the steep rock rib.

To climb the *Upper West Ramp*:

Exit left at the ¼" bolt (P6) by traversing left along small grassy steps, then up bushy ramps and 4th class ground westward until it eases and lands on the hikers trail. Or you can access the *Upper West Ramp* by climbing a short 5.6 slab crack directly above the belay at the 'good stance' at the top of pitch 5.

an enjoyable multi-pitch route that meanders up 600' of rock to the west side hikers' trail. Begin west and uphill about 30' of a prominent corner near the railroad tracks.

Pitch 1: Climb easy steps on clean rock 80' to a bolt belay at Snag Ledge.

Pitch 2: Traverse horizontally right (NE) along ledges 70' to another bolt anchor.

Pitch 3: Move up a slab to the left 12', then move right (crux) over a slight bulge to a small stance under a roof. Move up right along a steep right-facing slab corner system for 40'. When possible work up to the right to turn an exposed corner, then up to the Tree Ledge belay (bypassing the Young Warriors bolt anchor on the SE Buttress face).

Pitch 4: Follow a left leaning dihedral ramp system 160' to Grassy Ledges and set a belay.

Pitch 5: Wander up and left past a small fir tree through a short offwidth 'slot' move to a good stance and set a belay.

The Standard Exit for the Southeast Face (the popular method) is as follows:

Pitch 6: From the good stance continue up a right-facing low angle ramp system (¼" bolt at top of ramp) as it angles up right to an airy stance. From the airy stance climb straight up 30' to a notch and set up another belay.

Pitch 7: Continue up the steep rock rib for 160' and belay for the last time at a tree. A short scramble from here up in the forest ends at the paved summit hikers trail. Descend the hikers trail back to the car.

Note: Some of the pitches of the SE Face described above can be combined with use of a 60-meter or 70-meter rope. Also, the first two pitches have fixed belay stations, while on the remainder of the climb you will need to set up your own natural belay anchors. Reference photo Map #1, Inset Map #2 and Topo Map B for a closeup visual analysis of this route.

Note: Be vigilant when traversing across Grassy Ledges. Handle your rope with caution, because loose rock is easily disturbed by foot or rope. Dislodged rocks are a hazard to the rock climbers below. The belay anchors for the SE Face route above Grassy Ledges are not fixed and you will need to use natural protection at each belay stance.

27. Variation   5.9
25' (7m) in length, Pro to 2"

28. Desdichado   5.10c
40' (12m) in length, QD's and pro to 1½"
A unique short climb with poor hangers. Located about ⅓ of the way up the crux pitch of the Southeast Face on a slightly overhung corner.

29. Dynaflux   5.11b
50' (15m) in length, QD's and pro to 1½"
Up left from the second belay on the Southeast Face is a bulging face with a vertical crack in it.

Two bolts protect the hardest moves. Rappel from bolt anchor.

30. Jill's Thrill 5.9 ★ ★ ★

190' (58m) in length, Pro to 2"

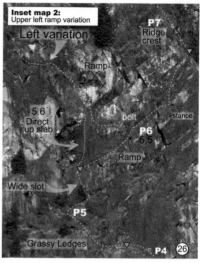

A fun route, especially the second half. Start at Snag Ledge belay. Climb a long corner up right with 2 fixed pitons. Belay at anchor on a ledge to the left at 80'. Step back to the right and continue 60' up a steeply angled flared crack system past a minor stance up another crack to a large ledge at a belay anchor. A 50' third pitch powers up a thin crack and ends on another ledge on Grassy Ledges.

Jill's Thrill is a common rappel on Beacon Rock that many climbers use to exit down from Grassy Ledges. There are other rope rappel options, but this one is conveniently oriented near the SE Face, and it can be done with a single 60-meter rope.

Map 2: *Upper West Ramp exit variation*

31. Tooth Faerie 5.10a

70' (21m) in length, Pro to 2" and #0 TCU recommended

Ascend a clean crack directly above belay anchor. At the overhanging flake, face climb up the left side of crack to join with Jill's Thrill.

32. To the Edge and Beyond 5.11b

70' (21m) in length, Pro to 2" including TCU's

Somewhat contrived, but challenging.

33. Fear of Flying 5.10b ★ ★ ★

160' (48m) in length, Pro to 1½"

A superb Beacon Rock climb. Step left from the Snag Ledge belay as if you are heading to Right Gull. Just before stepping onto a sloping wide stance, commence up a steep corner dihedral protected with 4 fixed pins (5.10a). As it eases slightly, power up another short crack to a flat ledge (65') and belay at Jill's Thrill anchor on right. Continue up a 5.10b thin crack (fixed pin) to a minor ledge and step right to join the remaining portion of Jill's Thrill.

34. Desperado 5.10d R

160' (48m) in length, Thin pro to 1½" and pitons

__. Crazy Horse

Pro: Nuts to 1" and cams to 4"

Start on Right Gull P2 and pull past the crux to a ledge, but avoid the next wide 5.8 part of Right Gull. Look for another wide crack and ascend up this crack corner (5.8ish) to a ledge, then up a face with a crack on the left. Climb over a minor bulge and step right and up to a large ledge where it lands on a gravelly bench low on Grassy Ledges. Expect some moss and friable rock in this area.

35. Right Gull III 5.10a (or 5.7 A0) ★ ★ ★

Multi-pitch, Pro to 3"

A very popular route with plenty of variety.

Pitch 1: From the Snag Ledge belay step left around a corner and enter a large right-facing corner. Climb this until it tops out on a pedestal, then gingerly move left to a bolt anchor.

3ʳᵈ pitch slab *SE Face* **4ᵗʰ pitch *SE Face*** **6ᵗʰ pitch *SE Face***

Pitch 2: Either A0 or free climb (5.10a crux) past 2 fixed pitons to a ledge. Above are several options. On the right is an offwidth (4"); in the center, a slightly dirty left leaning crack (5.8); or on your left is a 3" hand/fist crack (5.8). At the top of these options, step left to a bolt anchor on a comfortable ledge. Bluebird and several other routes end here as well.

Pitch 3: Continue up a wide crack pulling through an awkward bulge (5.8) to a rocky ledge with a small oak tree.

Pitch 4: Wander up behind the tree and leftward via a series of steps and belay on Grassy Ledges at a tree. Reference Topo C.

36. Vulcan's Variation 5.8
12' (3m) in length, Pro to ¾"
A rather convenient way to bypass the crux on Right Gull. Climb a thin crack to the right of the second belay and above a sharp ear of rock.

37. Muriel's Memoir 5.9
25' (7m) in length, Pro to 1½"
When Right Gull eases to the rocky ledge near a small oak tree, look to your left. This is the good looking clean corner crack. Rejoins with regular route.

The following 13 routes are located above Grassy Ledges beginning near Tree Ledge and ending at the top out point for Flying Swallow.

38. Synapse 5.10c
35' (10m) in length, Pro to 1"

39. Death and Taxes 5.12c ★
45' (13m) in length, QD's and minor pro to 1"
This short, premium quality face climb utilizes a series of incipient seams and edges. A very unusual climb to be found here at Beacon. It is located approximately 40' up and left of Tree Ledge (SE Face route).

40. Lost Variation II 5.8
Pro unknown
An indisputable route so named because numerous parties were unable to find it, yet it is rumored to be an interesting

7ᵗʰ pitch *SE Face*

climb.

41. Elusive Element 5.10d R ★

80' (24m) in length, Pro to 1½" including TCU's

A fabulous yet easily missed route roughly 100' up left from Tree Ledge. Lead up a right facing corner (crux) past 2 bolts to an easy slab. Continue up the crack to a short steep section (crux) and reach a bolt anchor just beyond. A really good climb except for the weird hangers and run out sections.

42. Cloud Nine 5.9

80' (24m) in length, Pro to 2"

A bit mossy, but still a neat crack climb on a long slab. Located immediately uphill and left of Elusive Element. No fixed belay at present.

43. High and Mighty 5.11b ★

80' (24m) in length, TCU's and wires to 1½" Needs bolts or fixed pins

An excellent route high above Grassy Ledges. Located up left from the easy 5th class offwidth move on Grassy Ledges (SE Face route). Climb a wandering set of seams on a steep smooth face until possible to turn a corner leftward then up a crack on a slab. No fixed belay anchor.

44. Sacrilege 5.10d ★★★

80' (24m) in length, QD's and minor pro to 1"

A fantastic face climb on very steep terrain. Incredible lead and one of the better upper wall Beacon classics. To the right of Diagonal Desperation is a large hidden terrace with an oak tree on it. Sacrilege is the route on the right side of this terraced ledge.

45. _____ 5.12+

80' (24m) in length (TR immediately left of the above climb)

__. Hibernal Hi-Jinx 5.7 C2

Pro: Nuts to 1", a hook, and cams to 6" if you have it

This aid climb adroitly assaults an overhung zigzagging crack and offwidth system just left of an oak tree starting on the little people's ledge.

46. Diagonal Desperation 5.11c R

160' (48m) in length, Pro to 2" & very small pro

Located just to the right of the upper pitches of Smooth Dancer. This free climb ascends a long left-leaning crack system, then branches up right under a small overhang. Surmount the overhang to easier terrain. Merges onto the upper west exit of SE Face.

47. _____

48. Riverside 5.10b

Multi-pitch, [P1 80' (24m)], Pro to 2½"

Steep sustained crack climbing that utilizes odd pods (half-body jams) up a left-leaning crack system located near the left end of Grassy Ledges. Rappel after 80' or continue up to the west side trail.

49. _____ 5.11+

80' (24m) in length (TR)

50. _____ 5.12+

80' (24m) in length (TR)

The following routes are described right to left beginning immediately left of the SE Face route.

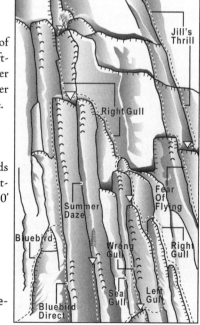

Topo C: *Right Gull*

51. Little Wing   5.8   ★ ★ ★
80' (24m) in length, Pro to 2"
Immediately left of the SE Face route is a fun little classic climb that begins up several reason-able slab steps. Follow this corner to a stance on a detached pedestal, then finish up a shallow well-protected crack until it is possible to step right at the Snag Ledge belay.

52. Broken Arrow   5.10a
60' (18m) in length, Pro to 1"

53. Unknown   5.12a
120' (36m) in length, QD's and pro to 1"
Uphill and left of the SE Face is a smooth face that offers several thin steep rock climbs. Climb (the right one) a very difficult steep face that has fixed bolts and pitons for 40' until you can reach over and use the outside corner of Right Gull. Lay back up this (2 bolts) until it is neces-sary to join the Right Gull route.

54. Magic Fingers   5.12c
110' (33m) in length, Pro to 2½"
Magic Fingers is the left climb, a serious and demanding 2 bolt seam on this steep face. The climbs eventually opens up to a crack and becomes the large wide chimney section on the last 20 ft. of Left Gull.

55. Wrong Gull   II 5.10c   ★ ★
110' (33m) in length, Pro to 2½"
No two ways about it, a terrific climb with excellent protection. Start in the minor corner near an old tree stump. Stem up 80' to a bolt anchor on a ledge. Then, if you're very bold, jam up the left side of a detached free standing pillar. Joins Right Gull.

56. Sorcerer's Apprentice   5.10c
40' (12m) in length, Pro to 1"
A thin seam crack immediately left of Wrong Gull.

57. Old Warriors Never Die   5.12b   ★
80' (24m) in length, QD's and minor pro to 1"
A great bolted climb located on the outside of a minor rounded corner. Climb 45' up the steep face and short dirty corner to a ledge. Belay at anchor. Rappel or continue up right (bolts) via dubious cracks to join with Wrong Gull at the bolt belay. Rappel.

The following three routes are great climbs that define what Beacon is all about...steep powerful stemming up thin crack corners. Hopefully there is a fixed belay anchor, but if not just wrap a long sling around the blocks and rappel.

58. Seagull   II 5.10c   ★ ★ ★
45' (13m) in length for P1, Pro to 1½" and cams suggested
This and the following two climbs are superb classics. They accurately portray Beacon stem climbing at its finest. The route ascends a double cornered crack system (5.10c) just to the right of a large boulder. Bolt belay on ledge (45'). Rappel or climb a thin crack above (5.10d) to join with Right Gull.

59. Ten-A-Cee Stemming   5.10c PG   ★ ★ ★
45' (13m) in length, Thin wires and pro to 1½"
An excellent thin crack and corner stemming problem.

60. Av's Route   5.10d   ★ ★
45' (13m) in length, Thin wires and pro to 2½"
A good stemming climb on thin but good protection. Ascends the corner system just to the

FIRST TUNNEL

A great selection of stout short climbs are available at the First Tunnel, such as Spring Fever, Winter Delight and Sufficiently Breathless. These tricky leads are a must for any solid 5.10 lead climber.

left of the large boulder. Beware of minor poison oak near the top of the climb.

61. Too Close for Comfort 5.12a
This is the outside corner next to Av's Route.

62. Left Gull III 5.10a or 5.8 A0
Multi-pitch, Pro to 3"
An unusual but fun climb. Some poison oak and chimney climbing to contend with. Starts up broken corners and ledges immediately right of the first tunnel and joins with Right Gull at its second belay on the pedestal. Reference Topo E.

63. Summer Daze 5.11c or C3 ★★
95' (28m) in length, Thin wires and TCU's to 2½"
Great climb with a desperate thin start. From the belay ledge at the top of Av's Route / Seagull step left then proceed up the seam (piton). The crack widens and passes a fir tree halfway up before it joins with Right Gull at a ledge belay.

64. Unknown 5.12
130' (39m) in length (TR)
An outside arête and face between Summer Daze and Bluebird.

65. Bluebird Direct 5.10d R ★
160' (48m) in length, Pro to 2½"
Directly above the first tunnel is a long dihedral. Commence up a thin seam on the tunnel's right side to a ledge 20' up. Stem up a poorly protected dihedral to where it joins with the standard Bluebird route. A good climb but a little run out.

The following five routes offer high quality and moderately difficult climbing with challenging characteristics.. Reference Topo D. These climbs are located at the First Tunnel.

66. Spring Fever 5.10a ★★
55' (16m) in length, Pro to 1½"
Ascend the thin seam just to the right of the first tunnel. At the small ledge 20' up step left and continue up a weird crack to a bolt anchor belay. Rappel.

67. Winter Delight 5.10b PG ★★★
55' (16m) in length, Pro to 1½" (#2 TCU required)
A prize worth attaining and a delight to climb. Climbs

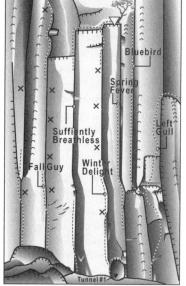

Topo D: *Winter Delight*

Kyle leading Sufficiently Breathless

a partly bolted seam immediately left of the first tunnel. Rappel from the bolt anchor.

68. Sufficiently Breathless 5.10a ★ ★ ★
55' (16m) in length, Pro to 1½" Doubles at ¾"
Superb route with excellent protection. Ascend via a minor crack and corner system just left of Winter Delight. Several fixed pitons. Exit right to the belay anchor.

69. Fall Guy 5.10d ★ ★
65' (19m) in length, 5 QD's and optional pro to ¾"
An exciting definitive face climb. Climb a shallow vertical corner to a sloping stance (loose rock just above) stepping up left and around corner to join with Aging Fags. Rappel from bolt belay.

70. Aging Fags 5.10d PG ★
65' (19m) in length, RP's, small wires and TCU's to 1"
A wide dihedral that is quite bold to lead. Starts off from a ledge 15' left of the tunnel.

71. Blownout Direct 5.10b
65' (19m) in length, Pro to 1½"
Climbs a free-standing thin flake, then pulls into a corner stance before ascending a piton protected seam. Rappel from bolt anchor.

72. Tombstone Territory 5.7
25' (7m) in length, Pro to 2½"

73. Bluebird II 5.10a ★
Multi-pitch, Pro to 4"
One of the original Beacon favorites with an excellent crux pitch. The old starting point was located at a fir tree next to the base of Wild Turkeys. From there it traversed rightward via brushy, sloping ledges and minor down steps. Otherwise climb one of a number of routes near the first tunnel to approach.

74. Variation 5.9
40' (12m) in length, Pro to 3"
Halfway up the crux pitch of Bluebird, step left onto a good ledge and finish up a deep dihedral choked with bushes.

75. Bridge of the Gods 5.12b
110' (33m) in length, Pro to 4"
High above the first tunnel is an impressive shallow corner system that eventually widens to an offwidth crack splitting an arête. Two rope rappel. Approach via one of the lower variations.

76. Pirates (aka Rock Pirates) 5.12a R
110' (33m) in length, Pro to 2" and run out
An unusually demanding climb on balancy holds. A very long lead with many fixed pitons. Approach via one of the lower variations. Two rope rappel.

77. Blownout II 5.10b ★ ★ ★
Multi-pitch, Pro to 2½" Doubles recommended
One of the ten supreme classics. Commence up Blownout Direct (or another nearby option) to a bolt belay. Move up left, then straight up a jagged hand crack to a belay in a protected

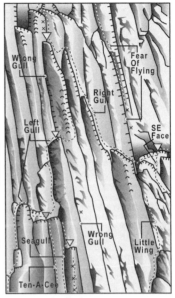

Topo E: *Left Gull*

Leading *Blownout*

Topo F: *Blownout*

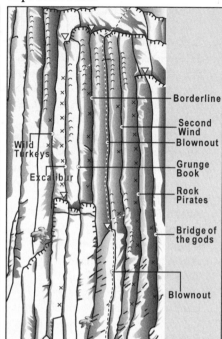

- Borderline
- Second Wind
- Blownout
- Grunge Book
- Rock Pirates
- Bridge of the gods
- Blownout

Wild Turkeys

Excalibur

corner beneath the great upper dihedral. Step forth and climb the obvious corner 120' (crux) until possible to exit right onto a gravelly ledge. Reference Photo Map #3 (Topo F).

78. Second Wind 5.11d ★ ★

100' (30m) in length, Pro to 2" and TCU's recommended

Twenty feet up the last pitch of Blownout (¼" bolt), traverse right around the arête and finish up a strenuous thin finger crack.

79. Borderline II 5.11b ★ ★ ★

80' (24m) in length, QD's and pro to 1½"

The second pitch is an impressively powerful climb. **Pitch 1:** Begin at the lone fir tree immediately right of the Wild Turkeys start. Climb up right onto a detached flake and climb (pitons) 40' up (5.10+) to a belay on the 'Beacon Towers' ledge. **Pitch 2:** Step right and embark up the beautiful second pitch (bolts and gear) via face climbing and lay back to the top. Pitch two is the primary portion that most hard core climbers aim to lead so avoid the first pitch by climbing Blownout Direct or a nearby alternative route.

80. Grunge Book III 5.10a A3

80' (24m) in length, Pins and pro to 1½"

Virtually all of this route (except 40') has been free climbed. The upper pitch has seen some 5.13- TR activity.

81. Excalibur 5.12b ★ ★ ★

80' (24m) in length, QD's, small wires, TCU's, and Cams to 2½"

Incredible! An extreme line and one of the more difficult established free climbs at Beacon Rock. Start on the 'Beacon Towers' immediately right of Wild Turkeys. Face climb straight up until it eases and widens gradually near the top.

Shane leading *Excalibur* 5.12b

82. Crankenstein 5.11a
35' (10m) in length (TR)

Immediately right of the start for Wild Turkeys is this minor dihedral corner.

83. Wild Turkeys III 5.10c A2
Multi-pitch, Pitons and pro to 1½"

One of the original Beacon aid routes. The popular first pitch goes free at 5.10c, but the second has still yet to be freed. Probably 5.12+. Ascend an interesting corner left of a fir tree. Climb 25' to a belay on a sloping ledge. Continue up right via easy steps to the 'Beacon Towers'. Belay then nail the seam left of Excalibur.

84. Unknown 5.12+
120' (36m) in length (TR)

From the first belay on Wild Turkeys commence directly up a shallow dihedral. It soon straightens to a vertical seam on a perfect smooth face.

The following climbs are above the Second Tunnel.

85. Psychic Wound 5.10b
80' (24m) in length, Pro to 1½"

This climb and the following several routes are located above the second tunnel. From a stance at a thin oak tree step up right and climb a left facing corner (piton) to a stance. Finish up a weaving corner system until possible to exit left to the Flying Dutchman bolt belay. The upper portion of this crack system is 5.12 TR.

86. Flying Dutchman 5.10b (P2 5.11b/c) ★★
80' (24m) in length for P1, Pro to 1½" Small wires and TCU's suggested

An enjoyable route. Excellent rock. Begin at the thin oak tree and climb up past two pitons to a stance. Continue straight up a left facing dihedral to the bolt anchor. The upper pitch has been free climbed at 5.11b/c to Grassy

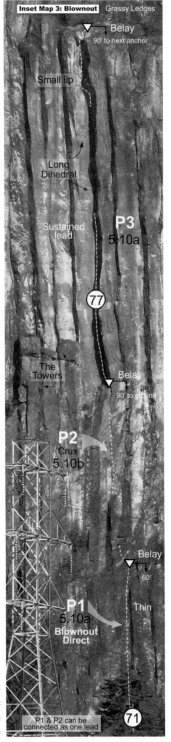

Inset Map 3: Blownout   Grassy Ledges
Belay
90' to next anchor
Small lip
Long Dihedral
Sustained lead
P3
5.10a
77
The Towers
Belay
90' to ground
P2
Crux
5.10b
Belay
60'
P1
5.10a
Thin
Blownout Direct
P1 & P2 can be connected as one lead
71

Map 3: *Blownout*

Ledges.

87. Bears in Heat II 5.11b ★★

80' (24m) for P1, Pro to 2½" and cams suggested

A great climb. The name describes accurately the second pitch bear hug. Start as for Flying Dutchman past the pitons to a stance. Step left, then ascend an unusual crack system to a crux move just short of the anchor. Rappel or continue up (35') the second pitch bear hugging and jamming to reach a final belay. Rappel.

88. Dirty Double Overhang III 5.7 A3

Multi-pitch, Pitons and pro to 1½"

A long, multi-pitch aid route immediately right of the great roofs in the center of the wall. The two pitches above Grassy Ledges offer good free climbing.

89. Smooth Dancer III 5.9 A2

Multi-pitch, Mostly thin KB, LA, RURPs, Pecker or birdbeak, pro #00 to 4", brass aid nuts

This is the other sustained two-pitch aid route on the central face. A cool nailing route for aid aficionados, yet still begging to see a free ascent.

__. Crack To Nowhere 5.8 C1 or A2

Pro: Nuts to 1", Cams to 3" including doubles, brass aid nuts, hook, Pecker or birdbeak, KB's

Located immediately right of Take Fist is a crack breaking through a roof which continues a short distance then stops. This climb ascends to that point, but a possible free extension could exist with the addition of bolts on the arête above the crack. Ascend Take Fist P1 and jump over right onto the crack system to punch through the large roof till the crack ends.

90. Take Fist III 5.10d

Multi-pitch, Pro to 3"

This wild climb leads through a fist crack in the 'great roof' area. A little brushy on the first pitch. Start near the twin oak trees angling up right to a vegetated dihedral. Commence upward and through the overhang to the top. Rappel via another established safer rappel on Grassy Ledges.

A series of overhangs exist about halfway up the vertical wall starting with Dirty Double Overhang and proceeding up leftward to Ground Zero. The crux for Ground Zero is turning the left side of the large overhang.

91. Ground Zero III 5.11d ★★

Multi-pitch, Small wires, TCU's and double sizes to 2½"

Seldom climbed in its entirety but one of the more challenging and unusually physical leads. Each pitch is more extreme than the previous culminating with a crux at the roof. Start near the

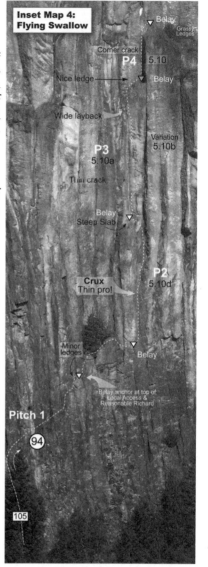

Map 4: Flying Swallow

Inset Map 4: Flying Swallow

Belay
Grassy Ledges
Corner crack
P4 5.10
Nice ledge
Belay
Wide layback
Variation 5.10b
P3 5.10a
Thin crack
Belay Steep Slab
P2 5.10d
Crux Thin pro!
Minor ledges
Belay
Belay anchor at top of Local Access & Reasonable Richard
Pitch 1
94
105

twin oak trees up easy 5.9 slabs to a piton belay 80'. Continue up to a small lip (5.10c) and some difficult climbing to a bolt anchor on the left 80'. Another 25' lead to an anchor underneath the roof. Smear left (crux) around the corner, then finish up a very steep crack to the top 50'.

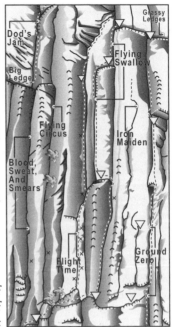

92. Nuke-U-Later   5.10c R

120' (36m) in length, Pro to 1½"

Start as for Ground Zero but a thin crack that leads up through flaky, hollow rock. Anchor just below a small overhang. Rappel.

93. Iron Maiden   III 5.11 A4

KB, LA, Baby Angles and Pro to ¾"

Step left from the Nuke-U-Later belay and nail up a seam on a blank face.

94. Flying Swallow   III 5.10d PG   ★ ★ ★

Multi-pitch, Pro to 3", Extra thin-to-medium wires and very small cams

One of the better Beacon Rock classics.

Pitch 1: The present route starts up the 5.6 section of Dod's Jam, then traverses rightward across to the top of Black Maria, Reasonable Richard and Local Access. But it is much more direct and fun to climb one of these three options mentioned above.

Topo G: *Flight Time*

Pitch 2: From that bolt anchor traverse up right to the base of a 60' dihedral. Belay, then have at it.

Pitch 3: This lead is unusually strenuous and involves difficult protection placements. Stem upward (crux) to a sloping ledge and bolt anchor.

Pitch 4: Above is a slightly overhung finger crack that opens to an offwidth. Climb this to another ledge and belay.

Pitch 5: Then continue up a nice left-facing corner 20' to a belay anchor on Grassy Ledges.

95. Variation   5.10b   ★

60' (18m) in length, Pro to 2½" Extra wires

96. Direct Start to Flying Swallow   5.11a

100' (30m) in length (TR)

The following three climbs are viable direct start options to Flying Swallow, Flight Time and Blood, Sweat and Smears.

97. Local Access Only   5.10a

110' (33m) in length, Pro to 1"

Wander up an unprotected slab to a small corner dihedral. A viable option for accessing the upper routes such as Flight Time. Another route called **Third Rail** (5.10-)is located immediately to the right of LAO. **Third Rail** ascends minor corners and tiny stances then angles left to end at the same belay anchor.

98. Reasonable Richard   5.9 PG

110' (33m) in length, Pro to 1½" and TCU's recommended

Commence up an unprotected slab to a stance, then embark up a minor crack (1 bolt) on a rounded face leading to a bolt anchor. A good climb but a bit bold [*unreasonable?*] to lead.

99. Black Maria   5.9+ PG

110' (33m) in length, Small wires, TCU's and cams to 3"

A minor corner directly below True Grunt and just left of Reasonable Richard. Start up easy slabs but work left from a stance into a dihedral. Continue up this until you can exit right to the anchor.

100. Flight Time   II 5.11c   ★★

Multi-pitch, Pro to 1½"

For the climber with strong wings here is a terrific and well-protected route. Move up right (from the belay at Reasonable Richard) along dirty ledges to a mostly fixed crack. This is the wild one. Desperately climb up using the right crack when necessary to a sloping ledge and belay. Step back left and continue up a stiff dihedral to a hanging belay. Rappel or continue up and exit out right under a roof to join with Flying Swallow just above the west edge of Grassy Ledges. See Topo G.

101. Flying Circus   III 5.10c R

Multi-pitch, Pro to 4" Extra set of wires

Above Reasonable Richard is a crack (with a small bush growing from it) that opens up to an offwidth. A long 50-meter lead. Joins Dod's Jam route in the great amphitheater.

102. Blood, Sweat, & Smears   II 5.10c   ★★★

165' (50m) in length, Pro to 3" Double set of wires

A most excellent route and one of Beacon Rock's finest. Traverse up left from Reasonable Richard belay. Enter and climb the dihedral passing through several small overhangs and thin sections. Belay on Big Ledge.

103. True Grunt   II 5.11a PG

165' (50m) in length, Pro to 2" Extra wires

A difficult and technical crux. Unique but seldom ascended. A very long lead.

104. Steppenwolf   IV 5.11+ A0 (5.10d to Big Ledge)   ★★★

165' (50m) in length for the 1st pitch, Pro to 2" Extra wires

This route is one of the best prizes at Beacon Rock. Start at the third tunnel up steep corners and steps on the lower 5.7 section of the Dod's Jam route. When possible, angle up right to a

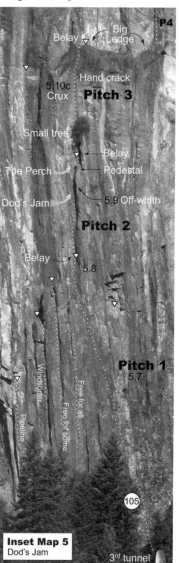

Map 5: Dod's Jam

P4

Belay — Big Ledge

5.10c Crux   Hand crack   **Pitch 3**

Small tree

Belay

The Perch   Redestal

Dod's Jam   5.9 Off-width

Pitch 2

Belay   5.8

Pitch 1
5.7

Windsurfer
Pipeline
Free for all
Free for some

105

Inset Map 5
Dod's Jam

3rd tunnel

THIRD TUNNEL

A stellar list of high quality climbs is available immediately past the Third Tunnel. Classics such as Dod's Jam, Free For All, Free For Some, Windsurfer, and Pipeline should always be on your hit list when visiting Beacon.

bolt belay under a roof. Step up right around the roof and climb a long exhilarating dihedral. Pull through a final overhung jam crack to Big Ledge. Above are two clean cracks that join halfway up and then angle to the right. The right crack is Steppenwolf, while the left is a continuation of Journey to the East (now Wishbone). Free climb up the right crack (5.11d/.12a) for 60' to a bolt anchor. Above are several more pitches of mixed free and aid climbing up the main headwall to the west side hikers trail.

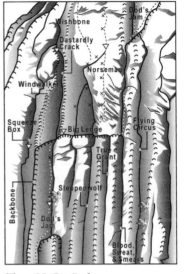

Topo H: *Big Ledge*

Dod's Jam route begins at the Third Tunnel.

105. Dod's Jam III 5.10c ★★★

Multi-pitch, Pro to 3"

One of the all time Beacon classics. Very popular, especially the lower portions. **Pitch 1:** Start up easy slabs (at the 3rd tunnel to the right of the large oak tree) leftward along a series of corners and small ledges. When you reach the base of the main dihedral (Free For All joins here) step up to the birds nest belay.

Pitch 2: Climb a crack that quickly becomes an offwidth (5.9) to a ledge aptly called 'The Perch'

Pitch 3: Climb up past a small tree via a crux (5.10c) jam crack to the famous Big Ledge belay.

Pitch 4: To continue the next pitch, step to the far right end of the ledge and into a deep corner system. Move up a series of wide cracks and offwidth chimneys (5.7 - 5.9) then angle up right along slabs to a sling belay about 40' directly above the west edge of Grassy Ledges. The original route bailed down to Grassy Ledges.

Pitch 5: To continue up, surmount a small bulge which leads up past some small ledges and short 5.8 sections before exiting onto the rocky slope near the west side trail. The upper portion has route finding challenges that require experience and diligence on steep, seldom climbed terrain.

Most climbers rappel from Big Ledge or climb Dastardly Crack because it offers a quality finish to the trail above.

Dod's Direct Finish: A good alternative climbing route is a direct finish located at the immediate right edge of the main upper headwall. Although seldom climbed it offers an unusually wide man-eating, overhanging (5.9) wide crack system that ends near the trail overlook. Reference Photo Map #5 (Topo H) for a visual detail.

106. Dod's Deviation 5.9 (variation) ★

45' (13m) in length, Pro to 3"

107. Wishbone III 5.12

Multi-pitch, Pro to 3½"

This line is the original **Journey To The East** IV 5.11 A4 aid line, but now established as a free climb. From a large oak tree follow a series of large flakes (5.9) and minor cracks. Cross over Dod's Jam to access a crack on the right side of Dod's Deviation. Climb this crack/face (5.12-) to Big Ledge. From the ledge climb a thin crack (5.12-) directly off the ledge till it merges with Steppenwolf at the tiny roof, then angle up left via a seam and lead (5.12) to the final belay. The original aid line continued to the hiker's trail, but the free version does not top out.

108.   Devil's Backbone   5.12a   ★★
80' (24m) in length, Pro to 1½"

Probably the finest example at Beacon of a crack that splits an arête. Approximately 20' above the first belay on Dod's Jam move left via under clings to an arête. Climb straight up to Big Ledge. An incredible climb!

109.   The Norseman   5.12b   ★★
60' (18m) in length, 5 QD's and minor pro to 1½"

This is the bolted route on the headwall buttress. From Big Ledge climb up Steppenwolf a few feet until possible to move right to a bolted rounded buttress. Ascend this to a bolt anchor. Excellent climb.

110.   Dastardly Crack   5.9   ★★
165' (50m) in length, Pro to 2"

Directly above Dod's Jam from Big Ledge is a large dihedral. Climb the obvious tight corner, then angle up left (passing the Windwalker belay anchor) on good edges to a bushy corner that leads to the west side hikers' trail.

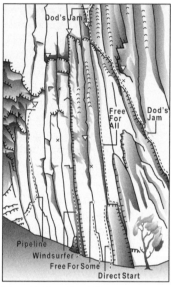

Topo I: *Free For All*

111.   Squeeze Box   5.10b PG   ★
165' (50m) in length, Pro to 2"

An interesting fist crack through a roof. From Big Ledge angle down left until possible to turn a corner. Climb a dihedral and overhangs to rejoin with Dastardly Crack.

112.   Windwalker   5.11d   ★★
90' (27m) in length, Pro to 3"

This is the arête immediately left of Dastardly Crack. Traverse left off from Big Ledge to the arête, then ascend directly up till you merge with Dastardly at a belay anchor.

Starting with the route Free For All and moving leftward to Pipeline you will find a superb selection of long challenging leads. This area is a popular destination for Beacon climbers. Depending on your skill level there are stellar rock climbs here for all expert levels from 5.8 to 5.11+.

113.   Free For All   5.8   ★★★
150' (45m) in length, Pro to 2"

Excellent route. A must for everyone! Just left of a large oak tree (left of the 3rd tunnel) is a detached free standing 25' pillar. The left side is the Direct Start (5.10a), while the right side is 5.8. Climb either. From the top of the pillar continue up the obvious crooked hand crack until it joins with Dod's Jam at

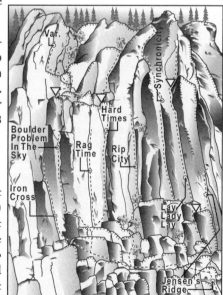

Topo J: *West Face*

the first belay. Reference Topo Diagram I for a visual detail.

114. Free For Some   5.11a PG ★★★

140' (42m) in length, Pro to 2"
TCU's recommended

A remarkable and demanding lead with excellent protection. Immediately left of Free For All is a thin seam. Climb this to a bolt anchor at 65' then ascend the second half (5.10c) or rappel.

115. Windsurfer 5.10b ★★★

120' (36m) in length, Pro to 3"
Double set of wires

A popular and exciting climb. To find this good route look for a left-facing dihedral with three small roofs. Begin up a wide crack that ends at a ledge and bolt belay.

116. Fresh Squeeze (aka Squeeze Box Direct) II 5.11c/d ★

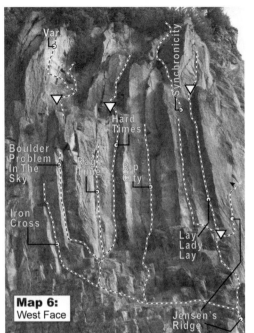

Map 6:
West Face

120' (36m) in length for the 1ˢᵗ pitch,
Pro to 2" and pins (P2 140')

On a face between Pipeline and Windsurfer are two crack systems. The right is Fresh Squeeze. Ascend the first pitch (5.11c) to a ledge and belay. The second pitch steps up above the anchor, moves right and climbs a vertical face broken by a seam. Eventually enters a dihedral and eases (5.10) until it joins with Squeeze Box.

117. Rise Up 5.10c

90' (27m) in length, Pro to 3"

This route begins immediately right of Pipeline and ascends a long discontinuous crack using gear till you pass a single bolt near a crux face section. Continue up a finger/hand crack to a large ledge where the Windsurfer belay anchor is also located. Rappel.

118. Pipeline 5.11b ★★★

60' (18m) in length, Pro to 1½"

Superb classic route. On the right side of the Arena of Terror is a thin, difficult layback finger crack that ends at a bolt anchor next to several small overhangs. A barndoor crux.

119. Pipe Dream 5.12a ★

160' (50m) in length for the 1st pitch, Pro to 3" and extra set of wires

Little is known about the quality of this route, but it looks incredible! The route has been free climbed in very bold style (ground-up). From the belay ledge for Fresh Squeeze (1ˢᵗ pitch) step left and ascend a remarkable crack on a smooth face to an anchor at the base of an easy dihedral. Rappel with 2 ropes or continue up and join with Dastardly Crack.

120. Pipeline Headwall III 5.11b

Multi-pitch, Pro to 2"

121. Silver Crow IV 5.10d A3 (or 5.10c free)

KB, LA, Rurps and pro to 4"

122. Axe of Karma   IV 5.10c A3
Multi-pitch, KB, LA and pro to 4"

The following six climbs are located left of the Arena of Terror. The left most is the regular (5.7) approach arête to Jensen's Ridge and the other west side routes.

123. Red Ice   5.10d ★
145' (44m) in length, Pro to 2½"
Just left of the Arena of Terror. Ascend easy ground to a loose, hollow section. Move up left and finish up a beautiful finger to hand crack in a dihedral. Bolt Anchor. Rappel with two ropes or ascend one of the upper climbs on the west face.

124. Doubting Thomas   5.10c
145' (44m) in length, Pro to 1½"
This climb (and the next three) are seldom ascended, but could provide a variable approach to climbs on the west face or an alternate to Jensen's Ridge upper pitches.

125. Boys of Summer   5.10b
145' (44m) in length, Pro to 2"

126. Fingers of a Fisherman   5.10b
145' (44m) in length, Pitons and pro to 2"

127. Crack of Dawn   5.9
145' (44m) in length, Pro to 2"
A short climb near the outer edge of the Jensen's Ridge approach buttress.

128. Jensen's Ridge   III 5.11a ★★
Multi-pitch, Pro to 4" including TCU's and big pro for OW
The physical crux is a thin tips crack on the second pitch, while the offwidth just beyond is certainly the psychological mind bender. Commence up an easy ridge (loose) to a bolt belay. Step right (nearly off the platform) and ascend the desperate thin crack 20' to a ledge. Enter into a deep dihedral that opens to a wide offwidth. Belay at bolts just where Lay Lady Lay joins. Continue to the hikers' trail via two options. Both are 5.9+.

___. Jensen's Rimjob   III A2+
Pro: Birdbeak or KB's, Hook, Double set of Nuts to 1", and Cams to 6"
From the top of Pipeline Headwall/Silver Crow launch onto vertical terrain via a crack corner system immediately right of the upper part of Jensen's Ridge route. Can reduce cam size to 5" if utilizing the upper section of standard Jensen's route.

129. Updraft to Heaven   III 5.10d R A1
160' (48m) in length, KB and pro to 6"

130. Mostly Air   5.10b PG
160' (48m) in length, Pro to 2½" (poorly protected)

Reference the West Face photo map #6 (Topo J) for an analysis of the following routes

131. Lay Lady Lay   II 5.10b ★★★
100' (30m) in length, Pro to 2½"
A quality route except for the poison oak that plagues the start of this and the following three routes.

132. Synchronicity   II 5.8 A2
Multi-pitch, KB, LA and pro to 4"

133. **Rip City** II **5.10a** ★★
    80' (24m) in length, Pro to 1¾"
    Poison oak plagues this route.

134. **Hard Times** II **5.10c**
    80' (24m) in length, Pro to 2½"
    Plenty of steep stemming.

135. **Rag Time** II **5.10c**
    80' (24m) in length, Pro to 2½"

136. **Boulder Problem in the Sky** II **5.10d** ★★
    Multi-pitch, Pro to 2½"
    Excellent stem problem with an exciting roof crack.

137. **Iron Cross (aka On the Move)** II **5.11b PG** ★
    Multi-pitch, Pro to 4"

138. **Variation** **5.9**
    80' in length, Pro to 2½"

Tyler Kamm leading *Free For Some*

NORTHWEST SECTION OF BEACON ROCK

VISUAL BIO

Northwest Section only: **12** Month **1** Min NW Shade PM Regs Trad

These emblems represent most of the Northwest Section of Beacon Rock. This area offers a shaded environment with limited afternoon sunshine. The right-most routes (such as Siege Tactics) are approximately a 3-minute approach.

The following addendum provides a detailed analysis of the northwest section of Beacon Rock and its diverse selection of routes ranging in difficulty from 5.8 to 5.12. Only at the Northwest area is the opportunity allowed by park policy for year-round rock climbing. The Northwest Area starts from the posted sign near a water spigot and picnic table at the north side near State Route 14. It extends rightward to another posted sign along the summit hiking trail as it encounters the main west wall of Beacon Rock before proceeding uphill on a paved walkway. The topo (Topo K, L & M) details two main sections which are separated by a spat of low angled brush covered slopes. The rock climbs on the NW side of Beacon are not frequently ascended mainly due to the technical difficulty, inobvious nature of the protection on certain climbs, and the lack of precise route information to adequately guide climbers to this area. Hopefully this database will encourage you to explore some of these lesser known rock climbs at Beacon Rock. Topo M is a closeup detail of the Large Alcove near Headcase. The upper portion of the

NORTHWEST SECTION OF BEACON

The *Northwest Area* is open year-round. It encompasses the area from immediately west of the water spigot next to the north face, and ends where the hiker's trail meets to cliff on the west side. There are posted signs explaining the exact boundaries. This area offers a substantial selection of routes ranging from 5.7 to 5.12, mixed bolt and natural protection routes. The enjoyable 5.8 mixed crack and face slab climb referred to as the *Iron Spike* route is definitely worth sending, especially the first 3 pitches. The third pitch sends the 1" thick iron rung spike ladders that are directly fixed to the wall. If not into foraging with poison oak just rappel off after the third lead.

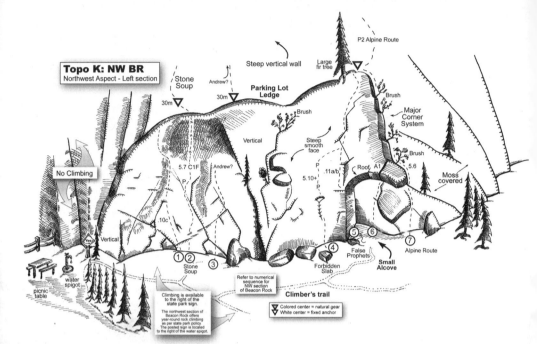

Refer to numerical sequence for NW section of Beacon Rock

two main NW section diagrams are not to exact scale.

1. _____ **5.10c**

100' (30m) in length, Pro to 1½" including cams

A steep face route with difficult to place protection that ascends criss-crossing seams and minor cracks. Exit up left onto easier terrain then continue to the anchor.

2. **Stone Soup   IV 5.9 C2F**

Multi-pitch, Pro: Double set of offset Nuts to 1", some Aliens, large cams to 5" (Two 3" cams), a Hook, small cams down to #00, and thin aid Nuts.

This route ascends challenging mixed nailing and free terrain on the less-traveled northwest section of Beacon. Portions of this wall have been explored by climbers many years ago as can be seen by the old fixed gear found on parts of this route. This extreme route was developed over a sustained period of time by a core group of active climbers seeking a rewarding experience on this particular well-featured section of the monolith. Stone Soup provides the all-encompassing multi-pitch spicey adventure climb with less of the political obligations found on the peregrine protected south face. Aside from some wet moss, grit, brush, insipient seams and pebbles this formidable route vies to add a rare dimension to the hard-core list of rock climbing routes found on the northwest section of Beacon Rock. See photographic Map 7 and Map 8 for a closeup analysis of the entire route.

P1 30m (5.7 C1F [5.11?]): Begin just inside the forest right of the water spigot in a trench. Move up right on an easy 5th class slab with edges to a steep crack. Aid up and left to another slab, then straight up on gear passing two pins and three bolts to end on Parking Lot Ledge at a bolt anchor. The first pitch has been climbed at 5.10c exiting up left or 5.11b top-rope direct.

P2 32m (5.7 C2F [5.10+?]): From the Parking Lot Ledge aid climb directly up a steep open flat face via angular leaning seams and minor cracks passing five pins and five bolts to an anchor at 3-Tree Ledge.

P3 25m (5.9): From belay at 3-Tree ledge aid an awkward crack up right and mantle over some blocks. Aid up and then right to an easy ramp. Move left along ramp passing a huge

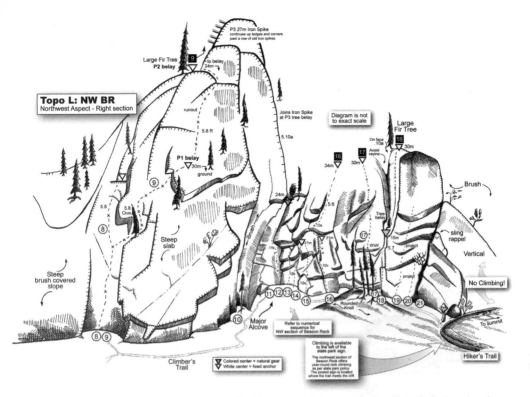

Topo L: NW BR
Northwest Aspect - Right section

slung tree. Climb a flaring awkward offwidth to small ledge. Ascend a 5" crack (bolt at base). The wide crack ends at the Alice-In-Wonderland Ledge (great bivi). Use a nearby fixed bolt and pin to set an anchor. *Other option:* Climb easy ramp on left, traversing across narrow grass ledge (5.9) back up rightward. *Note:* P3 & P4 can be linked in one lead.

P4 15m (5.6): From 'a/w ledge' aid (and hook) a 7-bolt vertical face up right to a large ledge. Step left to a 2-bolt anchor next to several trees on a large platform known as Swiss Family Ledge. *Alternative:* start off the far left end of the 'a/w ledge' and wander up 'Mike's Lark' variation on 5.6 terrain by a round-about method on nice rock.

P5 30m: Move belay from the bottom of Swiss Family Ledges to the top ledge, passing a fixed pin and 2 bolts on several ledgelets. Belay at top right edge of ledge from a slung tree and single bolt. Aid up and left to an arete, then aid up the arete mostly on reachy fixed pins and bolts to an overhanging crux below a small perch at a bolt. From the perch, free climb (5.6) up an easier arete till it steepens and move right to a hanging belay anchor.

P6 25m: Move up then over right a short distance and climb a short 5.6 section, then aid past four bolts and a piton, avoiding some hollow blocks on your immediate left. End at a 2-bolt anchor at a small stance called the 'phone booth' with a small tree on your right.

P7 30m (5.7): Move belay up 10m over low 5th class rock to intermediate fixed belay. Continue up 30m of grassy 3rd class (pass ancient relics of the old hiking trail) over a short 5.6 step and up to the trail near the summit. Best to walk off via hikers trail.

3. _____

100' (30m) in length, Pro ?

This face climb starts immediately left of a large boulder at the bottom of the pit. Sends a steep face using thin cracks and seams for protection. Likely one of Andrew's routes.

4. Forbidden Slab   5.10+ R

80' (24m) in length, Pro to 3"

Climb the face on the outer left side of the prow of the little alcove. This route is mostly a natural gear lead. Climb past two fixed pitons and angle up right to merge into route #5.

5. **False Prophet 5.11a/b** ★
80' (24m) in length, Pro to 3"
This line begins on the inside left face (2 bolts) of the tiny alcove. Power up several nice holds, then use hard smears and desperate side clings to gain a small edge above the roof at the beginning of a crack. Race up nice 5.10a broken cracks angling up right to the fir tree belay on a large ledge.

6. **Alcove Overhang   5.11 [?] or A2**
35' (10m) in length, Pro ?
This line ascends the very short but fiercely overhung crack in the roof of this tiny alcove.

7. **Alpine Route   5.6**
75' (23m) in length, Pro 3"
A major right facing corner system that ends at a giant fir on a ledge. P2 continues up broken mossy ledges and corners to land at 'three trees ledge' on Stone Soup.

8. **Genesis   5.8**
80' (24m) in length, Pro ?
This route branches directly up left from the first portion of Iron Spike but ends abruptly at a fixed anchor.

9. **Iron Spike   P1 5.8, P2 5.8, P3 5.7**   ★★
Multi-pitch, Pro to 3" including cams
This is a great route worth climbing...at least the first three leads. A bit mossy in places due to lack of use, but hopefully you will be encouraged to make the ascent regardless. This is a fairly long multi-pitch route where the first two pitches are well fixed with bolts requiring the occasional gear placement along the way.
P1 90' lead (5.8): Commence up a steep slab with edges placing gear when needed. At the second bolt traverse directly right to a thin fir tree, and then climb a tight vertical crux section (bolts) using small edges. Continue up right on smears past another bulge to a belay anchor at a stance.
P2 80' lead (5.8): Climb a steep slab using smears and edges with some runout sections. Ends on a nice ample ledge and a fixed anchor near a large fir tree.
P3 85' lead (5.7): Scramble upward into a dirty corner of brush and trees. At about 40' you will encounter the Iron Spike ladder. Ascend this (5.7) by slinging the 1" thick metal spikes or placing large cams in the crack corner. Ends at a large fir tree belay.
P4, P5 & P6 (5.5): Traverse south along a narrow path ledge system (poison oak) and up to a ledge at 60-meters. From a fir tree climb variable terrain (5.5) for several more leads ascending up various ledges. Rappel after the 3rd pitch to avoid the green itchy stuff.

Is It The Best Multi-pitch 5.10 At Beacon?

Try this route combination, and perhaps you will consider it to be one of the best multi-pitch 5.10 rock climbing routes at Beacon Rock.
Climb up **Free For All** using the direct start .10a on the left side of the pedestal. Continue up a long stellar 5.8 jam crack and merge with the 1st belay on **Dod's Jam**. Climb **Dod's** up to the perch, then past the small bush and up the precarious .10c jam to Big Ledge. Then launch up left onto a high quality 5.9 stem corner crack system called **Dastardly Crack**. Once you are past the initial 80' it eases to moderate 5.7 terrain that ends at the tree belay next to the hikers trail. Wow, is that a wild line! .

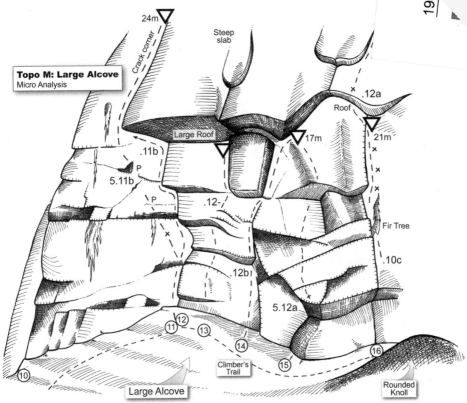

Topo M: Large Alcove
Micro Analysis

24m

Crack corner

Steep slab

.12a

Roof

Large Roof

17m

21m

.11b

P

5.11b

P

.12-

Fir Tree

.10c

.12b

5.12a

11 12 13

14

15

16

Climber's Trail

10

Large Alcove

Rounded Knoll

10. _____

Unclimbed corner system to the left of the major alcove.

See Topo M for a closeup detail of the Large Alcove. Headcase and Siege Tactics are located in this well-protected overhanging nook.

11. Head Case 5.11b ★

80' (24m) in length, Pro to 3½" including cams (has a fixed pin/bolt)

Starts in the very corner of a major alcove, but quickly launches out onto the face to exit up around the lip of the roof (crux) to a long dihedral crack corner system. Belay at a tree at 24-meters. Continue climbing a steep crack corner (P2) 5.10a for another lead.

12. Spiny Fish 5.11b

80' (24m) in length, Pro to 3½"

Also starts the same as for Headcase but literally stays in the very corner of this major alcove using the crack, then turns the lip crux rejoining there with Headcase. Continue up a crack system to a tree anchor. The climb takes mostly 2" pro except for the large stuff needed to surmount the roof.

13. _____   **5.12 [?]**

60' (18m) in length, Pro to ?

An unfinished 5.12 project that ascends the face immediately right of Headcase and ends at the giant roof.

14. Siege Tactics   5.12a

55' (17m) in length, Pro to 2½" (wires and cams)

This is the power line that ascends up through very steep ground on the right inner section of the alcove. At a large block move around it to the right, then up to the last main roof. A few moves up right is the anchor. Rappel.

15. _____   5.12b project

55' (17m) in length, Pro to ?

Unfinished project. This line sends the outside of the nose next to Siege Tactics by surmounting the overhang straight on. Continue up dicey face edges till it merges again with Siege Tactics anchor.

16. Dorian's Dilemma   5.10c 1ˢᵗ pitch   ★

55' (17m) in length 1ˢᵗ pitch to anchor under large roof

Pro: 2" wires and cams, small wires are useful

This climb ascends a crack, breaks through a small crux overhang and continues up past a small fir tree using a minor right facing corner (bolts) to a belay-rappel anchor immediately under the upper large roof. Crux is pulling roof; 2 bolts on upper face (10a or so) just below rap anchors.

Pitch two of Dorian's Dilemma is 5.12a. This second part powers through the crux large overhang (2 bolts) and then waltzes up an easy corner crack to an anchor at 24m. Rappel.

17. Gitmo Love Machine 5.12a ★

100' (30m) in length, Pro ?
Pro: QD's, small TCU's and wires to 1"

This is a stellar face climb on tenuous holds. Stick clip the first bolt. Powerful .10+ climbing to get off the ground then you hit a solid .12a crux immediately to pass the first bolt. Some hard face moves then surmount the second roof (TCU) which is a tricky .11d move. A long 15' run out above the second roof with several bolts and a single large midway jug. At the third roof (place small cam) power over this at .11c to another runout 5.8 slab to the anchor, and then rappel if you still have any energy.

18. Fireballs (P1) 5.7 to small tree, (P2) 5.10c

50' (15m) in length to small tree
100' (30m) in length when done as one full lead
Pro: gear to 1½" including cams (especially small cams)

This line ascends a corner crack to a tight slot in a roof where you must squeeze behind the constriction to end at the small tree belay. Avoid the upper ravine. Rappel or continue up right onto pitch 2 of Fireballs.

Pitch 2 continues past the small tree up right on a very steep angled crack that avoids the ravine. Ascend a steep vertical face via a 4-bolt line to a fixed anchor at 30 meters next to a large fir tree. Rappel.

19. _____

100' (24m) in length
A project?

20. _____

80' (24m) in length
Another project?

21. _____ 5.9 [?]

40' (12m) in length, pro to [?]

A wide offwidth crack system that smears up steep terrain past a slight overhang and ends on a minor sloped ramp at a sling rappel around a rock horn of a detached flake. Rappel.

A posted State Park sign limits rock climbing on the Northwest Section to the left of the hikers trail. The summit-bound hikers trail meets the west face of Beacon Rock at this point.

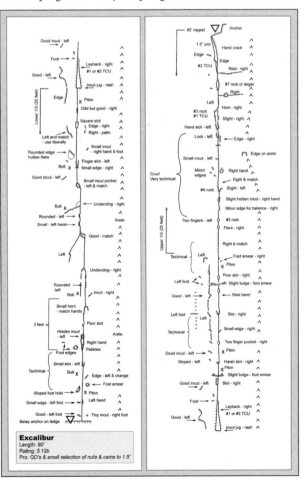

Excalibur
Length: 80'
Rating: 5.12b
Pro: QD's & small selection of nuts & cams to 1.5'

The Legend of Beacon Rock

Chances are, if you've climbed at Beacon Rock over the past three decades or so, you've met, talked to, heard about, or even tied in with one of the giants of Northwest climbing, Jim Opdycke. Born April 25, 1944, Opdycke first made it to the top of Beacon Rock when he was just five months old. Literally. A picture from the fall of 1944 shows baby Opdycke and his family atop the monolith after hiking all the way up the trail. But it wasn't until forty years later that Opdycke really began to make his mark at Beacon Rock.

In the interim, Opdycke grew up in Vancouver. In 1967, he hit the road, thumbing his way around the country for three years before returning home and joining the workaday world. An inveterate adventurer, Opdycke needed more, so in 1972 he started climbing mountains. Over the next four years, he embarked on some hardcore mountaineering, heading to the hills in the harshest of conditions to sharpen his skills and learn how to survive.

And then in 1976, Opdycke's friend, Jay Kerr, introduced him to rock climbing, first at Broughton Bluff near Troutdale and then at Beacon Rock. At Beacon, the two climbed all the way to the top via a wet, dirty 5.10c known as Seagull. Opdycke was hooked.

Though he continually climbed all around the west — Yosemite, Devil's Tower, Colorado, Arizona,

Alaska, Oregon, Idaho, and Washington — Opdycke eventually found his true calling at Beacon Rock. After being injured in a fall in 1984, Opdycke headed out to Beacon to find the rock dirty, overgrown, and largely silent. Many of the pioneers from earlier decades had backed off by then, but Opdycke saw that there was still plenty of trail to blaze at Beacon. He began solo aiding up some of the lines he'd always wanted to do, cleaning them all the way up, adding solid bases down below. He would take friends out to Beacon and turn them on to his routes; he'd also listen to what other climbers had to say about his routes, whether they were any good or not.

Over the ensuing years, Opdycke put up some of the most classic routes at Beacon Rock: Young Warriors, Little Wing, Jill's Thrill, Ground Zero, Stardust, and Cruisin' to name a few. In total, he has put up close to 4,000 feet of new routes at Beacon Rock.

Yet beyond just his climbing at Beacon, Opdycke is known as well for his stewardship of the place. Always friendly and encouraging to up-and-coming climbers — a mentor even — he has logged countless hours cleaning and tending to routes at Beacon. On opening day every year, he's almost always the one who cleans the Southeast Corner and gets it in shape for the season to come. And even if he's not climbing when he's at Beacon, Opdycke's likely doing something to make it better: battling poison oak, picking up trash, shoring up a base. It's what he loves to do, not only because he reveres Beacon Rock, but because he wants other people to be able to have the same adventures out there that he's had.

So the next time you head out to Beacon, keep your eyes and ears open for a wiry, mustachioed man with the hands of a climber and an easy, enthusiastic smile. He's part of the reason you're there.
Written by Jon Bell

BEACON ROCK

CHAPTER 8

FRENCH'S DOME

THOUGH TINY IN COMPARISON to many crags, the merits of French's Dome should not be overlooked. Many Portland area rock climbers have discovered that this miniature crag's rare qualities give it an enduring appeal. A visit to French's is sure to spark your enthusiasm, as well.

This unique and easily accessible dome of rock lies amongst a tall canopy of evergreen trees along the lower west side of Mt. Hood. There are at least a dozen climbing routes available ranging from 5.6 to 5.12. Most of the climbs are fixed with bolts, practically eliminating the need for natural protection. The overall height is 160 feet from the longest side and 80 feet on the road face.

The dome itself is *not* visible above the forests of Douglas fir trees, but it is just a short, one-minute walk to the crag. French's Dome is an interesting geological wonder of the Oregon woods and a perfect little area to escape from the city. Misty Slab is the visible sloping buttress of rock located 40 minutes uphill from French's, yet because of the approach, ascents there have been kept to a minimum.

The Dome seemed to languish for years after the intial four original routes were established. In the 1980s local summer ski school coaches became enthralled by the place and sought to establish a string of new routes that has literally set the place on edge. Hermann Gollner, Vance Lemley, Pat Purcell, Tom Sell, John Rust and Joe Reis put considerable time into cleaning and establishing the 5.11/.12 grade at the Dome. Their route development energy helped tremendously to make the Dome a premier climbing destination in the Mt. Hood National Forest.

Effective erosion control platforms have been built along the cliff base of French's Dome providing a long-term solution to a hillside that had been rapidly sliding away. With Forest Service trail building guidance and a volunteer workforce locals have built a legacy that will keep this place a perfect little Mt. Hood gem!

The routes at French's Dome are described symmetrically clock-wise, which you will find quite beneficial because the trail first encounters the crag at the routes facing the road. Beginning with the road face the list shown below details each rock climb as if you were to descend the perimeter trail around the crag to the left from the road face. Then from the lowest portion of the Dome the routes are described uphill ending with the Yellow Brick Road route as the last climb to be mentioned.

French's Dome is composed of olivine basalt and is a tall remnant of an old volcanic neck core after the surrounding softer material eroded away exposing the rock knob.

HOW TO GET THERE

Drive east from Gresham on U.S. hwy 26. Con-

Alan Blank leading *Straw Man* 5.7

French's Dome: Face Climbing Paradise

tinue through Sandy, Oregon until you are near the small community of Zigzag at the base of Mt. Hood. Turn north on the Lolo Pass Road. The crag is located 6¼ miles up the Lolo Pass road (U.S.F.S. 18) from its junction with U.S. 26 at Zigzag. Look for an unobtrusive dirt pullout on the right and the NW Forest Pass sign. A vehicle parking pass is required for all users at this site. You can obtain a daily or annual Northwest Forest Pass parking permit at their office in the small community of Zigzag.

VISUAL BIO

7
Month 1 Min Shade Trees   Regs   **Sport**

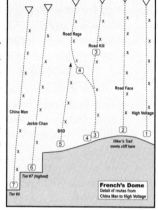

These emblems represent the French's Dome climbing site. French's is a giant round spherical dome encapsulated deep within a substantial green forest so there is generally no need for sunscreen lotion. French's Dome is a sport crag haven because the nature of the rock (crackless) lends itself to bolt protected climbing.

The routes in this section are numbered according to a descent made clockwise to the left from the road face area to the lowest portion of the Dome, and up the far side on the perimeter trail.

1. **High Voltage 5.12 b ★**
60' (18m) in length, 5 QD's
This line lies a few feet immediately right of the Road Face climb.

2. **Road Face 5.12a ★★★**
60' (18m) in length, 6 QD's
This is a classic route originally done as an aid line, but now is a popular and difficult free climb. If you have ascended the Giant's Staircase the summit rappel descends down to the base of the cliff at this point.

3. **Road Kill 5.12a ★★**
60' (18m) in length, 5 QD's
This is the direct finish from **Road Rage** that leads up to its own seperate anchor .

4. **Road Rage 5.12a ★★**
60' (18m) in length, 5 QD's
Climb the first 2 bolts then move left and continue up (*see diagram*).

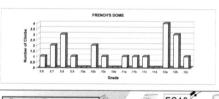

5. **BSD 5.12b**
60' (18m) in length, 6 QD's (BSD merges into Road Rage at 3rd bolt)
A steep climb located immediately above the upper tier platform.

6. **Jackie Chan 5.12b ★★★**
60' (18m) in length, 5 QD's

7. **China Man 5.11b ★★★**
60' (18m) in length, 7 QD's
An excellent climb on a slightly overhanging face with many small edges and finger holds.

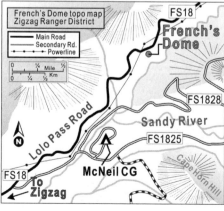

8. The Dark Side (aka The Seige) 5.12b ★★

60' (18m) in length, 6 QD's

9. Pumporama 5.12a/b ★★

60' (18m) in length, 6 QD's

The route is overhung for the entire distance, and ascends a black streak of rock. A series of thin holds low on the climb lead to a difficult sequence of moves from the 4th to 5th bolts.

10. Crankenstein 5.11c ★★★

60' (18m) in length, 5 QD's

An excellent climb and considered to be one of the best routes at the Dome. The technical crux is low on the climb, but the bulge near the end of the climb is surprisingly formidable to most people.

French's Donut Link-Up 5.13a/b

An unusually powerful link-up connects all the difficult crux sections of seven routes by traversing uphill at mid-height starting on Crankenstein. Once you reach Road Rage power through its thin crux moves and finish up to the anchor as the finale. This very sustained traverse was nearly sent by Ryan Palo in 2009, and finally freed in 2011 by Matt Spohn.

11. Dirty Deeds (aka Silver Streak) 5.10c ★★★

60' (18m) in length, 6 QD's

Another superb climb and a good one to quickly grasp the nature of edgy face climbing at the Dome.

12. Straw Man 5.7 ★★★

80' (24m) in length, 9 QD's

A very popular and classic rock climb that starts up easy holds, then passes a steep crux section near the 5th bolt. Additional new closely spaced bolts have made this climb more reasonable in nature.

13. Emerald City 5.8

Length: 60' (18m)

The top anchor and route were developed sometime in the year 2011 for climbing. Located between Straw man and Alpha.

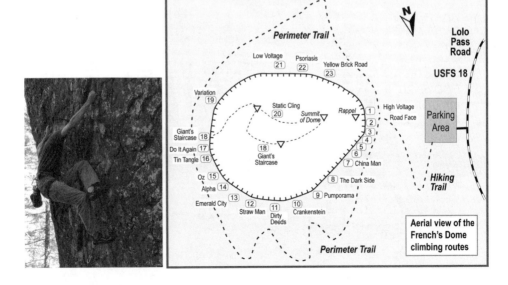

Aerial view of the French's Dome climbing routes

14. Alpha   5.8   ★★★

80' (24m) in length,   8 QD's

A great climb with a variety of small ledges, face climbing, and positive knobby hand holds near the crux. Climb up easy steps in a gully, then continue up a steep face to a short vertical section. The original left start is seldom climbed. Rappel from bolt anchors.

15. Oz   5.8   ★★

60' (18m) in length,   8 QD's

Ascends a ramp of large steps then embarks up and left on a steep face to a crux near the 4th bolt. and then large hand holds and edges on the upper portion near the bolt anchor.

16. Tin Man (aka Tin Tangle)   5.8   ★★★

60' (18m) in length,   5 QD's

This excellent and popular route climbs directly up the blocky rib. The best holds are near the blocky rib, while several bolts are located slightly to the right.

17. Do It Again   5.9   ★

50' (15m) in length,   4 QD's

This route travels up left of the blocky rib called Tin Tangle. Start at the same place as you would for Giant's Staircase, but ascend directly up to the first bolt, then angle slightly left of the rib.

Reference Map #1 for a photographic visual analysis of the routes near the east side start of Giant's Staircase.

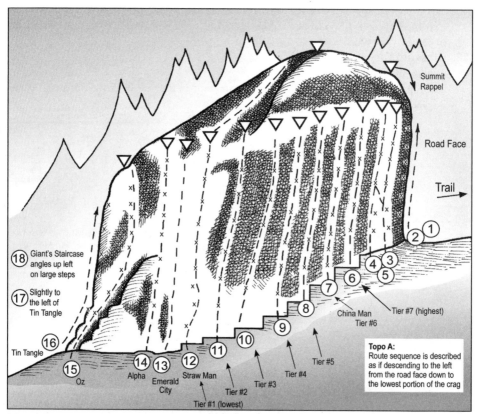

Topo Diagram A: *Descending left from Road Face*

18. Giant's Staircase 5.6 ★★★

Multi-pitch climb, QD's

This is a classic and original climb that ascends steps and ledges starting from the lower or longest side of the pinnacle. From the lowest point in the trail ascend up easy steps leftward (bolts) to a ledge and a bolt belay anchor. From the first belay traverse right (bolts) to bypass a vertical section, till you pass a minor ridge. Climb upward on good holds (bolts) into a large gully and belay at an anchor. Continue up the gully to the summit of the pinnacle and belay at a bolt anchor. To rappel descend west down to the road face 80-foot rappel station. This rappel descends down a section of cliff that is substantially overhung.

19. Giant's Direct 5.7

30' (9m) in length, QD's

This viable alternative direct start merges with Giant's Staircase at the first belay. Sports several additional bolts.

20. Static Cling 5.10b

60' (18m) in length, QD's

Interesting route with a short steep crux right out of the gate. Using the right side of the scoop will reduce the rating to 5.9. The upper portion of the route is easier but a bit crumbly.

21. Low Voltage 5.11a ★

60' (18m) in length, 4 QD's

An interesting long climb which is easier (5.10a) if you are climbing a bit to the right of the bolts. A bit gravelly on the upper section near the anchor.

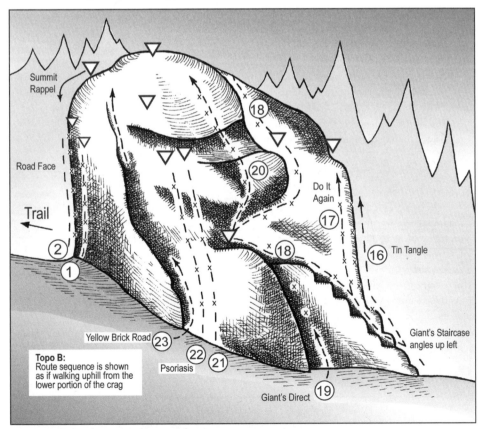

Topo Diagram B: *Ascending uphill from Giant's Staircase*

French's Dome
Map 1: Giant's Staircase

17 Do It Again

Alpha

Tin Tangle

Oz

Orig
Alpha

14

16

15

18

Giant's Staircase

22. Psoriasis 5.12d
60' (18m) in length, 5 QD's
A true power-enduro route that lacks a comfort jug. The business begins at 3rd bolt so get your rests where you can find them. Crux between 4th and 5th bolt, but is pumpy to the anchor.

23. Yellow Brick Road 5.10b R
180' (54m) in length, Pro to 3" and runout
Seldom climbed; runout and limited gear placements.

A Typical Day At The Dome

I was belaying Tymun on the Road Face route at French's Dome in the quiet early AM morning hours on a warm Spring day. The trail from the parking lot to the crag is a short one minute walk so climbers tend to let their kids or pups run down first to the crag.

Casually I peered up the trail looking beyond the trees and a minor thicket of shrubs. I noticed a rather large black dog lopping gently down along the trail toward the Dome. Oh great... here come the morning crowds.

As the creature moved a bit closer in my direction my thoughts abruptly sharpened when I realized, "Damn, that's no dog...it's a bear!"

At just about the same time I realized IT, the bear also realized that HE was not alone either. Immediately the bear busted off the side of the trail heading south past me and disappeared into the forest and brush. Then, it was quiet once again at French's Dome.

Story told by Dave Sowerby

FRENCH'S

CHAPTER 9

SALMON RIVER SLAB

S ALMON RIVER SLAB is a steep slice of exposed rock face located at a small road side pullout just a few short miles south of the tiny community of Zigzag. The rock climbs here provide a comprehensive cluster of well-bolted sport routes on a smooth flakey rock.

Salmon River Slab is a steep slice of exposed rock face located at a small road side pullout a few miles south of Zigzag. The climbs are a tiny cluster of well-bolted sport routes on a smooth but slightly flexible rock.

The rock bluff faces west and is shaded during the morning hours. The best time to visit here to climb is from May to October (on a sunny day!) so you can take advantage of the great Salmon River swimming hole just a few steps across the road from the rock climbs.

VISUAL BIO

6 Month 1 Min (W) PM **Sport**

These emblems represent Salmon River Slab. Approach time is essentially just parking the car and stepping out. Don't forget to bring a swimsuit; a brisk splash in the river is a must! This steep slab of rock is ideal for sport climbing.

HOW TO GET THERE

Drive east from Sandy, Oregon on US Highway 26 to the tiny community of Zigzag. Turn south onto the Salmon River Road (FS road 2618) and continue due south on this for 4 miles. The popular summer time swimming hole is on the west side of the road, while the tiny bluff is located on the left (east side) of the road at a small dirt pullout.

1. **Climbing Theme 5.6**
   45' (13m) in length, 6 QD's
   A basic minor rock climb, but it crosses several sections of loose poor quality rock.

2. **White Rice 5.9**
   50' (15m) in length, 9 QD's
   Considered to be one of the better climbs here. The crux is at the small overhung lip a few moves below the belay anchor.

3. **Camel Back 5.9**
   50' (15m) in length, 8 QD's
   A popular climb and an interesting lead.

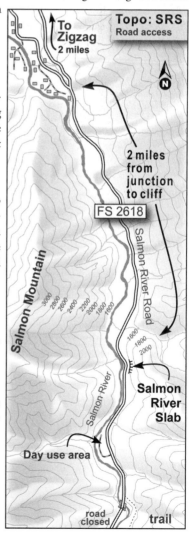

Topo: SRS
Road access

To Zigzag
2 miles

N

2 miles from junction to cliff

FS 2618

Salmon Mountain

3000 2800 2600 2400 2200 2000 1800 1600

Salmon River Road

1600 1800 2000

Salmon River

Salmon River Slab

Day use area

road closed trail

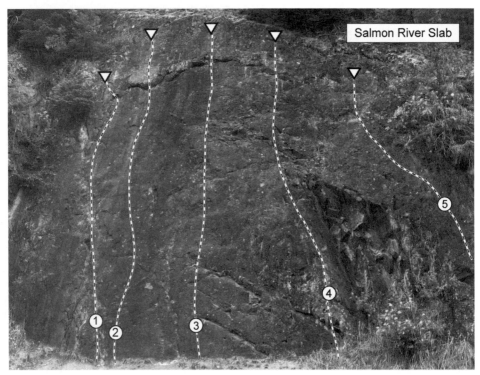

Salmon River Slab

4. Cave Man   5.7
50' (15m) in length, 6 QD's
Pull past a steep short bulge section for the initial opening moves, then cruise up a moderately easy steep slab using numerous edges to the belay anchor at the top of the cliff.

5. Salmon   5.5
45' (13m) in length, 7 QD's
Start on the right side of the cliff; power up an initial steep section while angling up leftward to easier ground. Numerous edges with some minor dirty sections to contend with.

Edges & Ledges 5.8

"Never measure the height of a mountain until you have climbed it."
~Dag Hammarskjold

SALMON RIVER SLAB

SELECTED BIBLIOGRAPHY

CLIMBING:

Ozone, Kevin Evansen & Associates, DHX Advertising, 2008

Oregon Rock, Jeff Thomas, The Mountaineers, 1983

Oregon High, Jeff Thomas, Keep Climbing Press, 1991

Rocky Butte Quarry, Mike Pajunas & Robert McGown, 1989

A Climbing Guide to Oregon, Nicholas Dodge, The Touchstone Press, 1975

Portland Rock Update, David Sowerby, 1997

Bouldering In Portland and the Columbia River Gorge, Greg Lyon, 2000

Washington Rock, Jeff Smoot, Falcon Publishing, 1999

Canyoneering, Christopher Van Tilburg, The Mountaineers, 2000

Rock Climbing Southwest Oregon, Greg Orton, Mountain N' Air Books, 2001

Oregon Rock Climbing, Volume 1 Willamette Valley, Greg Orton, Mountain N' Air Books, 2005

Weekend Rock Oregon, Ron Horton, The Mountaineers Books, 2006

Rock Climbing Oregon, Adam Bolf & Benjamin Ruef, Falcon Guide, 2006

Smith Rock State Park climbing guide, Alan Watts, Falcon Guide, 2010

Cascade Alpine Guide, Fred Beckey, The Mountaineers, 2nd Edition, 1979

Mountaineering: Freedom of the Hills, 5th Edition, The Mountaineers, 1992

Mazama Annual Publication, A Climbers Guide to the Columbia Gorge, Carl A. Neuburger, Vol. XL, No. 13, December 1958

Mazama Annual Publication, Brief Guide to the Apocalypse Needles, Bob Martin, Vol. XLV, No. 13, December 1963

Mt. Hood: A Complete History, Jack Grauer, Mazama Club Journal, 1975

HIKING:

Exploring Oregon's Wild Areas, William L. Sullivan, The Mountaineers, 1988

100 Hikes in the Central Oregon Cascades, William L. Sullivan, Navillus Press, Revised Edition 1995

Guide to the Middle and South Santiam Roadless Areas, 2nd Edition, Marys Peak Group, Sierra Club, 1977

35 Hiking Trails - Columbia River Gorge, Don & Roberta Lowe, The Touchstone Press, 1980

100 Oregon Hiking Trails, Don & Roberta Lowe, The Touch-

On lead at Trout Creek

Linda Schneider leading
Dracula 5.12a

stone Press, 1969

60 Hiking Trails-Central Oregon Cascades, Don & Roberta Lowe, The Touchstone Press, 1978

50 Hiking Trails - Portland & Northwest Oregon, Don & Roberta Lowe, The Touchstone Press, 1986

EARTH SCIENCES:

A Field Guide To Western Birds, Peterson Field Guide Series, Roger Tory Peterson, Houghton Mifflin, 1961

Wildflowers of the Columbia Gorge, Russ Jolley, Oregon Historical Society Press, 1988

Plants of the Pacific Northwest Coast, Pojar & MacKinnon, B.C. Ministry of Forests & Lone Pine Press, 1994

Field Guide to Pacific State Wildflowers, Peterson Field Guide Series, Theodore F. Niehaus & Charles Ripper, Houghton Mifflin Company, 1976

Field Guide to Rocks and Minerals, Peterson Field Guide Series, Frederick H. Pough, Houghton Mifflin Company, 5th Edition, 1996

Field Guide to North American Rocks and Minerals, The Audubon Society, Charles Chesterman, published by A. A. Knopf, Inc., 1979

Geology of Oregon, Ewart M. Baldwin, University of Oregon Bookstore, 1964

Earth: An Introduction to Physical Geology, Tarbuck & Lutgens, Prentice-Hall Inc., 1999

Tymun leading Gandalf's Grip 5.9

Hugh on crux pitch *SE Face Route 5.7,* Beacon Rock

APPENDIX B

Businesses, Organizations, and other Agencies

Climbing Equipment Stores:

The Mountain Shop
1510 NE 37th Avenue
Portland, Oregon 97232
503-288-6768
mountainshop.net

Mountain Hardwear
722 SW Taylor Street
Portland, Oregon 97204
503-226-6868
mountainhardwear.com

Next Adventure
426 SE Grand Avenue
Portland, Oregon 97214
503-233-0706
nextadventure.net

The North Face
1202 NW Davis Street
Portland, Oregon 97209
503-727-0200
thenorthface.com

Oregon Mountain Community
2975 NE Sandy Blvd.
Portland, Oregon 97232
503-227-1038
e-omc.com

US Outdoor Store
219 SW Broadway
Portland, Oregon 97205
503-223-5937
usoutdoor.com

Recreation Equipment Inc.
1405 NW Johnson Street
Portland, Oregon 97209
503-221-1938

7410 SW Bridgport Rd.
Tigard, Oregon 97224
503-624-8600

2235 NW Allie Avenue
Hillsboro, Oregon 97124
503-617-6072

12160 SE 82nd Avenue
Clackamas, Oregon 97266
503-659-1156
rei.com

Salem Summit Co.
246 State Street
Salem, OR 97301
503-990-7304
salemsummit.com

Peak Sports
207 NW 2nd Street
Corvallis, Oregon 97330
541-754-6444
peaksportscorvallis.com

Red Point Climbers Supply
8283 11th Street
Terrebonne, Oregon 97760
800-923-6207 or 541-923-6207
redpointclimbing.com

Outdoor Organizations:

Mazamas
527 SE 43rd Avenue
Portland, Oregon 97215
503-227-2345
mazamas.org

The Mountaineers
300 3rd Avenue W

Seattle, Washington 98119
206-284-6310
mountaineers.org

American Alpine Club
710 Tenth Street, Suite 100
Golden, Colorado 80401
303-384-0110
americanalpineclub.org

Santiam Alpine Club
P. O. Box 1041
Salem, Oregon 97308
santiamalpineclub.org

Obsidians
P.O. Box 322
Eugene, Oregon 97440
obsidians.org

The Chemeketans
P.O. Box 864
Salem, Oregon 97308
chemeketans.org

Crag Rats
Hood River, Oregon
503-386-4806

ACCESS & ACTIVISM:

Access Fund
P.O. Box 17010
Boulder, CO 80308
303-545-6772
accessfund.org

CLIMBING GYMS:

The Circuit Gym
6050 SW Macadam Avenue
Portland, Oregon 97239
503-246-5111

The Circuit Gym
410 NE 17th Avenue
Portland, Oregon 97232
503-719-7041
thecircuitgym.com

Clubsport Rock Gym
18120 SW Lower Boones Ferry Rd.
Portland, Oregon 97224
503-968-4500
clubsports.com/oregon

Portland Rock Gym
21 NE 12th Avenue
Portland, Oregon 97232
Phone: 503-232-8310
portlandrockgym.com

Stoneworks Climbing Gym
6775 SW 111th Avenue
Beaverton, Oregon
503-644-3517

The Source Climbing Gym
1118 Main Street
Vancouver, WA 98660
360-694-9096
sourceclimbing.com

Crux Rock Gym
401 W 3rd Avenue
Eugene, Oregon 97401
541-484-9535
cruxrock.com

In Climb Gym
550 SW Industrial Way #39
Bend, Oregon 97702
541-388-6764
inclimb.com

Stone Gardens Gym
2839 NW Market Street
Seattle, Washington 98107
206-781-9828
stonegardens.com

Vertical World
2820 Rucker Avenue
Everett, Washington
425-258-3431
verticalworld.com

GUIDE SERVICES:

Northwest Mountain Guides
10117 SE Sunnyside Rd., Ste. F-1170
Clackamas, Oregon 97015
503-698-1118
gotrek.com

Oregon Peak Adventures
P.O. Box 25576
Portland, Oregon 97298
877-965-5100
oregonpeakadventures.com

Northwest School of Survival
2870 NE Hogan Rd., Ste. E, #461
Gresham, Oregon 97030
503-668-8264
NWSOS.com

Timberline Mountain Guides
P.O. Box 1167
Bend, Oregon
800-464-7704
timberlinemtguides.com

Chockstone Climbing Guides
1533 NW Saginaw
Bend, Oregon 97701
877-254-6211 or 541-318-7170
chockstoneclimbing.com

First Ascent Climbing Services
1136 SW Deschutes Avenue
Redmond, Oregon 97756
800-325-5462 or 541-548-5137
goclimbing.com

Rainier Mountaineering, Inc.
30027 SR 706 East
P.O. Box Q
Ashford, Washington 98304
888-892-5462
rmiguides.com

Smith Rock Climbing Guides
9297 NE Crooked River Drive
Terrebonne, Oregon 97760
541-788-6225
smithrockclimbingguides.com

EDITORIAL:

Debra Peterson, Freelance Editor
debrapeterson@gmail.com
P.O. Box 1484, Sandy, OR 97055
PDQueue Desktop Services
(503) 668-0627

Jon Bell Ink
Freelance writer
(503) 290-4282
jbell@jbellink.com

MANAGING AGENCIES:

USFS Regional Office
319 SW Pine Street
P.O. Box 3623
Portland, Oregon 97208
503-221-2877

Mt. Hood National Forest
2955 NW Division Street
Gresham, Oregon 97030
503-667-0511

Gifford Pinchot National Forest
500 West 12th Street
Vancouver, WA 98660

360-891-5000

Col. River Gorge Nat. Scenic Area
902 Wasco Street, Ste. 200
Hood River, Oregon 97301
541-386-2333

Oregon & Washington State Parks
800-233-0321

Beacon Rock State Park
34841 State Route 14
Skamania, WA 98648
360-427-8265

Willamette National Forest
P.O. Box 10607
Eugene, Oregon 97440
503-687-6522

Bureau Of Land Management
Oregon State Office
825 NE Multnomah
Portland, Oregon 97208
503-231-6274

Washington State D.N.R.
SW Region
601 Bond Road
Castle Rock, Washington 98611
360-577-2025

RESCUE ORGANIZATIONS:

Portland Mountain Rescue
P.O. Box 5391
Portland, Oregon 97228-5391
503-222-7678
info@pmru.org

Silver Star Search & Rescue
1220 "A" Street
Washougal, Oregon 98671
360-835-3131
silverstarsar.org

WEATHER & CLIMATE CONDITIONS:

noaa.gov
weather.gov

APPENDIX C

The 'Routes By Rating' list provides a detailed analysis of climbing routes by technical difficulty rating which is subdivided again by the crag. A plus symbol [+] after the route name indicates that the climb may be harder. Many routes have additional risk factors such as PG, R or X, so read the full route beta in each chapter before launching onto a particular route of choice. A few climbs (like Hanging Gardens route) are listed twice; once under the 5.6 A0 rating and again under the 5.10a free rating.

5.4

Rocky Butte:
E-Z Corner
Carver:
Smooth Operator
Spear Fishing in Bermuda
Madrone:
Mountaineer's Route
Far Side:
Northern Passage Upper [+]

5.5

Carver:
Talent Show
Madrone:
Beginner's Luck
Far Side:
Dulcinea
Salmon Slab:
Salmon

5.6

Broughton:
Giant's Staircase
Hanging Gardens (A0)
Lickity Split
Pony Express
Rocky Butte:
Quarry Cracker
Passing Lane
Joe's Garden
Madrone:
Double Dutch Right
Screensaver

Sisters of Mercury
Ozone:
Bearded Lady
Night Owl
Stairway to Heaven
Love Supreme (P1)
Mountaineer's Route
Far Side:
MJ08
Birthday Surprise
Wounded Knee
Well Hung
31 Feet of Pleasure
41 Feet of Pain
Beacon:
Boardwalk
French's:
Giant's Staircase
Salmon Slab:
Climbing Theme

5.7

Broughton:
Prometheus Slab
Milestone
Arch de Triumph
Rocky Butte:
Miss Kitty
Flakey Old Man
Carver:
Sanity Assassin
Leaning Uncertainty
Great Barrier Reef
Madrone:

Double Dutch Left
Chicken
Electric Everything
Stamina
Ozone:
Old Toby
Bag Ends
Afternoon Delight [+]
Flayel Bop
Meth Rage
Far Side:
Silverdyke
Scary As...
Sweet Surprise
Left Cheek
Bill's Thrill
Northern Passage Lower
Wet and Dirty
Beacon:
Rhythm Method
Cruisin'

Southeast Face
Right Gull (A0)
Tombstone Territory
French's:
Straw Man
Giant's Direct
Salmon Slab:
Cave Man

5.8

Broughton:
American Graffiti[+]
Edges and Ledges
The Sickle
That's the Way
Toe Cleavage [+]
Split Decision
Tin Star
Rocky Butte:
The Joker
Captain She's Breaking Up
Urban Cowboy
Midnight Warrior
Superman
Ace
Eve of Destruction
Robotics
Orient Express
Speeding Down South
Carver:
New Generation

Shadow Fox
Passport to Insanity
Madrone:
Route Crafters
Chop the Monkey [+]
Slippery Sage
Life As We Know It
Exodus
Ozone:
Rude Boy
Eight is Enough
Chaos
Siddartha
Hang Up Your Hang Ups
Ivans Arête
Stigmata
Little Dipper
Numb Nuts
Far Side:
Introductory Offer [+]
Right Cheek
Adams Crack
White Lightning
Snake
Snake Buttress [+]
Happy Crack
The Martyr
Kinetic Flow
Dwarf Toss
The Far Side
Child Abuse
Beacon:
Stardust
Vulcan's Variation
Lost Variation
Little Wing
Left Gull (A0)
Free for All
French's:
Oz
Alpha Centauri
Emerald City
Tin Tangle

5.9

Broughton:
Frodo's Journey [+]

Traffic Court
Pipen's Direct [+]
Gandalf's Grip [+]
Risky Business
The Hammer [+]
Spud [+]
Chockstone Chimney
Loose Block Overhang
BFD
Sesame Street
Anastasia
Classic Crack
Physical Direct
Friction
Under Your Belt [+]
Spider Monkey
Seventh Sojourn
Shandor
True Grit
Rocky Butte:
Panama Red
Gunsmoke
Jack of Heart
Silver Bullet
Invisible Man
Stained Glass
Dream Weaver
Tiger's Pause
Kleen Korner
Lord of the Jungle
Ranger Danger
Dead Man's Curve
Little Arête
Blueberry Jam
Rob's Ravine
Vertical Therapy
Stiff Fingers
Espresso
Foot Loose
Carver:
Crack in the Mirror
Neptune
Battleship Arête
Blue Monday
Crimson Tide
Rubicon
Last of the Mohicans

Madrone:
Patrick's Dihedral
Into The Black
Graduation
Cornick's Corner
Wolf of the Steppes
Catharsis (P1)
Sultans of Swing
Domino Effect
Dirty Dancing
Lord of the Rings
Plywood Jungle
Dihedral of Despair
Gym Droids
American Girl
Primordial Soup
Punters in Paradise [+]
Cast of Characters
The Arête
Stampede
Ozone:
Brandywine
Leisure Time
Redhorn Gate
Helm's Deep
Before the Storm
Snake Face
Opdyke Crack
Kung Fu
Ganesh
Dirty Jugs
Trinity Crack
Back in the Saddle
Jacob's Ladder
Tip Top
There Yare
Rasta Arete
Ripper
Standing Ovation
Dad's Nuts
No Nuts
Far Side:
Monkey Moves[+]
The Trembling
2Trad4U
Closeout
'Je' Mapel Jon Phillip

French Intern [+]
Tribal Therapy
Fool's Rush In
Mark it Eight Dude [+]
Beacon:
Young Warriors
Couch Master
Jingus Jam
Lethal Ejection
SEF Variation
Jill's Thrill
Muriel's Memoir
Cloud Nine
Reasonable Richard
Black Maria
Dod's Deviation
Dastardly Crack
Crack of Dawn
Iron Spike
French's:
Do It Again
Salmon Slab:
White Rice
Camel Back

5.10a

Broughton:
Least Resistance
Hanging Gardens
Shining Star
Sheer Stress
Sheer Energy
Mystic Void
Plan B
Pride and Joy
Zimbabwe
Happy Trails
Rocky Butte:
Sundance Kid
Last Tango
Temporary Arête
Bikini
MTV
Panes of Reality
Head Bangers Ball
Naked Savage
Mind Games

Ghost Rider
Smears for Fears
Sheer Madness
Thunder Road
Reach for the Sky
Power Surge
Carver:
Red Dihedral
Jungle Safari
Eyes of a Stranger
Rats in the Jungle
Out on a Limb
Madrone:
Jackson's Daring Deeds
Feat of Clay [+]
Tangerine Dream
Save the Whales
Hungry for Duress
Rising Desperation
Direct Finish
Lost in the Delta...
Ant Abuse
Fits and Starts
Miss Adventure
Windows of Your Mind
Reinhold's Dihedral
Girl Crazy
Logjam
What's Your Motive?
Ozone:
Why Must I Cry

Variety [+]
Snake Roof
Party at the Moon Tower
Carrots for Everyone
Kamikaze
Love Supreme (P2)
Bitches Brew
Big Dipper
Small Nuts
Stepchild
Far Side:
Ur Baby's Daddy
The Lonesome Winner [+]
Solid Gold [+]
Day of Atonement
Lion of Judah
The Darkhorse
Boo Coup [+]
The Head Wall [+]
Sweet _____
Beacon:
Return to the Sky
Tooth Faerie
Right Gull
Broken Arrow
Left Gull
Spring Fever
Sufficiently Breathless
Bluebird
Local Access Only
Rip City
Fireballs

5.10b
Broughton:

Sweet Emotion
Hang 'Em High
Fruit Bat
The Spring [+]
Short Circuit
Dyno-mite
Well Hung
Rocky Butte:
Harlequin
Trivial Pursuit
Zeeva
Stranger Than Friction
Slavemaker
Tigers Eye
Emotional Rescue
"D" and Rising
Blackberry Jam
Lemon Twist
White Rabbit
Swiss Miss
Shadows in Space
Carver:
Shady Personality
Edge of the Reef
Riders of the Purple Sage
Madrone:
Identity Crisis
Back in 'Nam
Spectrum
Mixing It Up
Whatever Blows Your Skirt Up
Pillow Talk
Paleontologist
Red Sun Rising
Crystal Hunters
Chromesister
Dangerous Breed
Ozone:
Sweeping Beauty
May Day
Heaven's Sake [+]
Burrito Killa
Far Side:
The Pin [+]
Lizard Locks
Sheep Skinners Delight [+]
Freak Freely [+]

Center Squeeze [+]
Good vibrations [+]
Fall From Grace
Happy Ending [+]
Beacon:
Cosmic Dust
Fear of Flying
Riverside
Winter Delight
Blownout Direct
Blownout
Psychic Wound
Flying Dutchman (P1)
Squeeze Box
Windsurfer
Boys of Summer
Fingers of a Fisherman
Mostly Air
Lay Lady Lay
French's:
Static Cling
Yellow Brick Road

5.10c
Broughton:
Reckless Driver
Tip City
Lean Years
Sandy's Direct
Fun in the Mud
Circus Act
Peer Pressure
Dry Bones [+]
Red Eye
Shoot from the Hip
Walk on the Wild Side [+]
Short Fuse
Crime Wave
Touch and Go
Wild Wild West
Rocky Butte:
Fandango
Body Language
Lever or Leaver
Stranger than Friction [+]
Eye in the Sky
Boy Sage [+]

Highway Star
Claymation
Hot Tang
  Carver:
Tequila Sunrise
Hinge of Fate
Call to Greatness
King Rat
  Madrone:
Sheesh
Wild Blue Yonder
Cut and Dried
Superstrings
Scotty Hits the Warp Drive
Primary Gobbler
Cold Hand of Technology
Red Scare
Banana Belt
Gym Rats From Hell
Shattered Dreams
Sacrifice
Nouveau Riche
Eye of the Tiger
  Ozone:
Screaming For Change
Rauch Factor
There and Back Again
Meat Grinder
High Plains Drifter
Orion
Piton Variation
  Far Side:
Oracle
Squeeze Play
Sharpen your Teeth [+]
Exchange Student
  Beacon:
Pacific Rim
Rock Police
Rookie Nookie
Bladerunner
Repo Man
Desdichado
Synapse
Wrong Gull
Sorcerer's Apprentice
Seagull

Ten-A-Cee Stemming
Nuke-U-Later
Flying Circus
Blood, Sweat, and Smears
Dod' Jam
Rise Up
Doubting Thomas
Hard Times
Rag Time
Dorian's Dilemma (P1)
  French's:
Dirty Deeds (Silver Streak)

5.10d

Broughton:
Dynamic Resistance
Something
Hung Jury
Demian
Arcturas
Thai Stick
Physical Graffiti
Velcro Fly
Lost Boys
Mystic Pizza
Dark Shadows
Under the Yum Yum Tree
Gorilla Love Affair
Amazon Woman
Alma Mater
  Rocky Butte:
Centurion
Live Wire
The Wanderer
Great Wall of China
Chinese Finger Torture
Lethal Ethics
Spiritual Journey
Leading Edge
Bird of Paradise
Skywalker
  Carver:
Marqueritaville
Scotch and Soda
Sweat and the Flies
  Madrone:
Tangerine Direct

Midget Madness
Surfing with the Alien
Short but Sweet
Cult of Personality
Sisters of the Road
Extinction
It Takes a Thief
Winds of War
  Ozone:
Whine and Cheese
Rolling Thunder
  Far Side:
Wushu Roof [+]
Hollow Victories [+]
Naughty and Nice
Stewart's Ladder
  Beacon:
Icy Treats (aka Frozen Treats)
Levitation Blues
Desperado
Elusive Element
Sacrilege
Av's Route
Bluebird Direct
Fall Guy
Aging Fags
Take Fist
Flying Swallow
Steppenwolf (P1)
Red Ice
Boulder Problem in the Sky

5.11a

Broughton:
Hangover

Mr. Potato
Endless Sleep
On the Loose
Habitual Ritual
Hit the Highway
Free Bird
Hanging Tree
Superstition
Gold Arch
Static Cling
Father
Luck of the Draw
  Rocky Butte:
Poodle with a Mohawk
Bite the Bullet
Damaged Circuit
Wizard
Flight of the Seventh Moon
Lathe of heaven
Arch Nemesis
Simple Twist [+]
Hyper Twist [+]
Telegraph Road
Joy Ride
Competitive Edge
Time of Your Life
Mystic Traveler [+]
  Carver:
Smerk
  Madrone:

Verbal
Inner Vision
Red Fox
  Ozone:
House of Pain
Vicious
Short Straw
Getting Your Kicks
  Beacon:
Sky Pilot
Switchblade
No Balls No Falls
Crankenstein
Direct to Flying Swallow
True Grunt
Free for Some
Jensen's Ridge
  French's:
Low Voltage

5.11b
  Broughton:
Peach Cling
Grace and Danger
Main Vein
Hard Body [+]
Bust A' Move
Mowgli's Revenge
Pioneer Spirit
  Rocky Butte:
Body Bionics
Edge of Might
Phylynx
High Road to China
Secret Maze
Crack Warrior
Seamingly Endless
Holy Bubbles
Orange Spice
Lunge and Plunge [+]
Wisdom Tooth
  Carver:
Night Vision
Dreamscape
Challenger [+]
  Madrone:
Aerial Display

Trauma Center
Mr. Noodle Arm
Arm Forces
The Gift of Time
Rainman
Playing with Fire
Mind Games
PC
  Ozone:
Chain Mail
Gophers Gone Wild
  Far Side:
The Arête [+]
Tunnel Vision
The Warm Up [+]
  Beacon:
Fire and Ice
More Balls Than Nuts
Dynaflux
To the Edge and Beyond
High and Mighty
Borderline
Flying Dutchman (P2) [+]
Bears in Heat
Pipeline
Pipeline Headwall
Iron Cross (aka On the Move)
Head Case
Spiny Fish
  French's:
China Man

5.11c
  Broughton:
New Wave
Critical Mass
Mr. Bentley [+]
The Conspiracy [+]
Opus [+]
Edge of Eternity
Vampyr [+]
Promised Land
  Rocky Butte:
Persistence of Time
You'll Dance to Anything
Jealous Rage
Stump the Jock [+]

Drew leading the 1ˢᵗ pitch of
Superstition 5.10c

No Leverage
Be Bold or Not To Be
Close to the Edge [+]
Toothpick
Far from the Edge [+]
Red Zinger
White Rabbit Buttress [+]
Trix are for Kids [+]
Face Disgrace [+]
Spider Line [+]
Hang Loose [+]
   Carver:
Notorious [+]
Uncola
Rites of Passage
Chariots of Fire
   Madrone:
Beam me up Mr. Scott
Dr. Opus Goes Power Lunging
True Catharsis
Firing Line
Dancing in the Lion's Jaw
Cloudwalker
Fisticuffs
Divine Wind
Divine Direct
   Ozone:
Masterpiece Theater
SOS [+]
MD Route [+]
Route 66
Mrs. Norris
   Beacon:
Cruisin' Direct Finish
Rock Master
Diagonal Desperation
Summer Daze
Flight Time
Steppenwolf (P2) [+]
Fresh Squeeze (aka Squeeze
Box Direct) [+]
   French's:
Crankenstein

5.11d
   Broughton:
Face Not Friction

Pinhead
Jumping Jack Thrash
Bloodsucker
The Hunger
Twist and Crawl
Amazon Man
   Rocky Butte:
Toxic Waltz
Walk on Water
Harder Than Life
   Carver:
Cherry Cola
Burning From the Inside
   Madrone:
Mental Crisis
Talk Talk Talk [+]
Where the Wild Things Roam
Agent Orange
Catharsis (P2)
Full Spank Mode
Shining Wall
   Ozone:
Beyond the Glory
   Beacon:
Second Wind
Ground Zero
Windwalker

5.12a
   Broughton:
Cinderella
Black Prow
Kashmir
Eagle's Wing
Ground Effects [+]
Dracula
Danse Macabre
Closet Nazi
Slash and Burn
Rocky Butte:
Hard Contact [+]
Zenith
The Arête
Seventh Wave
   Carver:
Free Ride
Sea of Holes

Wally Street
Angular Motion
Penguins in Heat
   Madrone:
O.J.
Comfortizer
Scott Free [+]
Subway to Venus
Never Mind
Time To Kill
   Ozone:
The Crumbling
The Humbling
Hell Boy
   Beacon:
Stone Rodeo
Too Close for Comfort
Pirates (aka Rock Pirates)
Wishbone [+]
Devil's Backbone
Pipe Dream
Siege Tactics
Dorian's Dilemma (P2)
Gitmo
   French's:
Road Face
Road Rage
Road Kill [+]
The Dark Side (aka The
Seige) [+]

Pumporama [+]

5.12b
Broughton:
Skullduggery
Slapfest
The Haunting
Bad Omen
Bloodline
Remain in Light
Heart of Darkness
Mowgli Direct
Rocky Butte:
Pluto
Carver:
Wally Wedding
Madrone:
Severed Heads
Ozone:
Grace
Beacon:
Old Warriors Never Die
Bridge of the Gods
Excalibur
The Norseman
French's:
High Voltage
BSD
Jackie Chan

5.12c
Broughton:
Scorpion Seams
Bela Lugosi
Predator
Carver:
Sport Court
Ozone:
Dark Lord
Angle of the Dangle
Beacon:
Death and Taxes
Magic Fingers

5.12d
Broughton:
MF Reunion
Genocide [+]

Tarzan
Carver:
Smooth Torquer
Digital
French's:
Psoriasis

5.13a
Broughton:
Dark Tower
Rocky Butte:
Packin' Heat
Carver:
Plastic Monkey
Rip Grip

5.13b

5.13c
Broughton:
Fright Night

Nailing routes:
Broughton:
Go Back to the Gym
Recipe for Airtime
Out of Africa
Killer Pygmy
Beacon:
Grunge Book
Wild Turkeys
Dirty Double Overhang
Smooth Dancer
Iron Maiden
Silver Crow
Axe of Karma
Updraft to Heaven
Synchronicity

APPENDIX D

The following is a list of first ascent data for most of the climbs in this book. A special thanks to all of you who freely shared your part of this analogy. This database has been gathered from well over a dozen climbers and all of those individuals are a valuable part in this compilation. Certain portions of first ascent route data could not be attained by the time this edition went to print.

This information base in no way represent a perfectly accurate list. For example, a person who cleans and fixes pitons or bolts on the new climbing route may or may not be the same person who attains the first ascent. Given the considerable time and effort that goes into the development phase of climbing routes your level of commitment is greatly appreciated by all of us.

A partial list of persons who provided pertinent data for this section are: Jeff Thomas, Wayne Wallace, Robert McGown, Chuck Buzzard, Jim Opdycke, Bill Coe, Jon Stewart, Kevin Evansen, Tymun Abbott, Shane Polizzano, Dave Sowerby, Gary Rall, Greg Lyon, Mike Pajunas, Mark Cartier, Nathan Charlton, Steve Mrazek, Eric Linthwaite, Greg Murray and many others.

The following brief definitions will help readers to interpret the first ascent data:

FA (First Ascent): Aid ascent, attempted free ascent with tension, or an ascent.

FFA (First Free Ascent): Free ascent with NO tension, weighting of pro or falls.

FRA (First Recorded Ascent): It is likely that the climb was done previously, but no record exists as to who did it.

TR (Top-rope): Climbing a route with a rope that is anchored from above. The route may have been free climbed or aid climbed already, but is usually tope-roped.

GFA (Ground-up First Ascent): Without pre-inspection.

PPP (Pre-placed protection): Gear placed on rappel (some or all), then the climb was sent.

BROUGHTON BLUFF

North Face
1. Frodo's Journey: FFA 9-17-2006 Philip Scoles
2. Traffic Court: FFA (before) 8-87 Wayne Wallace, Robert McGown
     (Ascent after section of North Face collapsed) 8-22-92 Tim Olson
3. Pipen's Direct: (FFA after the cliff section collapsed) 8-22-92 Tim Olson
4. Gandalf's Grip: GFA (regular route) 1968 Steve Strauch, Jim O'Connell
     FFA (by variation) 9-28-69 Steve Strauch, John Hack
5. New Wave: FFA 1st pitch 7-87 R. McGown, W. Wallace
6. Peach Cling: GFA 1972 Jim Mayers, Gail Van Hoorn
     FFA summer 1978 Doug Bower and partner
7. Cinderella: FFA 7-24-93 Steve Elder
8. Risky Business: FA 7-87 Wayne Wallace, Robert McGown
9. Dark Tower: FA Philip Scoles, FFA 9-8-11 Matt Spohn
10. Reckless Driver: FFA 1st and 2nd pitch 2-7-87 Tim Olson
     FFA Complete (1,2,3) 7-15-87 Wayne Wallace, Robert McGown
11. Skullduggery: FFA early 2012 Phil Hranicka
12. Sweet Emotion: FA 8-87 Wayne Wallace, Robert McGown

13. American Graffiti: FA 10-87 Wayne Wallace

Hanging Gardens Wall - Left Half
14. Giants Staircase: FA Unknown
15. Edges and Ledges: FFA 8-92 Greg Murray
16. The Sickle: FRA 1972 Ancil Nance
17. The Hammer: FA Unknown
18. Prometheus Slab: FA 1965 Bob Waring, John Wells, Bruce Holcomb
19. Spud: FA Unknown
20. Tip City: FA 1979 Jim Olson, Jay Kerr
21. Lean Years: FA Unknown
22. Hangover: (TR) 1979 Jay Kerr, Jim Olson
23. Chockstone Chimney: GFA 1965 Bob Waring, John Wells, Bruce Holcomb
24. Milestone: FA Unknown

Hanging Gardens Wall - Right Half
25. Loose Block Overhang: FRA & probable FFA 1975 Monty Mayko, Jim Garrett
26. Grace and Danger: FFA 6-30-91 Dave Sowerby
27. Slapfest: FFA 1-12-92 Tim Olson, Cindy Long
28. Least Resistance: FRA 1971 Talbot Bielefeldt, Tim Carpenter, Bruce Weideman
    FFA Fall 1975 Roger Baker
29. Dynamic Resistance: FFA 7-9-88 Wayne Wallace, Robert McGown
30. Sandy's Direct: FA PPP 1977 Robert McGown, Mike Smelsar, Sandy Regan
31. Face Not Friction: FA 1975 Alan Campbell and partner
    FFA PPP 5-30-81 Mark Cartier
32. Hanging Gardens: FA 1965 Bob Waring, John Wells, Bruce Holcomb
    FRFA 1974 Rich Borich
33. BFD: FA 1975 Bruce Casey, Monty Mayko
34. Mr. Potato: FA 1972 or 1973 Alan Campbell and partner
    FFA 7-18-81 Bruce Casey, Jeff Thomas
35. From Something to Nothing: FFA 10-11-87 Wayne Wallace, Tim Olson
36. Fun in the Mud: FA 1977 Robert McGown, Terry Yates
37. Circus Act: FFA 9-19-87 Wayne Wallace, Tim Olson
38. Shining Star: FA 1977 Mike Smelsar, Robert McGown
    FFA complete 3-16-87 Robert McGown, Wayne Wallace
39. Hung Jury: FFA 5-87 Robert McGown, Wayne Wallace
40. Hang 'Em High: FFA 9-7-87 Robert McGown, Wayne Wallace
41. Main Vein: FFA 8-91 Chuck Buzzard, Steve Mrazek
42. Sesame Street: FA 1972 Alan Campbell, Gail Van Hoorn
    FFA 7-8-73 Dean Fry and partner
43. Demian: FA Fall 1976 Robert McGown, Mike Smelsar
    FFA Unknown
44. Endless Sleep: FA Spring 1977 Robert McGown, Mike Smelsar
45. Peer Pressure: FA 1972 or 73 Jim Mayers, Alan Campbell
    FFA PPP Spring 1977 Mike Smelsar, Robert McGown
46. Scorpion Seams: FA 1980 Robert McGown, Steve Hillanger, Mike Corning
    FFA on 8-7-96 Alex Russell
    Resurrection: FFA 7-11-93 Gary Rall

47. Black Prow: FA 1979 Robert McGown, Mike Simpson
    FFA 6-18-94 Dave Sowerby

Red Wall
48. Arch De Triumph: FA 1987 Wayne Wallace
49. Arcturas: FFA Tim Olson
50. Anastasia: FFA Tim Olson
51. Dry Bones: FFA Tim Olson
52. On The Loose: FFA 1978 Robert McGown
53. _____
54. Classic Crack: FA and FFA Unknown
    TR free in 1972 by Jim Mayers. Led free in 1975 by Doug Bower
55. Thai Stick: FA 1979 Robert McGown
56. Mr. Bentley: TR 1981 Ed Welter, Jack Goble
57. Sheer Stress: FA 1976 Bruce Casey, Monty Mayko
    FFA first 30' 1976 Ken Currens, Paul Landrum, Steve Strauch, Dan Foote
    FFA of complete climb Monty Mayko
58. Physical Graffiti: FA Summer 1977 Robert McGown, Mike Smelsar
    FFA Summer 1977 Doug Bower and partner
59. Habitual Ritual: FFA 2-5-92 Gary Rall
60. Physical Direct: FFA 11-18-90 Tim Olson, Cecil Colley
61. Hit the Highway: FA 1977 Bruce Casey, Monty Mayko
62. Kashmir: FFA (via Classic Crack) 11-18-90 Gary Rall
63. Red Eye: FA 1st pitch 1976 Monty Mayko, Bruce Casey
    FA complete 1978 Mark Cartier and partner
    FFA 10-3-78 Jeff Thomas, Paul Gleeson
64. Critical Mass: FA Summer 1981 Robert McGown, Scott Woolums
    Redirected via bolts; FFA on 9-5-90 by Gary Rall
    The Conspiracy: FFA 2-6-93 Gary Rall (2-bolt variation on left)
65. E. Pluribus Pinhead: FFA 8-91 Steve Mrazek, Chuck Buzzard
    FA variation (*see Oregon Rock*) that merges with Red Eye 1981 Jay Kerr, David Howe
66. Opus: FFA 2-5-92 Dave Sowerby
67. Sheer Energy: FA Fall 1979 Jim Olson or Alan Kearney
68. Hard Body: FFA 5-5-91 Tim Olson, Wayne Wallace
69. Shoot from the Hip: FFA 4-7-91 Tim Olson
70. No Friction: FA 7-88 Wayne Wallace
71. That's the Way: FA 7-88 Wayne Wallace

Bridge Cliff
72. Under Your Belt: FA 4-24-87 Wayne Wallace, Scott Tracy
73. Walk on the Wild Side: FA 1977 Jay Kerr, David Howe
74. Edge of Eternity: FFA 2-25-88 Wayne Wallace, Robert McGown, Tim Olson
75. Spidermonkey: FA 1977 Robert McGown, Mike Simpson
76. Fruit Bat: FA 1977 Robert McGown, Doug Bower
77. Seventh Sojourn: FA 1977 Robert McGown, Mike Simpson, Roger Baker
78. Shandor: FA 1-8-88 Wayne Wallace
79. Eagle's Wing: FFA 3-6-93 Dave Sowerby

Spring Rock

80. Toe Cleavage: FFA 11-6-87 Wayne Wallace
81. Velcro Fly: FFA 4-9-89 Tim Olson, Wayne Wallace
82. Free Bird: FFA 11-8-87 Wayne Wallace
83. Ground Effects: FFA Summer 1989 Greg Lyon
84. Jumping Jack Thrash: Top-rope 10-86 Jack Goble, Ed Welter, Mark Cartier
    FFA 9-5-90 Gary Rall
85. The Spring: FA 1977 Robert McGown, Bruce Casey
86. Short Fuse: FFA 6-28-92 Tim Olson, Cindy Olson
87. Dyno-Mite: FFA 11-27-87 Wayne Wallace
88. Short Circuit: FFA 3-28-93 Andrew Glasfeld

Bat Wall
89. Hanging Tree: FA PPP 6-2-77 Robert McGown, Jeff Thomas
90. Go Back to the Gym: GFA 10-28-90 Wayne Wallace, Tim Olson
91. Dracula: FA Unknown, FFA 5-20-90 Gary Rall
92. Bela Lugosi: FFA 9-16-90 Gary Rall
93. Fright Night: FA [free?] 7-12-91 Matthias Pausch
    FN Left Variation to the Pod: FFA 2010 Matt Spohn
94. The Haunting (old Snap-Crackle-Pop): GFA 1977 Bruce Casey, Monty Mayko
    FFA 1-2-92 Gary Rall
95. Bad Omen: FFA 12-16-90 Tim Olson
96. Danse Macabre: FFA 8-19-92 Dave Sowerby
97. Bloodsucker: GFA Summer 1977 Robert McGown, Mike Smelsar
    FFA 1-20-92 Jay Green
98. Bloodline: GFA 2-91 Wayne Wallace, Robert McGown
    FFA 1-19-92 Dave Sowerby
99. Predator: FFA 10-16-93 Dave Sowerby
100. Superstition: GFA 1977 Robert McGown, Scott Woolums, Jim Olson
    FFA 7-11-81 Jeff Thomas, Mark Cartier
101. Lost Boys: FA Unknown
    FFA complete 12-2-90 Wayne Wallace, Tim Olson, Jay Green, Mike Carter
102. Mystic Pizza: FFA 12-9-90 Wayne Wallace, Tim Olson
103. Mystic Void: FA 1977 Robert McGown, Scott Woolums
104. Well Hung: GFA 1977 Robert McGown, Mike Simpson
    FFA Unknown (4-1977 Dan Foote & Bruce Casey yo-yoed the route
105. Gold Arch: GFA 1978 Robert McGown, Doug Bower, Terry Yates
106. The Hunger: FFA 8-29-92 Dave Sowerby
107. Dark Shadows (Shadow Dancing): GFA 1979 Robert McGown, Jim Olson, Mike Simpson
    FFA 11-2-90 Dave Sowerby, Mike Sessions
108. _____
109. Manson Family Reunion: FA Unknown
    FFA 9-7-92 Steve Mrazek
110. Vampyr: FFA 9-26-94 Dave Sowerby
111. Remain in Light: FFA Dave Sowerby 11-22-93

Broken Rock
112. Static Cling: FFA Greg Murray and partner
113. Plan B: FFA Greg Murray and partner

114. Lickity Split: FFA Greg Murray and partner

Trinity Wall
115. Bust A Move: FFA 6-2-91 Wayne Wallace, Tim Olson
116. Father: FA 3-6-88 Wayne Wallace
      FFA 11-11-90 Wayne Wallace, Tim Olson
117. _____
118. _____

Berlin Wall
119. Closet Nazi: FFA 9-90 Jay Green
120. Recipe for Airtime: FA 1-29-95 Tim Olson, Harry King
121. Twist and Crawl: FA Spring 1991 Wayne Wallace, Tim Olson
      FFA 7-91 Mike Carter
122. Genocide: FA 1-7-95 Dave Sowerby
123. Pride and Joy: FFA 11-11-90 Tim Olson, Wayne Wallace
124. _____

Jungle Cliff
125. Zimbabwe: GFA 9-29-91 Dave Sowerby, Greg Carmichael
126. Slash and Burn: GFA 3-23-91 Wayne Wallace, Tim Olson
      FFA 11-7-92 Dave Sowerby
127. Under the Yum-Yum Tree: GFA 2-7-88 Wayne Wallace, Greg Lyon
128. Tarzan: FFA 3-13-92 Dave Sowerby
129. Crime Wave: FFA 6-13-92 Tim Olson, Cindy Olson
130. Gorilla Love Affair: FFA 2-9-92 Cindy Long and Tim Olson
131. Out of Africa: GFA 7-79 Scott Woolums, Robert McGown
132. Heart of Darkness: FFA 4-27-91 Dave Sowerby
133. Mowgli Direct: FFA 1-17-96 Dave Sowerby
134. Mowgli's Revenge: FFA 2-2-92 Dave Sowerby
135. Amazon Woman: GFA Fall 1991 Wayne Wallace, Tim Olson
      FFA 1-17-92 Heather Macdonald, Cindy Long
136. Amazon Man: GFA 7-79 Robert McGown, Levi Grey, Mike Simpson
137. Killer Pygmy: GFA (to Skull Ledge) 11-30-91 Wayne Wallace, Tim Olson
      GFA 2nd pitch 12-10-91 Wayne Wallace, Robert McGown
138. Mujahideen: GFA 11-27-87 Wayne Wallace

New Frontier Wall
139. Luck of the Draw: FFA 10-9-93 Greg Murray
140. Touch and Go: FFA 8-8-93 Greg Murray
141. Alma Mater: FFA 6-2-91 Wayne Wallace, Tim Olson
142. Split Decision: FFA 8-27-93 Greg Murray
143. Tin Star: FFA 9-6-93 Greg Murray
144. True Grit: FFA 8-27-93 Greg Murray
145. Pony Express: FFA 9-93 Greg Murray
146. Happy Trails: FFA 1-2-91 Dave Sowerby, Mike Smith
147. Wild Wild West: GFFA 2-23-91 Dave Sowerby, Ric Weaver, Tim Olson
148. Pioneer Spirit: FFA 8-18-91 Dave Sowerby
149. Promised Land: FFA 9-7-91 Dave Sowerby

ROCKY BUTTE

Poodle Pinnacle
  Poodle with a Mohawk: FFA 6-87 Gary Rall
Trivial Pinnacle
1. Harlequin: FFA 8-9-87 Tim Olson, Robert McGown
2. Trivial Pursuit: FA 8-9-87 Robert McGown, Tim Olson
3. The Joker: FA Unknown

Silver Bullet Bluff
4. Captain She's Breaking: Up FA 8-87 Robert McGown, Jim Mohel, Tim Olson
5. Unknown:
6. Sundance: Kid FA Unknown
     FRFA 7-87 Greg Lyon, Robert McGown, Chris McMullin
7. Panama Red: FFA 7-87 Greg Lyon, Chris McMullin, Robert McGown
8. Miss Kitty: FA 7-87 Robert McGown, Eric Simmons
9. Gunsmoke: FFA 7-20-87 Robert McGown, Tim Olson
10. Bite the Bullet: FFA 7-20-87 Robert McGown, Wayne Wallace, Tim Olson
11. Jack of Hearts: FFA 7-15-87 Wayne Wallace, Robert McGown, Tim Olson
12. Silver Bullet: FFA 7-20-87 Robert McGown, Tim Olson, Steve Wong
13. Urban Cowboy: FFA 7-20-87 Robert McGown, Tim Olson, Steve Wong
14. Last Tango: FFA 7-87 Robert McGown, Tim Olson
15. Fandango: FFA 7-13-87 Robert McGown, Tim Olson
16. Midnight Warrior: FFA 7-13-87 Robert McGown, Tim Olson
17. Superman Crack: FFA 7-25-87 Robert McGown, Tim Olson
18. Glenn's Route: FFA Glenn Collier, Bill Coe, John Frieh
19. Centurion: FA 7-15-87 Robert McGown, Tim Olson
     FFA 7-87 Wayne Wallace, Robert McGown
20. Invisible Man: GFA 7-87 Robert McGown, Jim Mohel
21. Temporary Arête: FFA 9-88 Ed and Vern Welter

Video Bluff
22. Body Language: FFA 6-11-87 Robert McGown, Tim Olson
23. Body Bionics: FFA 6-11-87 Robert McGown, Tim Olson
24. Ace: FFA 6-6-87 Dan Wright, Tim Olson
25. Eve of Destruction: FFA 6-5-87 Robert McGown, Tim Olson, Jim Wright, Eve McDermitt
26. Live Wire: FFA 6-5-87 Robert McGown, Tim Olson
27. Damaged Circuit: FFA 6-5-87 Robert McGown, Tim Olson
28. Robotics: FFA 6-6-87 Tim Olson, Dan Wright
29. Edge of Might: FFA 8-87 Mike Pajunas, Gary Rall
30. Hard Contact: FFA 6-88 Greg Lyon
31. Lever or Leaver: FFA 8-87 Mike Pajunas, Gary Rall, John Sprecher
32. Persistence of Time: FA Summer 1991 Chad Franklin
33. Zeeva: FFA 8-20-82 Tim Olson, Dan Wright
34. Bikini: FFA [?]
35. Flakey Old Man: FFA 5-29-87 Tim Olson, Robert McGown
36. MTV: FA McGown
37. Stranger Than Friction: FFA 5-29-87 Tim Olson, Robert McGown
38. Panes of Reality: FFA 5-29-87 Robert McGown, Tim Olson

39. Stained Glass: FFA 5-29-87 Tim Olson, Robert McGown
40. Toxic Waltz: FA 11-91 Chad Franklin
41. E-Z Corner: FA Unknown

Dream Weaver Wall

42. Dream Weaver: FFA 4-86 Mike Pajunas, R. Moody
43. Head Bangers Ball: FFA 10-9-88 Wayne Wallace
44. Tiger Pause: FFA 10-85 Mike Pajunas, Joe Parsley
45. Kleen Korner:

Wizard Wall

46. Naked Savage: FFA 6-4-87 Robert McGown, Tim Olson
47. Lord of the Jungle: FFA 6-2-87 Robert McGown, Tim Olson
48. Slavemaker: FFA 6-4-87 Robert McGown, Tim Olson
49. Grub: FFA 5-24-87 Robert McGown, Tim Olson
50. Eye in the Sky: FFA 6-2-87 Robert McGown, Tim Olson
51. Phylynx: TR 1987 Mike Craig, FFA 5-87 Robert McGown, Larry Jennings
52. Walk on Water: FA 6-87 Robert McGown, Wayne Wallace
53. Mind Games: FFA 5-26-87 Robert McGown, Tim Olson
54. Wizard FA: 5-26-87 Robert McGown, Tim Olson, Dan Wright

Far East Wall

55. Great Wall of China: GFA 4-87 Robert McGown and partner
56. High Road to China: FFA 4-87 Robert McGown, Wayne Wallace
57. Chinese Finger Torture: GFA 4-87 Robert McGown, Terry Simms
58. The Wanderer: FFA 9-87 Dan Wright
59. Ghost Rider: FFA 6-87 R. McGown, Tim Olson, Dan Wright
60. Flight of the Seventh Moon: FFA 5-87 Mike Pajunas
61. Orient Express: FFA 5-87 Mike Pajunas, Rita Hansen, Charlie Martin, Gary Rall
62. Secret Maze: FFA 6-87 Mike Pajunas, Robert McGown, Dan Wright
63. Tigers Eye: FFA 4-9-88 Tim Olson, Greg Lyon, Matt Papolski, Mike Larsen

Warrior Wall

64. Smears For Fears: FFA 8-85 Mike Pajunas, Jim Parsley
65.
66. Crack Warrior: FFA 8-85 Mike Pajunas, Jim Parsley
67. You'll Dance to Anything: (TR) 7-88 Greg Lyon
68. Shear Madness: FFA 7-87 Mike Pajunas, J. McCracken
69. Quarry Cracker: FA 1986 Mike Pajunas
70. Lathe of Heaven: FA 1989 Robert McGown and partner
71. Arch Nemesis: FFA 8-85 Robert McGown, Daryl Nakahira
72. Boy Sage: FA 5-87 Robert McGown, Roger Baker
73. Jealous Rage: FA 5-87 Robert McGown, Roger Baker
74. Emotional Rescue: GFFA 9-85 Mike Pajunas, Jim Parsley

Freeway Wall

75. Simple Twist: GFA 4-87 Robert McGown, Chris McMullin, J. Fredericks
76. Hyper Twist: FFA 5-87 Dan Wright
77. Passing Lane: GFA 5-87 Mike Pajunas
78. Speeding Down South: FA 5-87 Mike Pajunas

79. Ranger Danger: FFA 5-22-87 Robert McGown, Tim Olson
80. Telegraph Road: (TR) 5-87 Dan Wright
81. Highway Star: GFA 7-77 Doug Bower, Shari Kearney, Robert McGown
82. Dead Mans Curve: FFA 5-87 Robert McGown, Tim Olson

Mean Street
83. Thunder Road: GFFA 4-87 Robert McGown, Jim Opdycke
84. Lethal Ethics: FFA 6-87 Wayne Wallace, Dave Bloom
85. Spiritual Journey: FFA 4-87 Wayne Wallace, Robert McGown
86. Little Arête: FFA 6-87 Robert McGown, Wayne Wallace
87. Seamingly Endless: FFA 4-87 Robert McGown, Wayne Wallace
88. Holy Bubbles: GFA 1983 Gary Rall
    FFA
89. Pluto FA Summer: 1990 Chad Franklin
90. Stump the Jock: FA
91. Packin' Heat: FA 8-28-93 Dave Sowerby
92. No Leverage: FA 4-87 Mark Kerns
93. Be Bold Or Not To Be:
94. Claymation: FFA 4-87 Robert McGown, Wayne Wallace

Toothpick Wall
95. Reach For The Sky: GFA 4-87 Mike Pajunas, Gary Rall
96. Zenith: (TR) 7-88 Greg Lyon, Matt Pixler
97. Blueberry Jam: FA 1977 Robert McGown, Mike Smelsar
98. Joy Ride: FFA 4-24-94 Mike Boehlke, Josh Dearing
99. Leading Edge: FA 4-87 Robert McGown, Wayne Wallace
100. Close To The Edge: FA (FFA?) 7-77 Robert McGown, Doug Bower
101. Toothpick: FA 1978 Robert McGown, Jon Sprecher
102. Far From The Edge: (TR)
103. Rob's Ravine: FA 1978 Bill Antel, Robert McGown
104. Competitive Edge: GFA 4-87 R. McGown, W. Wallace, Darryl Nakahira, Charlie Carlson
105. Vertical Therapy: FA 1986 Joe Parsley, Dennis Hemminger
106. Power Surge: FFA 4-87 Wayne Wallace, Robert McGown
107. Stiff Fingers: FA 1986 Dennis Hemminger

Breakfast Cracks
108. "D" and Rising: FA 8-87 Robert McGown, J. Mohel
109. The Arête: FA Summer 1991 Chad Franklin
110. Blackberry Jam: FRA 1974 Jim Davis, T. Crossman
    FFA 1977 R. McGown, Mike Smelsar
111. Hot Tang: FA 1978 Ted Johnson, Robert McGown, F. Ziel
112. Expresso: FA 1977 Mark Simpson, Rich Warren, Scott Woolums
113. Red Zinger: FA 7-87 Robert McGown, Dan Wright
114. Orange Spice: FA 5-87 Robert McGown, Tim Olson, Dave Sagient
115. Lemon Twist: FFA 5-87 Robert McGown, Tim Olson, Dave Sagient
116. Lunge and Plunge: (TR) Bill Coe, Mike Kruger
117. White Rabbit: FRA 1977 Robert McGown, Mike Smelsar
118. White Rabbit Buttress: (TR) 1984 Darryl Nakahira, Bruce Casey
    FFA Unknown

119. Unknown:
120. Harder Than Life:
121. Bird of Paradise: FA 1979 Doug Bower, Robert McGown, R. Baker
122. _____
123. Wisdom Tooth: FA 1978 Robert McGown, Terry Yates, Jeff Alzner
124. _____
125. Trix are for Kids: (TR)
126. Time of Your Life: (TR)
127. Swiss Miss: FA Unknown

Wall of Shadows
128. Shadows in Space: FA 1986 Robert McGown, Mike Simpson
129. Face Disgrace: (variation) FA 1986 Robert McGown, Mike Simpson
130. Skywalker: GFA 1986 Robert McGown, Mike Simpson
131. Mystic Traveler: FA 7-85 Mike Pajunas
    FFA (?) Robert McGown, Mike Simpson
132. Spiderline: GFA 1986 Robert McGown, Mike Simpson
133. Foot Loose: FA 5-85 Mike Pajunas, Joe Parsley
134. Joe's Garden: FA 6-85 Joe Parsley, Mike Pajunas
135. Hang Loose: FFA 10-15-88 Wayne Wallace
136. Seventh Wave: FA (?) Mike Pajunas

CARVER BRIDGE CLIFF

Rockgarden Wall
1. Crack in the Mirror: FFA 9-21-87 Mike Pajunas
2. Unknown: FA Unknown
3. Notorious: FA 9-22-87 Mike Pajunas, Robert McGown, Gary Rall
    FFA 10-87 Mike Pajunas, Darryl Nakahira
4. Margueritaville: GFFA Fall 1987 Robert McGown, Darryl Nakahira
5. Cherry Cola: FFA 8-89 Gary Rall
6. Uncola: FA 9-30-87 Tim Olson, Robert McGown
    FFA Unknown
7. Neptune: FA 9-87 Tim Olson, Robert McGown
8. Smooth Torquer: FFA 5-89 Greg Lyon
9. Smerk FA: 1st pitch 9-7-87 Tim Olson, Robert McGown
    FFA complete 10-15-88 Tim Olson, Cecil Colley
10. New Generation: FFA 1st pitch 8-23-87 Chris McMullin, Tim Olson
    FFA complete 2-88 Tim Olson, Robert McGown, Greg Lyon
11. Free Ride: FFA 6-89 Greg Lyon
12. Scotch and Soda: FFA 9-7-87 Tim Olson, Robert McGown
13. Tequila Sunrise: FFA 1st pitch 9-87 Robert McGown, Tim Olson
    FFA complete 2-88 Tim Olson, Greg Lyon
14. Red Dihedral: FA Unknown
    FFA 6-11-88 Tim Olson, Matt Pixler
15. Unknown: (TR)
16. Jungle Safari: FFA (complete) 3-88 Wayne Wallace, Tim Olson
17. Night Vision: FA 11-8-87 Tim Olson, Greg Lyon
    FFA complete 2-88 Tim Olson, Wayne Wallace

18. Sanity Assassin: FFA 11-87 Greg Lyon, Tim Olson
19. Sea of Holes: FA 10-11-87 Tim Olson, Greg Lyon
    FFA complete 7-21-89 Wayne Wallace, Tim Olson
20. Sport Court: FFA Spring 1990 Greg Lyon
21. Shadow Fox: FFA 10-11-87 Tim Olson, Greg Lyon
22. Wally Street: FA 6-21-88 Bruce Casey
23. Wally Wedding: FFA 10-25-88 Darryl Nakahira
24. Sweat and the Flies: FFA 9-18-88 Tim Olson
25. Battleship Arete: FFA 8-89 Virgil Morresette, Tim Olson

Wall In Between

26. Passport to Insanity: FFA 3-88 Tim Olson, Greg Lyon, Wayne Wallace
27. Burning From The Inside: FFA 5-88 Greg Lyon
28. Hinge of Fate: FFA 3-88 Tim Olson, Greg Lyon, Robert McGown
29. Eyes of a Stranger: FFA 4-16-88 Tim Olson
30. Shady Personality: FFA 3-88 Tim Olson, Greg Lyon, Wayne Wallace
31. Rats in the Jungle: FFA 6-26-88 Tim Olson, Matt Papolski

Yellow Wall

32. Call to Greatness: GFA and FFA 2-88 Wayne Wallace, Tim Olson
33. Plastic Monkey: FFA 11-89 Gary Rall
34. Rites of Passage: FFA 1-88 Tim Olson, Robert McGown
    FFA complete Darryl Nakahira and partner
35. Digital: FFA 5-25-89 Greg Lyon
36. Angular Motion: GFA 1975 Jeff Alzner, Terry Jenkins
    FFA 4-27-88 Greg Lyon
37. Out on a Limb: FFA 12-87 Tim Olson, Robert McGown, Greg Lyon
38. Smooth Operator: FA Unknown
39. Talent Show: FA Unknown
40. Blue Monday: FA Unknown
41. Crimson Tide: FRA Summer 1976 Mark Simpson, Doug McMillan
42. Spearfishing in Bermuda: FRA Summer 1976 Mike Simpson, Doug McMillan
43. Leaning Uncertainty: FA Unknown
44. King Rat: FFA 7-7-88 Tim Olson, Mike Larson
45. Chariots of Fire: GFA 2-88 Wayne Wallace, Robert McGown
    FFA 7-6-89 Wayne Wallace or Blake Hankins
46. Dreamscape: GFFA Winter 1988 Robert McGown, Greg Lyon, Tim Olson
47. Rip Grip: FFA 6-13-88 Greg Lyon
48. Rubicon: FFA 2-88 Tim Olson, Greg Lyon
49. Edge of the Reef: FFA complete 3-14-89 Tim Olson, Greg Lyon
50. Great Barrier Reef: FA 1-88 Wayne Wallace
51. Penguins in Heat: FFA 5-2-90 Jay Green and partner
52. Challenger: FFA 4-88 Wayne Wallace, Greg Lyon
53. Last of the Mohicans: FFA 8-19-88 Tim Olson
54. Riders of the Purple Sage: FFA 1st pitch 8-21-88 Tim Olson, Cecil Colley
    FA 2nd pitch 8-88 Tim Olson, Robert McGown

MADRONE WALL

Left Corner Wall

1. Jackson's Daring Deeds: FFA 9-88 John Jackson, Patrick Jackson
2. Patrick's Dihedral: FFA 9-88 Patrcik Jackson, John Jackson
3. Sheesh: FFA 9-88 John Jackson, Patrick Jackson
4. Identity Crisis: FFA 4-15-89 Tim Olson, Cecil Colley
5. Mental Crisis: FFA 2-28-89 Greg Lyon
6. Into The Black: FFA 4-15-89 Tim Olson, Cecil Colley
7. Talk, Talk, Talk: FFA 3-90 Greg Lyon

Orange Wall

8. Verbal: FFA Spring 1995 Walter Anyan
9. Back In 'Nam: FFA 3-17-96 D. Sowerby, Mike Gilchrist, Ian Yurdin, James Hilger, Jeff Powers
10. Feat Of Clay: FFA Early 1994 Clay Nichols
11. Wild Blue Yonder: FFA 4-23-89 Wayne Wallace, Robert McGown
12. Where The Wild Things Roam: FFA 5-30-89 Wayne Wallace, Robert McGown
13. Tangerine Dream: FFA 3-13-89 Robert McGown, Keith Jackson
14. Direct Start: 7-89 Robert McGown, Keith Jackson
15. Agent Orange: FFA 3-20-89 Wayne Wallace, Robert McGown
16. O.J.: FFA 10-6-95 Dave Sowerby
17. Comfortizer: FFA 5-5-93 Dave Sowerby
18. Midget Madness: FFA 9-88 Chuck Buzzard, John Jackson, Patrick Jackson
19. Graduation: FFA 6-88 John Jackson and partner
20. Route Crafters: FFA 6-88 Chuck Buzzard, Jeff Turner
21. Chop The Monkey: FFA Spring 1989 Andy and Ellen Hatfield
22. _____ FFA Mike Pajunas [?]
23. Cornick's Corner: FFA 6-88 Curt Cornick, Chuck Buzzard
24. Surfing With The Alien: FFA 10-30-88 Wayne Wallace, Tim Olson
25. Cut And Dried: FFA GFFA 7-29-89 Wayne Wallace, Tim Olson
26. Severed Heads: FFA Spring 1991 Greg Lyon
27. Short But Sweet: FFA 9-87 Chuck Buzzard, John Long
28. Cult Of Personality: FFA 4-12-89 Wayne Wallace, Jim Wright, Eve Mcdermitt
29. Wolf Of The Steps: FFA 3-89 Robert McGown and partner
30. Slippery Sage: FFA 3-89 Robert McGown and partner

Madrone Wall - main section

31. Save The Whales: FFA 3-89 Robert McGown, Keith Jackson
32. Hungry For Duress: FFA 7-86 Scott Smith, Chuck Buzzard
33. Beam Me Up Mr. Scott: FFA 6-87 Chuck Buzzard
34. Scott Free: FFA 7-89 Darryl Nakahira, Bruce Casey
35. Rising Desperation: FFA 9-86 Chuck Buzzard, Scott Smith
36. Direct Finish: FFA 9-86 Chuck Buzzard, Scott Smith
37. Dr. Opus Goes Power Lunging: FFA 10-88 Chuck Buzzard, D. Pihlija
38. Spectrum: FFA 10-29-88 Wayne Wallace, Tim Olson
39. Aerial Display: FFA 8-88 Chuck Buzzard, John Jackson
40. Mixin It Up: FFA 8-86 Chuck Buzzard, John Jackson
41. Catharsis: FFA 8-88 Chuck Buzzard, Curt Cornick
42. True Catharsis: FFA 8-24-95 Dave Sowerby

43. Superstrings: FFA 1-10-89 Wayne Wallace, Robert McGown
44. Lost In The Delta Neighborhood: FFA 6-86 Chuck Buzzard, Jeff Frank
45. Sultans Of Swing: FFA 12-88 Robert McGown, Ricardo Suito
46. Double Dutch Left: FFA Unknown
     FRA 6-86 Chuck Buzzard, J. Turney
47. Scotty Hits The Warp Drive: FFA 8-87 Scott Smith, Chuck Buzzard
48. Subway To Venus: FFA 2-26-91 Gary Rall
49. Trauma Center: FFA 1st Pitch Chuck Buzzard
     FFA 2nd Pitch Chuck Buzzard, J. Turney
50. Double Dutch Right: FA 35' Unknown
     FRA 6-87 Chuck and Patty Buzzard
51. Primary Gobler: FA Chuck Buzzard, J. Turney
52. Never Mind: FFA 8-24-95 Dave Sowerby
53. Whatever Blows Your Skirt Up: FFA 6-87 Chuck Buzzard, John Long
54. Pillow Talk: FFA 12-25-88 Wayne Wallace, Mark Egge
55. Ant Abuse: FFA 6-87 Chuck Buzzard, John Jackson, Curt Cornick
56. Time To Kill: FFA 3-93 Walter Anyan, Dave Sowerby
57. Mr. Noodle Arms: FFA Fall 1986 Chuck Buzzard and partner
58. Sisters Of The Road: FFA Fall 1986 Chuck Buzzard, Jerry Radant
59. Full Spank Mode: FFA10-88 Chuck Buzzard
     Variation: Full Wank Mode FFA Phillip Hranicka
60. Arm Forces: FFA 6-88 Chuck Buzzard

Shining Wall
61. Cold Hand Of Technology: FFA 12-27-88 Tim Olson, Gary Rall
62. Red Scare: GFFA 12-29-88 Wayne Wallace, Tim Olson
63. Domino Effect: GFFA 10-30-88 Wayne Wallace, Tim Olson
64. Dirty Dancing: FRA 9-86 Chuck Buzzard, J. Frank
65. Firing Line: FFA 12-10-88 Wayne Wallace, Tim Olson, Robert McGown
66. Lord Of The Rings: FA Unknown
67. The Gift Of Time: FA 12-88 Robert McGown
     FFA Unknown
68. Dancing In The Lion's Jaw: FA 35' Unknown
     FFA Complete 6-9-89 Wayne Wallace, Robert McGown
69. Paleontologist: FFA 1st Pitch 2-12-89 Wayne Wallace, Robert McGown
     FFA 2nd Pitch 3-89 Robert McGown, Daryl Nakahira
70. Extinction: FFA _____
71. Rainman: FFA 2-15-89 Wayne Wallace, Tim Olson
72. Playing With Fire: FFA 11-8-88 Wayne Wallace, Tim Olson, Robert McGown
73. Shining Wall: FFA 1-28-89 Wayne Wallace
74. Cloud Walker: FFA 1-29-89 Wayne Wallace, Tim Olson, Robert McGown, Bill Dykstra
75. Banana Belt: FFA 2-15-89 Wayne Wallace, Robert McGown
76. Fits And Starts: FFA 9-86 Chuck Buzzard, Jeff Frank
77. Beginners Luck: FFA 9-86 Chuck Buzzard, Jeff Frank
78. Gym Rats From Hell: FFA 4-6-89 Wayne Wallace, Robert McGown
79. Plywood Jungle: FFA 3-17-89 Robert McGown, Wayne Wallace, K. Jackson
80. Dihedral Of Despair: FFA 3-18-89 Robert McGown, K. Jackson
81. Shattered Dreams: FFA3-18-89 Robert McGown, K. Jackson

Hardscrabble Wall

82. Sacrifice: FFA 9-26-92 Tim Olson, Cindy Olson
83. Inner Vision: FFA 6-89 Chuck Buzzard, Chris Surville
84. Mind Games: FFA 4-7-89 Tim Olson, Wayne Wallace
85. Chicken: FFA 4-6-89 Tim Olson, Greg Lyon
86. Gym Droids: FFA 1-21-90 Tim Olson
87. Life As We Know: It GFFA 4-7-89 Wayne Wallace
88. Red Sun Rising: FFA 1-16-90 Tim Olson, Robert McGown
89. It Takes A Thief: FFA 1-16-90 Robert McGown, Tim Olson
90. American Girl: FFA 1-10-90 Dave Sowerby, Mike Smith
91. Miss Adventure: FFA 1-10-90 Dave Sowerby, Jay Green
92. Primordial Soup: FA 10-89 Robert McGown, K. Jackson
93. Crystal Hunter: FA 10-89 Robert McGown, K. Jackson
94. Winds Of War: FFA 3-24-90 Tim Olson, Robert McGown
95. Mountaineers Route: FA Unknown
96. Punters In Paradise: FFA Winter 1990 Josh Baker
97. Red Fox: FFA 3-30-90 Dave Sowerby, Robert McGown
98. Windows Of Your Mind: FFA 2-14-89 Tim Olson, Greg Lyon
99. PC: TR in 1989 Greg Lyon
100. Screensaver: FFA 1989 Mike Sessions and partner
101. Electric Everything: FFA 1989 Josh Baker and partner
102. Cast Of Characters: GFFA 1-28-89 Wayne Wallace, Robert McGown
103. Nouveau Riche: FFA 1-19-89 Wayne Wallace and partner
104. Stamina: FA Tim Olson
105. Reinholds Dihedral: FA 3-89 Robert McGown, Reinhold _
106. Eye Of The Tiger: FA 3-89 Robert McGown
107. Fisticuffs: TR Tim Olson
108. Goldfingers: FA 1-26-89 Victor Goldman, Thomas Miller
     FFA 2-1-89 Thomas Miller, Jeff Staley
109. Girl Crazy: FFA before bolts 1989 Chuck Buzzard, C. Surville
     (ascent after bolts) 1-22-90 Wayne Wallace
110. Unknown: FA 6-89 Chuck Buzzard, C. Surville
111. The Arête: (TR)
112. Exodus: FFA 2-27-89 Robert McGown, Tim Olson
113. Divine Wind: FFA 4-5-89 Tim Olson
114. Tapestry: FFA 2-27-89 Robert McGown, Tim Olson
115. Direct Start: FFA on-sight 4-8-89 Chuck Buzzard
116. Sisters Of Mercury: FFA 2-26-89 Tim Olson, Wayne Wallace
117. Chrome Sister: FFA 2-27-89 Tim Olson, Greg Lyon
118. _____
119. Stampede: FFA 3-19-90 Tim Olson, Dave Sowerby, Greg Lyon
120. Logjam: FFA 3-19-90 Tim Olson, Dave Sowerby, Greg Lyon
121. Dangerous Breed: FFA 5-6-90 Tim Olson, Wayne Wallace, Gary Gallagher
122. What's Your Motive? FFA 2-15-89 T. Olson, Wayne Wallace, Greg Lyon, Robert McGown

OZONE

1. Bearded Lady: FFA 6-4-05 Jeanean and Kevin Rauch

2. Old Toby: FFA 6-05 Jon Stewart, Amy Stewart
3. Bag Ends: FFA 2-05 Jon Stewart, Kevin Evansen
4. Brandywine: FFA 6-05 Amy Stewart, Jon Stewart
5. Rude Boy: FFA 2-25-05 Mark Deffenbaugh, Jon Stewart
6. Why Must I Cry: FFA 2-19-05 Mark Deffenbaugh, Jon Stewart
7. Night Owl: GFFA 2-18-05 Mark Deffenbaugh, Jon Stewart
8. Leisure Time: FA 6-14-07 Bill Coe, Ujahn Davisson, Jim Opdycke
9. Variety: FFA 6-14-07 Bill Coe, Ujahn Davisson, Jim Opdycke
10. House of Pain: FFA 7-05 Kevin and Maggie Evansen, Jon Stewart
11. Redhorn Gate: FFA 1-2-05 Jon Stewart, Kevin Rauch
12. Helm's Deep: FFA 2-18-05 Jon Stewart, Mark Deffenbaugh, Kevin Rauch
    Retro-bolt start added on 6-18-05
13. Before The Storm: FFA 6-07 Bill Coe, Larry Jennings, Jim Opdycke
14. Snake Face: FFA 4-26-05 Kevin Rauch, Bryan Smith
15. Snake Roof: FFA 2-5-05 Kevin Rauch, Bryan Smith
16. Vicious: FFA 4-05 Bryan Smith, Kevin Evansen
17. Opdyke Crack: GFA 1984 Jim Opdycke, Mike Jackson
18. Party at the Moon Tower: FFA 9-05 Kevin & Maggie Evansen
19. Eight Is Enough: FA 1984 Jim Opdycke
20. Chaos: FFA 2-05 Kevin & Maggie Evansen
21. Siddartha: FFA 3-05 Jon Stewart, Amy Stewart
22. Masterpiece Theater: FFA 2-05 K. Evansen, M. Deffenbaugh, B. Smith, K. Rauch, Jason Kohler
23. Beyond The Glory: FFA 8-28-06 Dustin Brubaker, Martin Seidenschmid
24. Screaming For Change: FFA 8-9-05 Kevin Rauch, Jon Stewart
25. Afternoon Delight: GFA 5-07 Bill Coe, Jim Opdycke
26. Kung Fu: FFA 3-05 Kevin Evansen, Bryan Smith
27. Whine & Cheese: FFA 11-05 Jon Stewart, Amy Stewart
28. Ganesh: FFA 10-05 Jon Stewart, Kevin Rauch
29. Dirty Jugs: FFA 4-05 Kevin & Maggie Evansen, Bryan Smith
30. Sweeping Beauty: FFA 9-05 Kevin Evansen, Jaime Bohle
31. Carrots For Everyone: FFA 7-05 Kevin Evansen, Michael Kilbury
32. Trinity Crack: FFA 5-26-05 Jon Stewart, Kevin Rauch
33. Kamikaze: FFA 5-29-05 Kevin Rauch, Glen Hartman
34. SOS: FA 6-12-05 Bob Graham, Kevin Rauch
35. May Day: FFA 5-6-05 Kevin Rauch, Kevin Evansen
36. There & Back Again: FFA 9-21-05 Kevin Rauch, Jon Stewart, Glen Hartman, Jason Frick
37. Chain Mail: FFA 2-27-05 Kevin Rauch, Mark Deffenbaugh
37a. Chopped Suey: Top-rope only
38. MD Route: FFA 2-26-05 Mark Deffenbaugh, Kevin Rauch
39. Back in the Saddle: FFA 5-12-07 Jon Stewart, Jim Opdycke
40. Rauch Factor: FFA 2-3-07 Jon Stewart, Jason Frick, Kevin Rauch
41. Short Straw: FA 11-3-07 Dave Sowerby, Tymun Abbott, Shane Polizzano
42. Meat Grinder: FFA 4-11-06 Jon Stewart, Jim Opdycke
43. High Plains Drifter: FFA 4-2-06 Kevin Evansen, Bryan Smith, Bill Coe
44. Rolling Thunder: FFA 4-24-05 Kevin Rauch, Jon Stewart
45. Jacob's Ladder: FFA 4-05 Kevin Evansen, Jon Stewart
46. For Heaven Sake: FFA 6-11-06 Jon Stewart, Amy Stewart, Jim Opdycke

47. Stairway to Heaven: FFA 4-05 Jim Opdycke, Larry Jennings
48. Tipp Topp: FFA 4-2-05 Kevin & Jeanean Rauch
49. Buttito Killa: FFA 5-13-05 Kevin & Jeanean Rauch, Jon Stewart
50. There Yare: GFFA2-13-05 Kevin Rauch, Arent Wortel
51. Love Supreme: FFA 12-11-05 P1 Kevin & Jeanean Rauch
    FFA P2 1-22-06 Jon Stewart, Amy Stewart
52. Bitches Brew: FFA 3-19-06 Jon Stewart, Amy Stewart, Jim Opdycke, Larry Jennings
53. Hang Up Your Hang Ups: FFA 2-8-06 Jon Stewart, Amy Stewart
54. Mountaineer's Route: FFA 1990's Dave Dick
55. Ivan's Arête: FFA 10-26-07 Kevin Evansen, Erick Linthwaite
56. Rasta Arête: FFA 2-15-05 Mark Deffenbaugh
57. Flayel Bop: FA 1986 Jim Opdycke, FFA 1991 Dave Dick
58. Stigmata: FA 1986 Jim Opdycke, FFA 1991 Dave Dick
59. Ripper: FA 1984 Jim Opdycke, Mike Jackson
60. Little Dipper: FFA 2-12-06 Kevin & Maggie Evansen
61. Piton Variation: FA 1984 Mike Jackson, Jim Opdycke, FFA 5-06 M. Deffenbaugh, J. Stewart
62. Orion: FFA 3-1-06 Kevin Evansen, Jon Stewart
63. Big Dipper: FA (TR) 2-06 Kevin Evansen, Bryan Smith. FFA 5-07 Mich Tannebaum
64. Standing Ovation: FFA 4-06 Kevin Evansen, Larry Jennings, Michael Kilbury
64a. Standing O. orig. ascent exits left at last 3 bolts: FFA 2-06 Kevin Evansen, Michael Kilbury
65. Gopher Gone Wild: FFA 2009 Tymun Abbott
66. Numb Nuts: FFA 5-08 Karl Seidenschmid, Martin Seidenschmid
67. Small Nuts: FFA 5-08 Karl Seidenschmid, Martin Seidenschmid
68. No Nuts: FFA 5-08 Karl Seidenschmid, Martin Seidenschmid
69. Dad's Nuts: FFA 5-08 Karl Seidenschmid, Martin Seidenschmid
70. Getting Your Kicks: FFA 5-10-09 Tymun Abbott, Shane Polizzano
71. Route 66: FFA 6-11-06 Phillip Hranicka, Kevin Evansen
72. Meth Rage: FFA 9-06 Kevin Evensen, Phillip Hranicka
73. Mrs. Norris: FA 8-12-08 Andy Davis
74. The Crumbling: FFA Spring 2005 Jason Kohler, Kevin Evensen
75. The Humbling: FA (TR) Fall 2005 Jason Kohler, Kevin Evensen
    FFA 2-07 Ryan Palo
76. Stepchild: FFA 2006 Dustin Brubaker, Martin Seidenschmid
77. Hellboy: FFA 3-2009 Tymun Abbott
78. Grace: FFA 2-2009 Shane Polizzano, Dave Sowerby, Tymun Abbott
    Slack Face (link up to DL): FFA 4-7-2009 Shane Polizzano
79. Dark Lord: FFA 3-26-09 Shane Polizzano
80. Angle of the Dangle: FFA 9-25-07 Kelton Rappleyea

THE FAR SIDE

1. Silverdyke: FA 6-26-08 Kyle Silverman, Jim Opdycke
2. Monkey Moves: FA Chad Ellers and Bill Coe 01/02/2011
3. The Pin: FA 2-7-09 Kyle Silverman, Bill Coe, Jim Opdycke
4. The Trembling: FA 3-30-09 Bill Coe, Ujahn Davisson, Kenny Allen, Jim Opdycke
5. Introductory Offer: FA Ujahn Davisson, Jim Opdycke, Bill Coe
6. The Arete: FA Ujahn Davisson, Bill Coe and Jim Opdycke
   FA Kelton Rappleyea overhanging 5.12 version to the right

7. Lizard Locks: FA Bill Coe, Jim Opdycke, Ujahn Davvison

8. MJ08: FA 2-7-09 Kyle Silverman, Bill Coe, Adam Winslow, Phil Guidotti, Ujahn Davisson, Jim Opdycke

9. Birthday Surprise: FA 4-25-09 Kyle Silverman, Bill Coe

10. Wounded Knee: FA 4-11-09 Kyle Silverman, Bill Coe, Jim Opdycke

11. Dulcinea: GFA 2-28-09 Bill Coe, Ujahn Davisson, Scott Peterson and Jim Opdycke

12. Sheep Skinners: Delight FA 2-7-09 Ujahn Davisson, Bill Coe, Kyle Silverman

13. Scary As...: FA 3-18-09 Kenny Allen, Dan Crump

14. Sweet Surprise: FA 3-11-09 Kenny Allen, Jim Opdycke

15. Right Cheek: FA 4-4-09 Adam Winslow, Phil Guidotti, Bill Coe, et al

16. Adams Crack: FA 1-31-09 Adam Winslow, Bill Coe, Jesse Hudson

17. Left Cheek: FA 4-17-10 Adam Winslow, Bill Coe, Jeff Thomas, Jim Opdycke

18. Bill's Thrill: FA 2-27-2010 Kyle Silverman, Bill Coe, Justin Pattison

19. White Lightning: FA 6-28-08 Kyle Silverman, Bill Coe, Jim Opdycke, Bryan Schmidt

20. Snake: FA 8-8-08 FA Kyle Silverman, Bill Coe

21. Snake Buttress: FA Bill Coe, Kyle Silverman, Jim Opdycke

22. Happy Crack: FA 8-18-08 Bill Coe, Jim Opdycke, Kyle Silverman

23. 2Trad4U: FA Spring 2008 Jon Stewart Bryan Smith

24. Ur Baby's Daddy: FA Fathers Day '08 Ryan Sund, Jon Stewart

25. Freak Freely: FA 4-08 Bill Coe, Jim Opdycke

26. The Lonesome Winner: FA Summer '07 Jon Stewart, Ryan Sund

27. Wushu Roof: FA 6-08 Joseph Healy, Ryan Sund

28. Oracle: FA 7-13-2008 Arent Wortel, Mark Deffenbaugh
    FFA 7-15-08 Arent Wortel, Mark Deffenbaugh

29. Solid Gold: FA on sight 6-28-08 Bryan Schmidt, Bill Coe

30. Hollow Victories: FA 6-08 Joseph Healy, Hanmi Hubbard

31. Day of Atonement: FA 1985 Jim Opdycke, Mike Jackson
    FA complete direct extension 6-08 Joseph Healy

32. Lion of Judah: FA 1985 Jim Opdycke, Mike Jackson

33. Naughty and Nice: FFA 5-4-08 Bryan Smith, Jason Frick, Kevin Evanson
    FA of upper dihedral 1985 Jim Opdycke, Mike Jackson

34. Squeeze Play: FA 5-08 Joseph Healy

35. Tunnel Vision: FA 6-18-08 Bryan Smith, Mark Deffenbaugh

36. The Darkhorse: TR FA harder right var. 6-18-08 Bryan Smith, Joseph Healy
    FFA 2-15-09 Bryan Smith, Kevin Evansen

37. Center Squeeze: FA Bill Coe, Jim Opdycke

38. Boo Coup: FA Bill Coe, Jim Opdycke

39. Sharpen your Teeth: FA 3-10 Tyler Kamm, Bryan Smith

40. Good Vibrations: GFA Spring '08 Arent Wortel, Jon Stewart

41. Closeout: FA 8-07 Jon Stewart, Ryan Sund

42. The Martyr: FA 7-06 Jon Stewart, Mark Deffenbaugh

43. Step and Fetch It: FA Joseph Healy

44. The Head Wall: FA Bill Coe, Jim Opdycke

45. Shoulder Hop: FA Bill Coe, Jim Opdycke

46. Sweet _____: FA Bill Coe, Kenny Allen, Jim Opdycke

47. 'Je' Mapel Jon Phillip: GFA Summer '08 Jon Stewart, Jim Opdycke, Glen Hartmen Summer

48. French Intern: FA 9-20-08 Mark Deffenbaugh, Jon Stewart

49. Exchange Student: FA 9-20-08 Mark Deffenbaugh, Jon Stewart
50. Stew's Ladder: FA Jon Stewart and Bill Coe, onsite GFA 6-28-08 Bryan Schmidt, Bill Coe
51. Northern Passage Lower: FA Bill Coe, Jim Opdycke
52. Kinetic Flow: FA Bill Coe, Jim Opdycke
53. The Warm Up: GFA Bill Coe, Ujahn Davisson, Jim Opdycke
54. Northern Passage Upper: FA Bill Coe, Eric Lindthwaite, Jim Opdycke
55. Senior Moment: FA Joseph Healy free solo
56. Well Hung: FA Bill Coe, Jim Opdycke
57. ___: FA 3-6-10 Bill Coe, Kyle Silverman, Jim Opdycke, Molly and Justin Pattison, Wes Reed
58. Tribal Therapy: FA 3-6-10 Bill Coe, Kyle Silverman, Jim Opdycke, Justin Pattison, Wes Reed
59. Dwarf Toss: FA 3-13-10 Bill Coe, Ujahn Davisson
60. The Far Side: FA 11-16-08 Jon Stewart 11-13-08 FFA Jon Stewart, Mark Deffenbaugh
61. Gas Station Fashion: FA Jon Stewart
62. Fall From Grace: FFA 8-10 Tyler Kamm, Arent Wortel
63. Fool's Rush In: FFA 5-10 Tyler Kamm, Bryan Smith
64. Mark it Eight Dude: FA to the bolts 3-10 Tyler Kamm and John Stewart
FA from bolts to top 5-8-10 Arent Wortel, Tyler Kamm
65. Child Abuse: FA 11-28-09 Bill Coe, Jeff Thomas, Shaun Coe, Jim Opdycke
66. Happy Ending: FA 4-21-10 Bryan Smith, Tyler Kamm
67. Kiddy Litter: GFA 4-26-09 Adam Winslow
68. Wet and Dirty: GFA 3-20-09 K. Silverman, B. Coe, A. Winslow. Direct by Adam Winslow
69. 31 Feet of Pleasure: GFA -3-20-09 Adam Winslow, Bill Coe, Kyle Silverman
70. 41 Feet of Pain: FA 4-4-09 Adam Winslow et al.

BEACON ROCK

1. Pacific Rim: FFA 9-10-89 Wayne Wallace, Tim Olson
2. Rhythm Method: FFA 1990s [?] Bill Coe and partner
3. Boardwalk: FFA Fall 1985 Bill Coe, Bob McMahon
4. Young Warriors: FFA
5. Stone Rodeo: FA 5-87 Wayne Wallace, Robert McGown
   FFA 6-87 R. McGown, Dan Wright (prior free ascent by Joe Healy, Tangen Foster?)
5a. Obnoxious Cubbyhole: FA 1977 Dick Morse, Chet Sutterlin
6. Rock Police: FFA 9-11-89 Wayne Wallace, Robert McGown
7. Return to the Sky: GFA 7-84 Robert McGown, Mark Simpson
8. Sky Pilot: GFA 4-85 Robert McGown, Scott Woolums
9. Couchmaster: GFA 1985 Bill Coe, Gary Rall, Jim Opdycke
10. Jingus Jam: FA 4-85 Scott Woolums, Robert McGown
11. Cruisin' Direct Finish: FA 1-6-87 Robert McGown, Wayne Wallace
12. Cosmic Dust: FA 1985 Robert McGown, Scott Woolums
    FFA [?] Darryl Nakahira
12. Cruisin': FA 1985 Dennis Hemminger, Jim Opdycke
14. Stardust: FA 1985 Scott Tracy, Jim Opdycke
15. Rock Master: FA 1985 Bill Coe, Jim Opdycke, Gini Hornbecker
    FFA 1985 Bruce Casey and partner
16. Rookie Nookie: FA 1985 Scott Woolums, RobertMcGown
    FFA 1986 Scott Tracy, Jim Opdycke
17. Icy Treats: FFA 12-84 Mark Cartier, Darryl Nakahira

18. Switchblade: GFA 3-85 Robert McGown, Guigi Regis
19. Bladerunner: GFA 3-85 Robert McGown, Guigi Regis
    FFA 7-14-86 Jeff Thomas
20. Fire and Ice: FFA 6-30-90 Tim Olson, Jim Yoder
21. More Balls Than Nuts: FFA Spring 1985 MarkCartier, Darryl Nakahira
22. No Balls No Falls: FFA Spring 1986 Scott Tracy, Jim Opdycke
23. Levitation Blues: GFA 1985 Jim Yoder, Robert McGown, Jim Opdycke
24. Repo Man: FA Summer 1985 (?) Robert McGown, Mark Simpson
25. Lethal Ejection: FA 1985 Ron Allen, Jim Opdycke
26. South East Face: GFA 4-29-54 John Ohrenschall, Gene Todd
27. Variation: FA 1974 Steve Lyford and partner
28. Desdichado (var.): FFA 10-89 Wayne Wallace, Tim Olson
29. Dyna Flux: FA 10-89 Robert McGown and partner
30. Jill's Thrill: GFA 1985 Robert McGown, Jim Opdycke, Jill Green
31. Tooth Faerie: FFA 7-26-92 Tim Olson, Cindy Olson
32. To The Edge: And Beyond FFA 8-88 Wayne Wallace, Reinhold Buche
33. Fear of Flying: GFA 1985 Robert McGown, Guigi Regis
34. Desperado: FA 1975 Robert McGown, Jim Opdycke
35. Right Gull: GFA 1965 Dean Caldwell, Chuck Brown
    FFA 10-72 Dean Fry
36. Vulcans Variation: FFA 9-86 Tim Olson
37. Muriel's Memoir: FFA 7-77 Muriel Lodder (Sharp), R. McGown
38. Synapse: FFA 8-90 Robert McGown, Wayne Wallace
39. Death and Taxes: FFA 8-2-90 Wayne Wallace
40. Lost Variation: GFA 5-10-58 Charlie Carpenter, Paul Resta
41. Elusive Element: FFA 6-22-90 Robert McGown, Wayne Wallace
42. Cloud Nine: FFA 10-24-87 Wayne Wallace, Tim Olson
43. High and Mighty: FA 6-5-89 Wayne Wallace, Tim Olson
44. Sacrilege: FFA 9-18-90 Tim Olson
45. _____
__. Hibernal Hi-Jinx: 1-23-09 Eric Linthwaite and associates
46. Diagonal Desperation: FA 1978 Robert McGown, Scott Woolums
    FFA 8-30-96 Dave Sowerby, Ryan Daudistel
47. _____
48. Riverside: FA 10-13-77 Jeff Thomas, Jim Dunavant
49. _____
50. _____
51. Little Wing: FFA 1985 Jim Opdycke, Robert McGown, Mark Cartier
    FA 2nd-3rd pitch Robert McGown, Scott Tracy
52. Broken Arrow: FA 1975 Robert McGown, Jay Green
53. _____ FA 1985 Robert McGown
    FFA Summer 1985 Mark Cartier
54. Magic Fingers: FA 1985 Jim Yoder, Robert McGown, Jim Opdycke
55. Wrong Gull: FA 1970s (?) Avery Tichner
    FFA 8-31-77 Jeff Thomas, Shari Kearney, Jack Holmgren
56. Sorceror's Apprentice: FA 1980 Robert McGown, Jim Olson
57. Old Warriors Never Die: FFA 1990 Jim Yoder

58. Seagull: GFA 1st pitch 9-3-77 Robert McGown, Jeff Thomas
    FA complete 10-4-77 Jeff Thomas, Jim Dunavant
59. Ten-A-Cee Stemming: FFA 1983 Avary Tichnor, Marlene Ford, John Haek
60. Av's Route: FFA 1979 Avery Tichner, Marlene Ford 1983
61. Too Close for Comfort: FFA 8-27-88 Wayne Wallace, R. Buche
62. Left Gull: GFA 1965 Dean Caldwell, Chuck Erwin
    FRFA 7-6-73 Jeff Thomas, Steve Lyford
63. Summer Daze: GFA 1975 (?) Avery Tichner, Robert McGown
    FFA Spring 1985 Mark Cartier, Darryl Nakahira
64. _____
65. Bluebird Direct: FA 10-16-77 Jeff Thomas, Bruce Casey
66. Spring Fever: FA Spring 1986 Scott Tracy, Jim Opdycke
67. Winter Delight: FFA 1988 Ron Allen, Mike Jackson
68. Sufficiently Breathless: FA Summer 1977 Scott Woolums, Terry Yates, R. McGown
69. Fall Guy: FFA Fall 1990 Ron Allen, Scott Tracy
70. Aging Fags: FFA Summer 1985 Avery Tichner
71. Blownout Direct: FFA Fall 1990 Scott Tracy, Jim Opdycke
72. Tombstone Territory: FA Fall 1990 Jim Opdycke, Mike Simpson
73. Bluebird: GFA 1972 Jeff Elphinston, Dave Mention
    FFA 9-11-76 Jeff Thomas, Monty Mayko, Ed Newville
74. Variation: FA (original finish) 1972 Jeff Elphinston, Dave Mention
75. Bridge of the Gods: GFA 1987 Robert McGown, Wayne Wallace, Scott Woolums
    FFA __
76. Pirates: FA Robert McGown
    FFA July 1985 Mark Cartier, Darryl Nakahira
77. Blownout: FA 1-19/20-69 Steve Strauch, Danny Gates
    FFA 10-16-76 Jeff Thomas, Ken Currens
78. Second Wind: FA Fall 1981 Ted Johnson, Bill Strayer
79. Borderline: FFA 1st pitch 6-1-89 Tim Olson, Tim Wolfe, Neal Olson
    FFA 2nd pitch 6-4-89 Tim Olson, Wayne Wallace
80. Grunge Book: GFA 5-70 Wayne Haack, Steve Strauch
81. Excalibur: FFA PPP 7-8-90 Tim Olson, Wayne Wallace
82. Crankenstein:
83. Wild Turkeys: FA Summer 1970 Brian Holcomb, Neal Olson, Glen Kirkpatrick
84. _____
85. Psychic Wound: FFA Spring 1985 Scott Tracy, Jim Opdycke
86. Flying Dutchman: GFA Fall 1984 Bob McMahon, Jim Opdycke, Bill Coe
    FFA Fall 1984 Mark Cartier
87. Bears in Heat: FFA Summer 1985 Mark Cartier, Darryl Nakahira
88. Dirty Double Overhang: GFA 7-73 Alan Kearney, Dave Henry, Malcolm Ulrich
89. Smooth Dancer: GFA Summer 1974 Alan Kearney, Les Nugent, Malcolm Ulrich
90. Take Fist: GFA Spring 1981 Ted Johnson, Mike Pajunas
    FFA 6-29-81 Mark Cartier, Jeff Thomas
__. Crack To Nowhere: FA
91. Ground Zero: GFA Summer 1984 Jim Opdycke, Bill Coe, Jay Bergren
    FFA 1985 Darryl Nakahira, Mark Cartier
92. Nuke-U-Later: FFA 1987 (?) Ron Allen, and partner

93. Iron Maiden: GFA 3-85 Robert McGown, Jeff Alzner
94. Flying Swallow: FA 1965 Kim Schmitz, Earl Levin, D. Caldwell
    FFA 8-10-77 Jeff Thomas, Del Young
95. Variation: FA 8-10-77 Jeff Thomas, Mark Cartier
96. Direct Start: (to Flying Swallow) TR
97. Local Access Only: FFA 8-89 Nathan Charleton, Eric Freden
98. Reasonable Richard: FFA 9-89 Tim Olson, Neal Olson, Jim Davis
99. Black Maria: FFA 9-23-89 Tim Olson, Eric Freden, Nathan Charleton, Tim Doyle
100. Flight Time: FA 1st pitch 7-77 Jeff Thomas, Mark Cartier
    FFA 1st pitch 8-1-81 Jeff Thomas, Mark Cartier
    FFA 2nd pitch 1984 Jim Olson
    FA 3rd pitch 1977 Robert McGown, B. Antel
101. Flying Circus: FA 1st pitch 6-18-77 Jeff Thomas, Neal Olson
    FA complete 6-22-1977 Jeff Thomas, Mike Smelsar
102. Blood Sweat and Smears: FA 7-20-77 Jeff Thomas, Robert McGown
103. True Grunt: FA 7-77 Jeff Thomas, Mark Cartier
    FFA (to Big Ledge via intial 1st pitch Steppenwolf) 6-12-77 R. McGown, Mike Smelsar
104. Steppenwolf: FA 5-71 Les Nugent, Bill Herman, Bill Nickle
    FFA (to Big Ledge via Dod' Jam start) 5-77 Robert McGown, Levi Grey
    FA (above Big Ledge) 7-78 Robert McGown, Doug Bower
    FFA (above Big Ledge for 80') 1982 or 83 Alan Lester, Mark Cartier
105. Dod's Jam: GFA (to Big Ledge) Summer 1961 Eugene Dod, Bob Martin, Earl Levin
    FA (to Grassy Ledges rappel) 1965 Kim Schmitz, Earl Levin
    FA complete 5-72 Jeff Thomas, Dean Fry
    Virtual free ascent (with tension) Summer 1972 Wayne Arrington, Jack Barrar
    FA Direct Finish Variation 1972 Wayne Arrington, Jack Barrar
106. Dod's Deviation: FA 6-12-77 Robert McGown, Mike Smelsar
107. Wishbone: FFA Eric Vining [Journey to the East GFA Spring 1983 McGown]
108. Devil's Backbone: FA 1989 Nathan Charleton, Ron Allen
109. The Norseman: FFA 7-14-88 Mark Cartier
110. Dastardly Crack: FA 1965 Bob Martin, Kim Schmitz, Gerald Bjorkman
    FFA 7-6-73 Jeff Thomas, Steve Lyford
111. Squeeze Box: FA 7-20-77 Robert McGown, Jeff Thomas
112. Windwalker: FFA Fall 2003 Mark Deffenbaugh, K. Rauch, Meaghan Woodruff, Hartman
113. Free For All: FA 8-73 Dean Fry, Steve Lyford
114. Free For Some: FRA Summer 1977 Robert McGown, Mike Smelsar
115. Windsurfer: FA 9-86 Robert McGown, Scott Woolums
116. Fresh Squeeze: FA Summer 1989 Nathan Charleton, Eric Freden
117. Rise Up: FFA Fall 2003 Mark Deffenbaugh, Kevin Rauch, Glen Hartman
118. Pipeline: FA Summer 1977 Robert McGown
    FFA 8-2-81 Ted Johnson, Charlie Priest
119. Pipe Dream: GFA 5-84 Robert McGown, B. Antel
    FFA 7-84: Jim Olson, M. Dennuci
120. Pipeline Headwall: FFA 5-85 Robert McGown, B. Antel
121. Silver Crow: GFA 5-82 McGown, Simpson, FFA 2003 M. Deffenbaugh, M. Woodruff
122. Axe of Karma: GFA 4-86 Robert McGown, Bob Scarborough
123. Red Ice: GFFA 2-86 Robert McGown, Scott Woolums

124. Doubting Thomas: FA Unknown
125. Boys of Summer: FFA 5-86 Robert McGown, Mike Simpson
126. Fingers of a Fisherman: GFFA 5-86 Robert McGown, R. Krukowski
127. Crack of Dawn: GFA 1986 Robert McGown, R, Krukowski
128. Jensen's Ridge: GFA 1968 Bob Martin, Dave Jensen
    TR 7-28-73 Dean Fry
    FFA 4-13-74 Jeff Thomas
___. Jensen's Rimjob: FA Eric Linthwaite and Kenny Allen
129. Updraft to Heaven: GFA 6-77 Robert McGown, Levi Grey
130. Mostly Air: GFA Summer 1981 Robert McGown, Mike Simpson
131. Lay Lady Lay: FA 6-77 Robert McGown, Mike Simpson
132. Rip City: FA 7-9-77 Jeff Thomas, Mike Smelsar
133. Hard Times: FA 7-3-77 Jeff Thomas
134. Ragtime: FA 11-12-76 Jeff Thomas, Willis Krause
    FFA 1981 Ted Johnson, Del Young
135. Synchronicity: FA Summer 1982 Robert McGown, Jim Olson
136. Boulder Problem in the Sky: FA 4-7-74 Jeff Thomas, Tim Miller
    FFA 11-11-76 Jeff Thomas, Chet Sutterlin
137. Iron Cross (On the Move): GFA 7-8-77 Robert McGown, Muriel Lodder
138. Variation: FA 10-22-76 Del Young, Jeff Thomas

Northwest section of Beacon Rock
1. _____
2. Stone Soup: FA multi-month effort 2-2010 to 4-8-2010. Eric Linthwaite, Justin Pattison, Kenny Allen, Bill Coe, Mike Reddig, Geoff Silverman, Pat Gallagher, Josh Kaplan, K. Silverman
3. _____ FA Andrew [?]
4. Forbidden Slab: FA Robert McGown and partner [?]
5. False Prophet: FA Andrew [?]
6. Alcove Overhang: FA unknown
7. Alpine Route:
8. Genesis:
9. Iron Spike:
10. _____
11. Head Case: FFA 11-5-2007 Shane Polizzano
12. Spiny Fish:
13. _____
14. Siege Tactics: FFA 6-30-2008 Shane Polizzano
15. _____
16. Dorian's Dilemma: GFA 6-3-09 Shane Polizzano, Dorian Parker
17. Dorian's: P2 GFA 6-3-09 Shane Polizzano, Dorian Parker
18. Gitmo Love Machine: FFA 6-2-09 Shane Polizzano
19. Fireballs: FFA 2008 Shane Polizzano
20. _____
21. _____
22. _____

French's Dome
1. High Voltage: FFA Hermann Gollner

2. Road Face: FA 1966 Phil Dean, Steve Heim, Jan Cummins
   FFA Hermann Gollner
3. Road Rage: FFA Gollner [?]
4. Road Kill: FFA 7-13-2008 Dave Sowerby, Tymun Abbott
5. BSD: FFA Dave Sowerby
6. Jackie Chan: FFA 5-27-2007 Tymun Abbott, Dave Sowerby
7. China Man: FFA Vance Lemley, Tom Kingsland, and ____
8. The Dark Side (aka The Seige): FFA
9. Pumporama: FFA Hermann Gollner
10. Crankenstein: FFA Vance Lemely, Tom Kingsland
10a. French's Donut Link-Up 5.13a/b: FFA Matt Spohn 8-20-11
11. Dirty Deeds (aka Silver Streak): FFA late 1990s Patrick Purcell
12. Straw Man: FA 1970 Steve Strauch, Wayne Haack
13. Emerald City: John Rust
14. Alpha: FFA 10-12-92 Tim Olson, Robert McGown
15. Oz: FFA John Rust
16. Tin Tangle (Tin Man): FA 1968 Jim Nieland rope-solo
17. Do It Again: FFA 1990s Bill Price, Tim Olson
18. Giant's Staircase: FA 1958 Ray Conkling, Leonard Conkling, Keith Petrie
19. Giant's Direct: FA Unknown
20. Static Cling: FFA Bob McGown and partner
21. Low Voltage: FFA [?]
22. Psoriasis: FFA 7-1-10 Phillip Hranicka
23. Yellow Brick Road: FA 1966 Bill Cummins, Steve Heim, Jan Cummins

FIRST FREE ASCENT
DON'T BE A ROCK CLIMBER WITHOUT A CAUSE

PORTLAND ROCK CLIMBS
ALL FOR THE SPORT OF ROCK CLIMBING

Index

ABOUT THE AUTHOR

As a long-time resident of the Pacific Northwest, Tim Olson has taken his passion for extreme rock climbing and ice climbing to great heights. His zest for adventure led him to explore the unique and seldom-climbed treasures found in the rugged Cascade Range and the scenic Columbia River Gorge.

The desire to share his knowledge and love of the sport with other climbers inspired Tim to embark on a new adventure. In 1993, as a novice writer, he published the first edition of Portland Rock Climbs, a guidebook about the sport of rock climbing in the Northwest. The second edition followed in 2001, and the third edition in 2007.

These days Tim enjoys rock climbing on a lighter note, with his digital camera—especially those high-altitude scrambles on the majestic slopes of Mt. Hood.

IMAGE ONE PORTLAND ROCK CLIMBS

International Rock Climbing Grades

The international rock climbing grading scale is a well established method of systemology. This chart provides climbers from diverse countries the opportunity to compare the standard YDS climbing grades against other popular grading systems.

The grades at our local climbing crags may vary slightly in letter grade which can produce slightly 'soft' or 'hard' ratings, but as a whole the YDS grades used at each climbing site will be comparable to the ratings shown on is chart.

YDS	British	French	Australian
5.3	VD 3b	2	11
5.4	HVD 3c	3	12
5.5	MS/S/HS4a,	4b	12/13
5.6	HS/S 4a	4c	15-17
5.7	HS/VS 4b	4c	15-17
5.8	VS 4c/5a	5a	18
5.9	HVS 5a/5b	5b	19
5.10a	E1 5a/5b	5c	20
5.10b	E1 5b/5c	6a	20
5.10c	E2 5b/5c	6a+	21
5.10d	E2/E3 5b/5c	6b	21
5.11a	E3 5c/6a	6b+	22
5.11b	E3/E4 5c/6a	6c	22
5.11c	E4 5c/6a	6c+	23
5.11d	E4 6a/6b	7a	24
5.12a	E5 6a/6b	7a+	25
5.12b	E5/E6 6a/6b	7b	26
5.12c	E6 6b/6c	7b+	27
5.12d	E6 6b/6c	7c	27
5.13a	E6/E7 6b/6c	7c+	28
5.13b	E7 6c/7a	8a	29
5.13c	E7 6c/7a	8a+	30
5.13d	E8 6c/7a	8b	31
5.14a	E8 6c/7a	8b+	32
5.14b	E9 6c/7a	8c	33
5.14c	E9 7b	8c+	34
5.14d	E10 7b	9a	35
5.15a	...	9a+	...
5.15b	...	...	...

CLIMBING NOTES

CLIMBING NOTES

CLIMBING NOTES

CLIMBING NOTES

CLIMBING NOTES

CLIMBING NOTES